CATALOGUE OF
ENGLISH POST-CONQUEST
VERNACULAR DOCUMENTS

TO MY PARENTS

CATALOGUE OF ENGLISH POST-CONQUEST VERNACULAR DOCUMENTS

DAVID A. E. PELTERET

THE BOYDELL PRESS

First published 1990 by The Boydell Press, Woodbridge

The Boydell Press is an imprint of Boydell & Brewer Ltd
PO Box 9, Woodbridge, Suffolk IP12 3DF
and of Boydell & Brewer Inc.
Wolfeboro, New Hampshire 03894–2069, USA

ISBN 0 85115 259 7

British Library Cataloguing in Publication Data
Pelteret, David A. E. (David Anthony Edgell), *1944–*
    Catalogue of English post-conquest vernacular documents.
    1. Incunabula – Catalogues, indexes
    I. Title
    011'.42
    ISBN 0–85115–259–7

Library of Congress Cataloging-in-Publication Data
Pelteret, David Anthony Edgell, 1944–
    Catalogue of English post-conquest vernacular documents / David
A.E. Pelteret.
        p.   cm.
    Includes bibliographical references.
    ISBN 0–85115–259–7 (alk. paper)
    1. English language – Middle English, 1100–1500 – Texts – Manuscripts –
Union lists. 2. Great Britain – History – Norman period, 1066–1154 –
Sources – Manuscripts – Union lists. 3. Great Britain – History – Henry II,
1154–1189 – Sources – Manuscripts – Union lists. 4. Manuscripts, English
(Middle) – Union lists. 5. Catalogs, Union – Great Britain.   I. Title.
Z6605.E5P44   1990
[PE505]
016.941 – dc20   89–25462
                                                                            CIP

This publication is printed on acid-free paper

Printed in Great Britain by
St Edmundsbury Press, Bury St Edmunds, Suffolk

CONTENTS

INDICES

PREFACE

This study was initiated over a decade ago at the behest of the late Professor Angus Cameron, who asked me to search out post-Conquest documents composed in Old English to supplement the list of texts he had compiled for his planned Dictionary of Old English (Cameron 1973). In a review of this list Mr Terry Hoad had added some texts and suggested that more could be found (Hoad 1975), as indeed proved to be the case. I am grateful to both of them for inadvertently sending me on a most interesting quest. When passing through London in 1979 I happened to check BL, Add. 29436, where I discovered an unrecorded version of 31. This led me to the conclusion that a full catalogue based on primary sources was needed.

The consequences of that conclusion appear in the following pages. Being dean of a large university residence of young men over the past decade has provided me with a stimulating atmosphere but not one that is conducive to tranquillity of mind or singleness of scholarly purpose. This project could not have been pursued had not Professors Robert Lockhart and Edward Chamberlin, successive Principals of New College in the University of Toronto under whom I have had the privilege to serve, had the understanding and generosity to permit me to take a number of weeks off from my administrative duties in 1981, 1985 and 1987 to examine manuscripts in British libraries. Professor Chamberlin secured for me a leave of absence for the 1988–9 academic year, which enabled me to bring the work to fruition. To both I am immensely grateful. My colleagues at New College have always been supportive, notably Mrs Clara De Abreu, who has given me invaluable assistance over the eight years we have worked together; Mrs Elaine Nascimento, who has displayed immense patience in helping me with two different word-processing systems; and Mrs Norma Bliss, who has shown me great kindness.

Inevitably a work of this compass has involved me in many other personal debts for which this book will be but a poor recompense. Miss Cecily Clark and Professor Jim Holt took time from their other commitments to look at a late draft of my manuscript: I was grateful for their suggestions and crave their indulgence for the occasions when I have not followed their advice. They must not, of course, be held accountable for any errors of commission and omission in the text: for those I alone am responsible. Professors Angus McIntosh, Robert Tittler and Andrew Watson, Mr Peter Kitson and Drs David Bates, David Dumville, Simon Keynes, Margaret Laing, Emma Mason, Malcolm Parkes and Nigel

Ramsay have all provided me with information and assistance. The Revd Mr
Nigel Hodge, curate of Machen, Gwent, told me something about the region
round Bassaleg (see 58) and presented me with a copy of E. T. Davies' book on
the ecclesiastical history of the area. The late Dr Ashley Amos and Dr Antonette
Healey afforded me the use of the resources of the Toronto Old English Dictionary project. My cousin, Mr Arthur Pelteret, has uncomplainingly provided me
with accommodation in London over the years; Dr and Mrs Christopher Chip-
pindale, Dr and Mrs Mark Cleary, Mrs Gladys Hines, Ms Marian Hoey, Dr
Jürgen Kopp, Ms Helen Rowett, Dr Alan Sked and Dr and Mrs Lyndon Wood-
ward have also been generous and kindly hosts. Drs David Howlett and Richard
Sharpe were most helpful to me during my stay in Oxford during 1988–9, as well
as being congenial interlocutors in numerous discussions.

Librarians and archivists make it possible for medievalists to pursue their
academic interests. I met with uniform courtesy, interest and assistance wherever
I went, which was one of the major pleasures of the undertaking. I wish to thank
the following: Professor R. I. Page, The Parker Library, Corpus Christi College,
Cambridge; Mr R. E. Trebilcock and Mrs P. A. Judd, Pembroke College Library,
Cambridge; Dr J. A. Cremona, Trinity Hall Library, Cambridge; the staff of
Trinity College Library and of the University Library, Cambridge; Miss Anne
Oakley and the staff of the Dean and Chapter Library, Canterbury; Mr Martin
Snape, Dean and Chapter Muniments, Durham Cathedral; Mrs Audrey Erskine,
Exeter Cathedral Library and the staff of the Devon Record Office, Exeter; the
staff of the Reading Room and the Students' Room, the British Library, London;
Mr Robert Yorke, College of Arms Library, London; Miss Betty Masters, Mr
James R. Sewell and the staff of the Corporation of London Records Office; the
staff of the Guildhall Library, Lambeth Palace Library and the Public Records
Office, London, especially Miss Margaret Condon and Mr N. Evans; Dr G. R. C.
Davis and the staff of the Royal Commission on Historical Manuscripts, London;
Mr J. H. Hopkins and Mr Bernard Nurse, Society of Antiquaries Library, Lon-
don; the staff of the Institute for Historical Research, University of London; the
staff of Westminster Abbey Library, London; Mr Nigel Yates and the staff of
Kent County Archives Office, Maidstone; the staff of the John Rylands Library,
Manchester; the staff of the Northamptonshire Records Office, Northampton;
the staff of the Ashmolean Archaeology Library, the Bodleian Library and the
English Faculty Library, Oxford; the staff of the Pontifical Institute of Mediaeval
Studies Library, Toronto; the staff of the John P. Robarts Library and the Rare
Book Room, University of Toronto; Mr L. S. Colchester and Mrs F. Neale, Dean
and Chapter Library, Wells; Canon (now Dean) Jefferey Fenwick, formerly
Librarian of Worcester Cathedral Library; and the staff of the Borthwick
Institute, York. My thanks also to those numerous stack attendants who anony-
mously fetched books, manuscripts and rolls for me.

My initial work for the Dictionary of Old English was funded by the Canada
Council. I was grateful to receive support for two of my research trips from the

Research Board of the University of Toronto, who were administering monies received from the Canadian Social Sciences and Humanities Research Council.

I dedicate this volume to my late father, Arthur Joseph Pelteret, and to my mother, Emily Mary Pelteret, who afforded me the university education they themselves were unable to experience.

Toronto
July 1989

INTRODUCTION

The year 1066 has rightly signified a boundary between two political and cultural eras in English history. Such precisely datable political events which bring in their train significant changes can often blind us, however, to equally significant continuities. Students of early Medieval England have in recent years become increasingly aware of this and have sought to explore the idea of continuity at both the beginning and the end of what has traditionally been regarded as the Anglo-Saxon period. The catalogue that follows should be seen as fitting into that general development.

By the eleventh century England possessed a highly-developed governmental and administrative infrastructure.[1] Administration utilizes patterns of documentation that are frequently conservative in form and content. Much of the Anglo-Saxon material has been lost, with only a few texts surviving as representatives of what must have been whole classes of document.[2] We must turn, therefore, to the more plentiful post-Conquest material not merely if we wish to assess to what degree the administrative patterns that developed in Norman England were influenced by pre-Conquest diplomatic but also if we want to gain additional information about Anglo-Saxon diplomatic practices themselves.

More than any other contemporary Western-European people, the Anglo-Saxons made use of the vernacular for the recording of their legal and administrative documents. Such activity did not cease with the Norman Conquest. This continuity has been masked because the bibliographical aids have not addressed themselves to its existence. N. R. Ker's immensely valuable *Catalogue of Manuscripts Containing Anglo-Saxon* (Oxford, 1957) concentrates on literary and philological manuscripts. Dr Ker deliberately omitted cartularies and single-leaf charters. He lists a numbers of manuscripts written well into the twelfth century,[3] but most of these are copies of originals of nearly two centuries before and thus only by implication do we learn that English remained in use as a written medium well after the Conquest. P. H. Sawyer's *Anglo-Saxon Charters: An*

---

[1]   Aspects of this are discussed in Harvey 1971, 753–73; Campbell 1975, 39–54 (= 1986, 155–70); and Campbell 1979, 119–35 (= 1986, 139–54).

[2]   Examples are to be found in Robertson 1939 (= 1956).

[3]   Ker 1957, xviii–xix. Exceptions composed after A.D. 1066 are the Laud *Chronicle* and the Thorney *Liber Vitae* (Ker 1957, 424–6, no. 346 and 163, no. 131.) Ker 163, no. 131*b* has been excluded because it is not certainly post-Conquest. Ker notes some pre-1200 cartularies on p. xiv n. 2. Schlemilch 1914 used only a handful of the vernacular legal and administrative texts in his study of English between A.D. 1000 and 1150.

Annotated List and Bibliography, Royal Historical Society Guides and Handbooks 8 (London, 1968) rendered a signal service to scholars by providing a full catalogue and bibliography of the charters of the period prior to the Conquest; the list stops, however, at 1066 and in any case its terms of reference exclude certain categories of administrative documents. Angus Cameron's 'A List of Old English Texts' in A *Plan for the Dictionary of Old English*, ed. R. Frank and A. Cameron, Toronto Old English Series 2 (Toronto, 1973) provides a useful catalogue based on the contents of the extant vernacular texts but it draws heavily on Ker and Sawyer; the later A *Microfiche Concordance to Old English* by R. L. Venezky and A. di P. Healey (Toronto, 1980) supplied omitted texts but neither work aimed at examining all the manuscripts or citing all the editions. Those looking for post-Conquest vernacular documents can gain some assistance from the *Regesta Regum Anglo-Normannorum*, 4 vols. (Oxford, 1913–69). As its title indicates, this calendar is limited to royal documents. The first volume under the general editorship of H. W. C. Davis drew heavily on W. H. Hart's work on Public Record Office documents.[4] Nevertheless, it still was a pioneering work when it appeared in 1913 and should be accorded due credit. It is, however, a frustrating volume to use since it does not consistently record whether a document is in Latin, in English or is bilingual. Its bibliographical details are incomplete and its mode of citation erratic.[5] The subsequent volumes are much more informative but they contain only a few vernacular documents.

This catalogue lists all legal and administrative documents that I have been able to trace containing continuous material in English which appears, or purports, to have been composed after the death of King Harold up to the end of King Henry II's reign in 1189.[6] Documents written primarily in Latin that contain lists of legal franchises such as *flymenafirmth* or *hamsocn* are included if the list *as a whole* is unambiguously expressed in English.[7] Excluded are texts containing occasional words introduced by such phrases as 'quod Anglice nominatur...'[8] and the odd vernacular sentence or phrase imbedded in a Latin text such as Archbishop Ealdred's famous anathema of the Norman sheriff Urse d'Abbetot:

[4] See Hart 1868.

[5] He records a class of documents in the Public Record Office called 'Exchequer Transcripts' which does not exist (cf. no. 31 below). Dr David Bates is preparing a new edition of Vol. 1 of the *Regesta.*

[6] The act itself may be pre-Conquest: no 138 below is a text composed after the Conquest that records a manumission that took place c. A.D. 1045. No. 60, an allegedly papal document which includes a vernacular rights clause, purports to date from the reign of Henry II, though it was probably confected at some point after A.D. 1264. One should not deduce from this record, therefore, that the chancery of Pope Alexander III possessed a command of English!

[7] Thus texts containing, for instance, 'on lande and on strande, on wude and on felde...' are included but not ones that replace *and/ond* with *et* or the ambiguous *nota*. Some of the Old English legal terms are discussed in Hurnard 1949, 289–323 and 433–60. On *hamsocn*, see Colman 1981, 95–110.

[8] Such English words can, of course, be of considerable philological interest; see Pelteret 1978, 56–65.

'Hattest þu Urs, haue þu Godes kurs.'[9] It does not follow that the documents are genuine, i.e., record legal acts that really took place, or that they are recorded in language contemporary with the act. Many of the Christ Church, Canterbury, writs, for example, may well be spurious and they certainly appear to descend from a writ of Cnut's of A.D. 1020;[10] it is likely also that some of the diplomas in Latin drew on pre-Conquest documents to provide them with their vernacular bounds.[11] Most of the royal documents are extant as *inspeximus* charters that date from some centuries after the deed was allegedly composed and thus contain scribal errors and phonological transformations. The purpose of this catalogue is not, however, to make such judgments but to provide the raw material with which diplomatists, historians, philologists and onomasticians can undertake their own investigations.

The catalogue draws heavily on the reference works already cited. In form it is closest to Sawyer's *Anglo-Saxon Charters*, though there are a number of differences. Like Sawyer, I have excluded 'literary' texts composed after 1066 such as the *Anglo-Saxon Chronicle*, the poem called *Durham*[12] and certain homilies; notes are similarly omitted,[13] as are glosses and glossaries. The catalogue does, however, include memoranda of various kinds such as lists of guild members and manumission-documents[14] in addition to the kinds of documents classified by Sawyer as charters. Translations have been given a separate section. I have not followed Sawyer in having a section entitled 'Comments'; instead I simply supply references to secondary publications, sometimes supplemented by a brief indication of their contents.

The catalogue may be considered to fall into two major sections: charters and grants, and miscellaneous records. Texts in the first part are listed in approximate chronological order, based on their latest possible date of issue. Once they have been examined more closely by specialists, greater precision in the dating of many of them may be expected. The records in the miscellaneous section in many cases can at present only be dated within fairly wide palaeographical limits. In some of the manuscripts documents have obviously not been entered in chronological order, notably the memoranda recorded in the prefatory folios of the Exeter Book (Exeter, Cathedral, 3501). It seemed wiser, therefore, to list the records in this section according to the centre with which they were associated (or the person, in the case of no. **145**) and then in the order in which they

---

[9] Hamilton 1870, 253 (Bk III, 115).
[10] Harmer 1952, 173–5; cf. ibid., 171. On the use of English at Christ Church in the post-Conquest period, see Clark 1976a, 5–6.
[11] For example, no. **58** below.
[12] For the continuation of the Anglo-Saxon intellectual and poetic traditions after the Conquest, see Howlett 1976, 289–93.
[13] See, for example, the notes from the latter half of the twelfth century edited in Crawford 1923 and also the recently discovered note bearing the name 'Coleman' in Stoneman 1987.
[14] I use this, perhaps cumbersome, compound word to distinguish the legal document recording a manumission from the act itself.

appear in each manuscript. This may not be intellectually tidy but it should facilitate the user's finding the relevant entry when working from a manuscript or facsimile.

That the latest document listed dates from the reign of Henry II is not meant to imply that vernacular documents ceased thereafter.[15] But the volume of primary material increases exponentially after that date and there was the risk that after all the labour but a 'ridiculus mus' would be born.

Each entry contains, where relevant, the following information:

(1) The date of the act[16] and a full abstract of the contents of the document are supplied. Incidental information not contained within the text but relevant to its understanding is enclosed in Roman type within parentheses. How to handle proper names (which often include toponymic by-names) is a peculiarly difficult problem in this period of rapid linguistic and cultural change.[17] Rather than striving for a completely logical consistency, I have sought to present the material so that it will be of use to scholars working in a range of disciplines. Personal names are thus given in a normalized West-Saxon or, if appropriate, Scandinavian or Continental Germanic form in order to facilitate consultation of onomastic dictionaries.[18] Names that have not been found in the main dictionaries are printed in the calendar in the form in which they appear in the manuscript(s).[19] It seems unnecessarily pedantic, however, to ignore the long-standing practice of using the modern form of certain very common names still in use

[15]   There is, for example, the famous proclamation of A.D. 1258 by Henry III: see Ellis 1868–9, 1–135. (Professor Holt has observed to me that the latter text should, however, be seen as a recognition of the importance of English by the Anglo-Norman élite rather than a continuation of the Anglo-Saxon vernacular charter tradition.) There are likely to be few pre-Conquest documents omitted from Sawyer's *Anglo-Saxon Charters* apart from texts discovered since 1968 and the manumission-documents. The latter are conveniently listed by Max Förster in Förster 1933, 45 nn. 4–7, supplemented in Förster 1941, 794 n. 3. The interesting list of serfs on fol. 162 of Maidstone, Kent Archives Office, DRc/R1, should also be noted. For a facsimile, see Sawyer 1957; it is edited in Pelteret 1986.

[16]   It should be noted that this is not necessarily the date of the composition of the entry. See, for example, no. 138 (n. 6 above).

[17]   The difficulties are well presented in Clarke 1976a, 1–34; Clark 1976b, 294–309; and Clark 1978, 223–51.

[18]   See the papers cited in the previous note and also Clark 1987, 18–19 for a comprehensive bibliography of the relevant onomastic literature. The following onomastic studies have been particularly helpful in compiling this catalogue: Anderson 1934 and 1939, Björkman 1910, Forssner 1916, Insley 1982 and 1985, Fellows Jensen 1968, Morlet 1968–85, Redin 1919, Tengvik 1938 and Von Feilitzen 1937.

[19]   Miss Cecily Clark posited several interpretations of names that I have recorded in the catalogue: *Gottune* = ?*Gotsune* 'Good Son' or 'Godson'(21), *Wiederic* = ?*Theodric* (56), *Fulquio* = *Folcwig* (67), *Malcorn* = ?'Cruel Horn' (69), *Inna Bure* = ?'In (the) Cottage' (93); *Spalla* = ?'Deputy' (95), *Gyldeberd* = ?'Golden Beard' (98); *Ruold* = ?*Hroaldr* and *Unfreig* = ?*Humphrey* (99), *Gollein* = ?*Goslen* (100), *Cotes sune* = ?*Coces sune* (102), *Uyceste* = *Touycestre* (haplography) (142); and *wunge* = ?*iunge* 'Young' (144). In addition I am grateful to her for a number of corrections and identifications of names that I have silently incorporated into the text.

today. Thus Alice (*Athelicc*), Aubrey (*Alberic*), Cnut (*Knutr*), Edith (*Eadgyth*), Geoffrey (*Godefrith*, etc.), Gilbert (*Gislebert*), Herbert (*Herebert*, etc.), Hugh (*Hugo*), John (*Johannes*), Mathilda (*Mahthild*), Peter (*Petrus*), Ralph (*Radulf*, etc.), Randolph (*Rondwulf*, etc.), Robert (*Rodbert, Ro[t]bert*), Theobald (*Theudobald*) and William (*Willelmus*) appear in their modern forms. The version(s) of the names as they appear in the manuscripts have been supplied in italics within parentheses in all cases with two exceptions: 'William' may be assumed to have the form *Willelm(us)* in a manuscript unless otherwise indicated and manuscript readings are generally excluded if they have the same form as the normalized name or its latinized equivalent. By-names provide one of our best opportunities for learning about the colloquial language of the day – but colloquial speech, being allusive, ironic, local and ephemeral, presents especial interpretive difficulties. Where a plausible translation can be provided, this is given with the manuscript reading in italics following within parentheses; where such is not possible, the by-name simply follows the name in italicized form. Where toponymic by-names and place-names can be identified, they are given in their modern form since this is how such names are listed in dictionaries; unidentified or lost place-names appear in italics. Usage has sanctioned the spelling of the toponymic by-name of Geoffrey de Mandeville (*recte* Magneville). Where a text presents a possible ambiguity, the relevant word or phrase is supplied in italics within parentheses. Manuscript expansions of both names and other words appear in roman. All names occurring in witness lists are recorded. If a document is bilingual or appears in both Latin and English versions, this is reported.

(2) Manuscripts are listed in alphabetical order of the city and library where they are housed, except that originals or pretended originals are placed first. Every attempt has been made to provide the current location, catalogue number and foliation. All manuscript copies, including modern ones,[20] have been noted since these in themselves may provide linguistic or historical information. Thus the numerous *inspeximus* copies of royal charters may contain phonological transformations[21] and William's first charter to London, which has been transcribed in every century from the thirteenth to the nineteenth,[22] illustrates the fierce regard

---

[20] The Corporation of London Records Office houses three sumptuous illuminated vellum volumes containing texts and translations of London charters (ChT 10–12). Bound in red calf and stored in loose red calf wrappers, they were transcribed at the request of the Corporation by Thomas Duffus Hardy in 1833–4. Of the medieval cartularies listed in the present volume, only London, British Library, Add. 15350 may be said to match them in splendour.

[21] This is even more likely to apply to non-Chancery texts; the numerous transcripts may well also prove to be of interest to historians. For the philological value of later transcripts, especially those made in regions outside London, see McIntosh 1976, 36–49, especially pp. 41–2, and Benskin 1977, 500–14. I am grateful to Professor McIntosh for supplying me with offprints of these two papers.

[22] There must be many more allusions to William's first charter to London (no. 8 below), for instance, than I have had time to trace. Proportionate to its size (6in. x 4in.), this bids fair to being the most transcribed and discussed English historical document.

the citizens of London have always had for their liberties.[23] A full list of the manuscripts consulted is given after the Bibliography below.[24] Facsimiles are indicated in parentheses, as is also the approximate date of the transcript.

(3) and (4) Printed texts, their source(s) where possible to determine, and translations are listed in abbreviated form.[25] (Full citations of all secondary authorities cited in the catalogue are given in the Bibliography at the beginning of the volume.)

(5) References to secondary works then follow. I certainly do not claim to have read the whole of Anglo-Norman historiography. (This would doubtless be an improving exercise, but Time's wingèd chariot has been espied hurrying near.) The intention has been merely to attempt to include many of the major authorities that may serve to assist newcomers to the field. Catalogues of manuscript collections have generally only been cited if they describe the specific text being discussed.[26] To keep the references within reasonable bounds, secondary references to the manuscripts in which texts are to be found have been excluded unless they make mention of texts contained within this catalogue.[27]

There are probably more texts in the Public Record Office and other collections still to be discovered. I hope that this catalogue will encourage others to bring such texts to light.

---

[23] See, for example, Levin 1969. I understand that recently a member of the Corporation wished to borrow William's first charter to wave about in the Council Chamber in order to reinforce an argument. Sadly, antiquarian zeal to preserve the original document led to a denial of the request.

[24] Apart from PRO, Exchequer Transcripts, no. 4, which has so far defeated both my efforts and those of several members of the staff of the Round Room to locate (cf. n. 5 above), only one other manuscript listed has eluded me: Cheltenham, Phillipps 26641 (*olim* 2777), which was sold in the 1970s. Neither the British Library nor the Bodleian, who attempt to record the migrations of manuscripts from the Phillipps Collection, know its current location. Other manuscripts examined but found not to include material relevant to this catalogue are: Cambridge, Trinity College, O. 2. 41 and R. 5. 33; Canterbury, D & C, Ch. Ant. series and Register P; London, BL, Cotton Tiberius A. vi, Cotton Vitellius D. ix and Harl. 6968; and London, Society of Antiquaries, 38 and 777.

[25] I hope to publish elsewhere some of the unprinted texts from the Exeter Book containing names and I am working on an edition of the manumission and quittance documents.

[26] In addition to printed catalogues, it should be noted that several libraries have valuable unprinted catalogues of the manuscripts in their possession: for Canterbury Cathedral see Bunce 1804–6 elucidated by Ramsay 1985, for Rochester Cathedral see Oakley 1970 (copies to be found in the Kent County Archives Office at Maidstone and in Canterbury Dean and Chapter Library) and for Worcester Cathedral see Benedikz and Brock 1980 and Brock 1981.

[27] Thus Chambers 1911 and the studies listed in Förster 1933, 10 n. 2 on London, British Library, Add. 9067 have been omitted.

BIBLIOGRAPHY
AND BIBLIOGRAPHICAL ABBREVIATIONS

ABBREVIATIONS

BÉC   *Bibliothèque de l'École des Chartes*
DCNQ   *Devon and Cornwall Notes and Queries*
EHR   *English Historical Review*
HMSO   Her/His Majesty's Stationery Office
JBAA   *Journal of the British Archaeological Association*
PRS   Publications of the Pipe Roll Society
PSANHS   *Proceedings of the Somersetshire Archaeological and Natural History Society*
RCP   Record Commission Publications
RS   Rolls Series
RTDA   *Report and Transactions of the Devonshire Association*
SS   Publications of the Surtees Society
TCBS   *Transactions of the Cambridge Bibliographical Society*
VCH   Victoria History of the Counties of England

BIBLIOGRAPHY

Allen 1827   Thomas Allen, *The History and Antiquities of London, Westminster, Southwark, and Parts Adjacent*, 5 vols. (London, 1827–37). [8, 23]

Allen 1935   Hope E. Allen, 'The Three Daughters of Deorman', *Publications of the Modern Language Association* 50 (1935), 899–902. [23]

Anderson 1934   Olof S. Anderson [now Arngart], *The English Hundred-Names*, Lunds Universitets Årsskrift, N.F., Avd. 1, Bd 30, Nr 1 (Lund, 1934). [Introduction, Index B]

Anderson 1939   O. S. Anderson [now Arngart], *The English Hundred-Names: The South-Western Counties*, Lunds Universitets Årsskrift, N.F., Avd. 1, Bd 35, Nr 5 (Lund and Leipzig, 1939). [Introduction, 96, 108–9, 123, 140, Index B]

Anonymous 1680 (= 1682)   *The Abridgement of the Charter of the City of London; Being Every Free-man's Privilege....* (London, 1680) = *The Priviledges of the Citizens of London: Contained in the Charters, Granted to Them by the Several Kings of This Realm, and Confirmed by Sundry Parliaments*...., ptd and publ. by Langley Curtis (London, 1682) [with same pagination]. [8]

Anonymous 1765 *The Laws and Customs, Rights, Liberties and Privileges of the City of London* (London: ptd for R. Withy and W. Griffin, 1765). [8]

Arnold ?1503 (= ?1521 = 1811) [Richard Arnold], *In this booke is Conteyned the names of yᵉ baylifs Custos mairs and sherefs of the cite of londo' from the tyme of king richard the furst. 7 also thartycles of the Chartur and libarties of the same Cyte* (Antwerp: A. van Berghen, ?1503); *In this boke is conteined yᵉ names of the baylyfs, Custose mayers and sherefs of yᵉ cyte of london*.... (London: Peter Treveris, ?1521); *The Customs of London, Otherwise Called Arnold's Chronicle*...., rptd from the first edition with the additions included in the second, [ed. Henry J. Ellis] (London, 1811). [8]

Arnold 1890 *Memorials of St. Edmund's Abbey*, ed. Thomas Arnold, 3 vols., RS 96 (London, 1890–96). [28]

Atkins 1940 Ivor Atkins, 'The Church of Worcester from the Eighth to the Twelfth Century. Part II', *Antiquaries Journal* 20 (1940), 1–38 and 203–29. [63, 78, 146–7]

Baddeley 1924 Welbore St Clair Baddeley, *A History of Cirencester* (Cirencester, 1924). [4, 9]

Ballard 1913 *British Borough Charters 1042–1216*, ed. Adolphus Ballard (Cambridge, 1913). [8]

Baring 1902 F. Baring, 'The Hidation of Northamptonshire in 1086', *EHR* 17 (1902), 79–83. [142]

Barlow 1963 (= 1979) Frank Barlow, *The English Church 1066: A Constitutional History* (London, 1963); 2nd ed. subtitled *A History of the Later Anglo-Saxon Church* (1979). [120–2, 124–34]

Barlow *et al.* 1972 F. Barlow, Kathleen M. Dexter, Audrey M. Erskins & L. J. Lloyd, *Leofric of Exeter: Essays in Commemoration of the Foundation of Exeter Cathedral Library in A.D. 1072* (Exeter, 1972). [17]

Bates 1982 David Bates, 'The Origins of the Justiciarship', *Proceedings of the Battle Conference on Anglo-Norman Studies IV – 1981*, ed. R. Allen Brown (Woodbridge, 1982), pp. 1–12 and 167–71. [25]

Battely 1703 William Somner, *The Antiquities of Canterbury*, 2nd ed., by Nicholas Battely (London, 1703); rptd with a new intro. by William Urry, Classical Town Histories (Wakefield, Yorks., 1977). [90]

Benedikz & Brock 1980 *Worcester Cathedral Library, Catalogue of Muniments, Class A*, compiled Benedikt S. Benedikz and Susan L. Brock, Cyclostyled ([Worcester], 1980). [Introduction]

Benham & Welch 1901 William Benham and Charles Welch, *Mediaeval London* (London, 1901). [8]

Benskin 1977 Michael Benskin, 'Local Archives and Middle English Dialects', *Journal of the Society of Archivists* 5.8 (October 1977), 500–14. [Introduction]

Bentley 1836   *Abstract of Charters and Other Documents Contained in a Cartulary of the Abbey of St. Peter, Westminster, in the Possession of Samuel Bentley* (London, 1836). [12]

Besant 1908   Walter Besant, *Early London: Prehistoric, Roman, Saxon and Norman*, Survey of London 1 (London, 1908). [8, 23].

Birch 1873   Walter de Gray Birch, 'The Great Seals of King Henry I', *JBAA* 29 (1873), 233–62. [46, 51]

Birch 1878   W. de G. Birch, 'On the Seals of King Henry the Second, and of his Son the So-called Henry the Third', *Transactions of the Royal Society of Literature*, 2nd ser., 11 (1878), 301–37 + 2 pls. [51]

Birch 1887   *The Historical Charters and Constitutional Documents of the City of London*, Rev. ed., ed. with intro., appendix and copious index by W. de G. Birch (London, 1887). [8, 23]

Bishop 1928–29   H. E. Bishop, 'Bishop Leofric's Burial Places', *DCNQ* 15 (1928–29), 53–4. [103]

Bishop 1953   Terence A. M. Bishop, 'Notes on Cambridge Manuscripts. Part I', *TCBS* 1 (1949–53), 432–41. [28]

Bishop 1955   T. A. M. Bishop, 'Notes on Cambridge Manuscripts. Part III: MSS. Connected with Exeter', *TCBS* 2 (1954–58), 192–9. [91, 102]

Bishop 1960   T. A. M. Bishop, *Scriptores Regis: Facsimiles to Identify and Illustrate the Hands of Royal Scribes in Original Charters of Henry I, Stephen, and Henry II* (Oxford, 1960). [46–8, 51, 54]

Bishop 1971   T. A. M. Bishop, *English Caroline Minuscule*, Oxford Palaeographical Handbooks (Oxford, 1971). [46]

Bishop & Chaplais 1957   *Facsimiles of English Royal Writs to AD 1100 Presented to Vivian Hunter Galbraith*, ed. T. A. M. Bishop and Pierre Chaplais (Oxford, 1957). [8, 22–3]

Björkman 1910   Erik Björkman, *Nordische Personennamen in England in alt- und frühmittel-englischen Zeit: Ein Beitrag zur englischen Namenkunde*, Studien zur englischen Philologie 37 (Halle, 1910). [Introduction]

Blair 1984   John Blair, 'Saint Beornwald of Bampton', *Oxoniensia* 49 (1984), 47–55. [17]

Blake 1970   D. W. Blake, 'The Church of Exeter in the Norman Period', Exeter M.A. diss., 1970. [17, 101, 103]

Blake 1972   D. W. Blake, 'Bishop William Warelwast', *RTDA* 104 (1972) 15–33. [103]

Boggis 1922   Robert J. E. Boggis, *A History of the Diocese of Exeter* (Exeter, 1922). [91–2, 101, 135, 137]

Bohun 1702 (= 1723) William Bohun, *Privilegia Londini: Or, The Rights, Liberties, Privileges, Laws, and Customs, of the City of London....* (London, 1702); 3rd ed. (1723). [8]

Brady 1690   Robert Brady, *An Historical Treatise of Cities, and Burghs or Boroughs....* (London, 1690). [8]

Brayley 1829   Edward W. Brayley, *Londiniana; Or, Reminiscences of the British Metropolis....*, 4 vols. (London, 1829). [8]

Brock 1981   *Worcester Cathedral Library: Catalogue of Muniments Class B 1–2000*, compiled by Susan L. Brock (Birmingham: University Library, 1981). [Introduction]

Brooke 1975   Christopher N. L. Brooke assisted by Gillian Keir, *London 800–1216: The Shaping of a City*, History of London (London, 1975). [8, 23]

Brown 1904   Cornelius Brown, *A History of Newark-on-Trent, Being the Life Story of an Ancient Town*, 2 vols. (Newark, 1904–7). [41]

Brown 1984   Reginald Allen Brown, *The Norman Conquest*, Documents of Medieval History 5 (London, 1984). [8]

Browning and Kirk 1890–1   A. Giraud Browning and R. E. G. Kirk, 'The Early History of Battersea', *Surrey Archaeological Collections* 10 (1890–1), 205–54. [2]

Brunner 1896a   Heinrich Brunner, 'Pollock and Maitland's History of English Law', *Political Science Quarterly* 11 (1896), 534–44. [English version of the greater portion of Brunner 1896b.] [145]

Brunner 1896b (= 1931)   H. Brunner, Review of Pollock and Maitland, *The History of English Law Before the Time of Edward I*, *Zeitschrift der Savigny-Stiftung für Rechtsgeschichte, Germanistische Abteilung* 17 (1896), 125–35; rptd in H. Brunner, *Abhandlungen zur Rechtsgeschichte: Gesammelte Aufsätze*, ed. Karl Rauch, 2 vols. (Weimar, 1931). [145]

Bunce 1804–6   [Cyprian R. Bunce], 'Chapter Library, Christ Church, Canterbury, Catalogue of MSS.', 4 manuscript vols. in 6 parts [Canterbury, *c.* 1804–6]. [Introduction]

Calthrop 1908   Muriel M. C. Calthrop, 'Abbey of Abbotsbury' in *The Victoria History of the County of Dorset*, Vol. II, ed. William Page, VCH (London, 1908), pp. 48–53. [26]

Cam 1944   Helen M. Cam, *Liberties and Communities in Medieval England: Collected Studies in Local Administration and Topography* (Cambridge, 1944). [96, 109, 123, 140]

Cameron 1973   Angus Cameron, 'A List of Old English Texts' in *A Plan for the Dictionary of Old English*, ed. Roberta Frank and A. Cameron, Toronto Old English Series (Toronto, 1973). [Introduction, 22, 57, 61, 70–89, 91–140, 145–6]

Campbell 1975 (= 1986)   James Campbell, 'Observations on English Government from the Tenth to the Twelfth Century', *Transactions of the Royal Historical Society*, 5th ser., 25 (1975), 39–54; rptd in J. Campbell, *Essays in Anglo-Saxon History* (London and Ronceverte, WV, 1986), pp. 155–70. [Introduction, 142]

Campbell 1979 (= 1986)   J. Campbell, 'The Church in Anglo-Saxon Towns' in *The Church in Town and Countryside*, ed. Derek Baker, Studies in Church History 16 (Oxford, 1979), pp. 119–35; rptd in J. Campbell, *Essays in Anglo-*

Saxon History (London and Ronceverte, WV, 1986), pp. 139–54. [**Introduction, 4, 9, 120–2, 124–34**]

Campbell 1980 (= 1986)   J. Campbell, 'The Significance of the Anglo-Norman State in the Administrative History of Western Europe' in *Histoire Comparée de l'Administration (IVe–XVIIIe Siècles)*, Actes du XIVe Colloque Historique Franco-Allemand, Tours, 1977, *Beihefte der Francia 9*, ed. Werner Paravicini and Karl F. Werner (Munich, 1980), pp. 117–34; rptd in J. Campbell, *Essays in Anglo-Saxon History* (London and Ronceverte, WV, 1986), pp. 171–89. [**142**]

Chambers 1911   Raymond W. Chambers, 'The British Museum Transcript of the Exeter Book (Add. MS. 9067.)', *Anglia* 35 (1911), 393–400. [**Introduction**]

Chambers 1933   *The Exeter Book of Old English Poetry*, with introductory chapters by R. W. Chambers, Max Förster and Robin Flower (London, 1933). [**Introduction, 91–134**]

Chanter 1914–15   J. F. Chanter, 'Exeter Cathedral Library', *DCNQ* 8 (1914–15), 175, no. 147. [**91**]

Chaplais 1966   Pierre Chaplais, 'The Authenticity of the Royal Anglo-Saxon Diplomas of Exeter', *Bulletin of the Institute of Historical Research* 39 (1966), 1–34. [**17**]

Chaplais 1987   Pierre Chaplais, 'William of Saint-Calais and the Domesday Survey' in *Domesday Studies: Papers Read at the Novocentenary Conference of the Royal Historical Society and the Institute of British Geographers, Winchester, 1986*, ed. James C. Holt (Woodbridge and Wolfboro, NH, 1987), pp. 65–77. [**64, 142**]

Clanchy 1979   Michael T. Clanchy, *From Memory to Written Record: England 1066–1307* (London, 1979). [**46, 62**]

Clark 1910   *Cartae et alia munimenta quae ad Dominium de Glamorgancia pertinent*, ed. Godfrey L. Clark, Vol. I (Cardiff, 1910). [**58**]

Clark 1976a   Cecily Clark, 'People and Languages in Post-Conquest Canterbury', *Journal of Medieval History* 2 (1976), 1–34. [**Introduction, 90**]

Clark 1976b   C. Clark, 'Some Early Canterbury Surnames', *English Studies* 57 (1976), 294–309. [**Introduction**]

Clark 1978   C. Clark, 'Women's Names in Post-Conquest England: Observations and Speculations', *Speculum* 53 (1978), 223–51. [**Introduction**]

Clark 1987   C. Clark, '*Willelmus Rex? Vel alius Willelmus?*', *Nomina* 11 (1987), 7–33. [**Introduction**]

Clarke *et al.* 1816   *Foedera, Conventiones, Litteræ et cujuscunque generis Acta Publica*, Vol. I, Part 1, ed. Adam Clarke and Frederic Holbrooke, RCP 11, HMSO (London, 1816). [**42, 44, 145**]

Clarke 1912   Kate M. Clarke, 'Records of St. Nicholas' Priory, Exeter', *RTDA* 44 (1912), 192–205. [**101**]

Clarke 1985   Howard B. Clarke, 'The Domesday Satellites' in *Domesday Book: A Reassessment*, ed. Peter H. Sawyer, (London, 1985), pp. 50–70. [**142**]

Cockayne 1864   Thomas O. Cockayne, *The Shrine. A Collection of Occasional Papers on Dry Subjects*, nos. 1–13 (London, 1864–70). [142]

Colman 1981   Rebecca V. Colman, 'Hamsocn: Its Meaning and Significance in Early English Law', *American Journal of Legal History* 25 (1981), 95–110. [Introduction]

Conway Davies 1960   *The Cartae Antiquae Rolls 11–20: Printed from the Original MSS. in the Public Record Office*, ed. James Conway Davies, PRS 71 (n.s. 33) (London, 1960 for 1957). [19]

Conybeare 1826   John J. Conybeare, *Illustrations of Anglo-Saxon Poetry*, ed. William D. Conybeare (London, 1826). [91]

Coote 1865–9   Henry C. Coote, 'Notices of Deorman of London, a Domesday Tenant in Capite', *Transactions of the London and Middlesex Archaeological Society* 3 (1865–9), 153–6. [23].

Coote 1876–80   Henry C. Coote, 'A Lost Charter; the Tradition of London Stone', *Transactions of the London and Middlesex Archaeological Society* 5 (1876–80), 282–92. [8].

Cowley 1977   Frederick G. Cowley, *The Monastic Order in South Wales, 1066–1349*, Studies in Welsh History 1 (Cardiff, 1977). [58]

Cox 1907   J. C. Cox, 'Religious Houses' in *The Victoria History of the County of Suffolk*, Vol. II, ed. William Page, VCH (London, 1907), pp. 53–155. [20, 28]

Craster 1925   Herbert H. E. Craster, 'Some Anglo-Saxon Records of the See of Durham', *Archaeologia Aeliana*, 4th ser., 1 (1925), 189–98. [61]

Crawford 1923   Samuel J. Crawford, 'The Late Old English Notes of MS. (British Museum) Cotton Claudius B. IV', *Anglia* 47 (1923), 124–35. [Introduction]

Crawley 1976   Charles W. Crawley, *Trinity Hall: The History of a Cambridge College 1350–1975* (Cambridge, 1976). [6]

Cronne 1957–8   Henry A. Cronne, 'The Office of Local Justiciar in England under the Norman Kings', *University of Birmingham Historical Journal* 6 (1957–8), 18–38. [13, 15]

Dale 1911   *Warren's Book*, ed. Alfred W. W. Dale (Cambridge, 1911). [6]

Dalrymple 1757 (= 1768)   John Dalrymple, *An Essay Towards a General History of Feudal Property in Great Britain....* (London, 1757); 3rd ed. (1768). [8]

Darlington 1933   Reginald R. Darlington, 'Æthelwig, Abbot of Evesham', *EHR* 48 (1933), 1–22 and 177–98. [4, 13, 15, 78]

Darlington 1968   *The Cartulary of Worcester Cathedral Priory (Register I)*, ed. R. R. Darlington, PRS 76 (n.s. 38) (London, 1968 for 1962–3). [63, 78]

Davidson 1881   James B. Davidson, 'On the Early History of Dawlish', *RTDA* 13 (1881), 106–30. [17, 91]

Davidson 1883   J. B. Davidson, 'On Some Anglo-Saxon Charters at Exeter', *JBAA* 39 (1883), 259–303. [17]

Davies 1953   Ebenezer T. Davies, *An Ecclesiastical History of Monmouthshire. Part I. Down to the Beginnings of the Reformation* (Risca, Mon., 1953). [58]

Davies 1982   Wendy Davies, 'The Latin Charter-Tradition in Western Britain, Brittany and Ireland in the Early Mediaeval Period' in *Ireland in Early Mediaeval Europe: Studies in Memory of Kathleen Hughes*, ed. Dorothy Whitelock, Rosamond McKitterick and David Dumville (Cambridge, 1982), pp. 258–80. [73, 87, 89, 135–40]

Davis 1905 (= 1949)   Henry W. C. Davis, *England under the Normans and Angevins 1066–1272*, A History of England 2, ed. C. W. C. Oman (London, 1905); 13th ed. (1949). [8]

Davis 1909   H. W. C. Davis, 'The Liberties of Bury St. Edmunds', *EHR* 24 (1909), 417–31. [19–20]

Davis 1925   H. W. C. Davis, 'London Lands and Liberties of St. Paul's 1066–1135' in *Essays in Medieval History Presented to Thomas Frederick Tout*, ed. Andrew G. Little and Frederick M. Powicke (Manchester, 1925), pp. 45–59. [36]

Davis 1958   Godfrey R. C. Davis, *Medieval Cartularies of Great Britain: A Short Catalogue* (London, 1958). [12, 21, 42, 49, 52, 55, 59]

Davis 1972   Ralph H. C. Davis, 'The College of St Martin-le-Grand and the Anarchy 1135–54', *London Topographical Record* 23 (1972), 9–26. [10]

Delisle 1906   Léopold V. Delisle, 'Mémoire sur la chronologie des chartes de Henri II Roi d'Angleterre et Duc de Normandie', *BÉC* 67 (1906), 361–401. [54]

Delisle 1907a   L. V. Delisle, 'Notes sur les chartes originales de Henri II Roi d'Angleterre et Duc de Normandie au British Museum et au Record Office', *BÉC* 68 (1907), 272–314. [51, 54]

Delisle 1907b   L. V. Delisle, *Les Formules Rex Anglorum et Dei Gratia Rex Anglorum: Lettre à M. J. Horace Round, M.A., Ll.D.*, (Chantilly: privately ptd, August 1907), 12 pp. + 1 p. post-scriptum + 1 pl. [54]

Delisle 1908   L. V. Delisle, 'Recueil de 109 chartes originales de Henri II Roi d'Angleterre et Duc de Normandie rassemblées et photographiées par le Rev. H. Salter', *BÉC* 69 (1908), 541–80. [51, 54]

Denholm-Young 1954 (= 1964)   Noel Denholm-Young, *Handwriting in England and Wales* (Cardiff, 1954); 2nd ed. [with same pagination], (1964). [51]

Denton 1970   Jeffrey H. Denton, *English Free Chapels 1100–1300: A Constitutional Study* (Manchester, 1970). [10]

Dickins 1950   Bruce Dickins, 'The Beheaded Manumission in the Exeter Book' in *The Early Cultures of North-West Europe (H. M. Chadwick Memorial Studies)*, ed. Cyril Fox and Bruce Dickins (Cambridge, 1950), pp. 361–7 + 1 pl. [102–3]

Dickinson 1876   Francis H. Dickinson, 'The Sale of Combe', *PSANHS* 22, (n.s. 2), Part II (1876), 106–13. [56]

Dickinson 1877   F. H. Dickinson, 'The Banwell Charters', *PSANHS* 23 (n.s. 3), Part II (1877), 49–64. [11]

DNB   *The Dictionary of National Biography*, ed. Leslie Stephen, 21 vols. (London, 1885–90). [4–5, 8–9, 20, 28, 56, 78]

Dodsworth & Dugdale 1655   *Monasticon Anglicanum*, ed. Roger Dodsworth and William Dugdale (vols. 1–2) and by Dugdale alone (vol. 3), 3 vols. (London, 1655–73). [26, 63, 91]

Douglas 1932   *Feudal Documents from the Abbey of Bury St. Edmunds*, ed. David C. Douglas, British Academy, Records of the Social and Economic History of England and Wales 8 (London, 1932). [4–5, 10, 17–20, 28, 143]

Douglas 1964   David C. Douglas, *William the Conqueror: The Norman Impact upon England* (London, 1964). [4, 6–9, 11–13, 15–17, 19, 21, 24]

Doyle 1949   Anthony Ian Doyle, 'Two Medieval Calendars and Other Leaves Removed by John Bowtell from University Library MSS.', *TCBS* 1 (1949–53), 29–36. [27]

Drage 1978   Elaine M. Drage, 'Bishop Leofric and Exeter Cathedral Chapter (1050–1072): A Re-Assessment of the Manuscript Evidence', Oxford D. Phil diss., 1978. [17, 91–2, 135–40]

Dugdale 1658 (= 1818)   William Dugdale, *The History of St. Paul's Cathedral in London, From Its Foundation untill These Times....* (London, 1658); 2nd ed. with a continuation and additions by Henry Ellis (1818). [27, 39]

Earle 1888   John Earl, *A Hand-Book to the Land-Charters, and Other Saxonic Documents* (Oxford, 1888). [11, 51, 73–7, 79–89, 91–101, 103–14, 120–2, 124–40]

Edmonds 1899   Revd Canon Edmonds, 'The Formation and Fortunes of Exeter Cathedral Library', *RTDA* 31 (1899), 25–50. [91]

EHD II   *English Historical Documents 1042–1189*, ed. David C. Douglas and George W. Greenaway, 2nd ed., EHD 2 (London and New York, 1981). [1, 4, 8–9, 11, 142]

Ellis 1833   Henry Ellis, *A General Introduction to Domesday Book*, 2 vols., RCP, HMSO (London, 1833). [142]

Ellis 1868–9   Alexander J. Ellis, 'The Only English Proclamation of Henry III, 18 October 1258....', *Transactions of the Philological Society* 1868–9, 1–135. [Introduction, 8, 23]

Ellis 1879–80   Alfred S. Ellis, 'On the Landholders of Gloucestershire, Named in Domesday Book', *Transactions of the Bristol and Gloucestershire Archaeological Society* 4 (1879–80), 86–198. [4, 9]

Entick 1766   John Entick, *A New and Accurate History and Survey of London, Westminster, Southwark, and Places Adjacent....*, 3 vols. (London, 1766). [8, 23]

Evans 1976   Babette Evans, 'The Collegiate Church at Cirencester: A Critical Examination of the Historical Evidence', in *Studies in the Archaeological History of Cirencester*, ed. Alan McWhirr, British Archaeological Reports, British Series 30 (Oxford, 1976), pp. 46–59. [4, 9]

Eyton 1878   Robert W. Eyton, *Court, Household, and Itinerary of King Henry II. Instancing Also the Chief Agents and Adversaries of the King in His Government, Diplomacy, and Strategy* (London and Dorchester, 1878). [51]

Eyton 1881   R. W. Eyton, 'The Staffordshire Chartulary, Series I. of Ancient
Deeds', *Collections for a History of Staffordshire Edited by the William Salt Archaeological Society* 2 (1881), 178–276. [69]

Farrer 1914   *Early Yorkshire Charters*, ed. William Farrer, 3 vols. (Edinburgh,
1914–16). [14, 16]

Fellows Jensen 1968   Gillian Fellows Jensen, *Scandinavian Personal Names in
Lincolnshire and Yorkshire*, Navnestudier udgivet af Institut for Navneforskning
7 (Copenhagen, 1968). [Introduction, Index A]

Finberg 1943a (= 1969)   Herbert P. R. Finberg, 'Church and State in Twelfth-
Century Devon: Some Historical Illustrations', *RTDA* 75 (1943), 245–57;
rptd in *West-Country Historical Studies* (Newton Abbot, 1969), pp. 89–103.
[59]

Finberg 1943b   H. P. R. Finberg, 'Abbots of Tavistock', *DCNQ* 22 (1942–6),
174–5. [59]

Finberg 1944   H. P. R. Finberg, 'The Bounds of Abbotsham', *DCNQ* 22
(1942–6), 201–2. [59]

Finberg 1947   H. P. R. Finberg, 'Some Early Tavistock Charters', *EHR* 62
(1947), 352–77. [59]

Finberg 1951 (= 1969)   H. P. R. Finberg, *Tavistock Abbey: A Study in the Social
and Economic History of Devon*, Cambridge Studies in Medieval Life and
Thought, n.s. 2 (Cambridge, 1951); 2nd ed. (Newton Abbot and New York,
1969). [59]

Finn 1971   R. Welldon Finn, *The Norman Conquest and Its Effects on the
Economy: 1066–86*, Domesday Studies (London, 1971). [142]

Förster 1913 (= 1949)   Max Förster, *Altenglisches Lesebuch für Anfänger*, Ger-
manische Bibliothek, Abt. 1, Reihe 3, Bd 4 (Heidelberg, 1913); 5th ed., ed.
Wilhelm Streitberg (1949). [8, 23]

Förster 1930   M. Förster, 'Die Freilassungsurkunden des Bodmin-Evangeliars'
in *A Grammatical Miscellany Offered to Otto Jespersen on His Seventieth Birthday*, ed. Niels Bøgholm, Aage Brusendorff and Carl A. Bodelsen (Copenhagen
and London, 1930), pp. 77–99. [87–9]

Förster 1932   M. Förster, 'Ae. *bam handum twam awritan*', *Archiv für das Studium der neueren Sprachen und Literaturen* 162 (1932), 230. [92]

Förster 1933   M. Förster, 'The Donations of Leofric to Exeter' and 'The Pre-
liminary Matter of the Exeter Book' in *The Exeter Book of Old English Poetry*,
With Introductory Chapters by Raymond W. Chambers, M. Förster and
Robin Flower (London, 1933), pp. 10–32 and 44–54. [Introduction, 91–134]

Förster 1938   M. Förster, 'Die Heilige Sativola oder Sidwell. Eine Namen-
studie', *Anglia* 62 (1938), 33–80. [102]

Förster 1941   M. Förster, *Der Flussname Themse und seine Sippe*, Sitzungsbe-
richte der Bayerische Akademie der Wissenschaften, Phil.-hist. Abt.,
Jahrgang 1941, Bd 1 (Munich, 1941). [Introduction]

Footman 1894   John Footman, *History of the Parish Church of Saint Michael and
All Angels, Chipping Lambourn* (London, 1894). [141]

Forssner 1916   Thorvald Forssner, *Continental-Germanic Personal Names in England in Old and Middle English Times*, Inaugural Dissertation (Uppsala, 1916). [**Introduction**]

Freeman 1867   Edward A. Freeman, *The History of the Norman Conquest of England, Its Causes and Its Results*, 6 vols. (Oxford, 1867–79). Vols 1–2 cited from 3rd ed. (1877–9), 3–4 from 2nd ed. (1870–6), 5–6 from 1st ed. (1867). [**2, 8, 10–11, 13, 23, 91**]

Freeman 1870   E. A. Freeman, *History of the Cathedral Church of Wells as Illustrating the History of the Cathedral Churches of the Old Foundation* (London, 1870). [**11**]

Freeman 1876   [E. A. Freeman], 'A Sale in 1072', *Saturday Review* 42 (1876), 688–9. [**11, 56**] [On the authorship of the article, see Taylor 1905, 48.]

Galbraith 1920   Vivian H. Galbraith, 'Royal Charters to Winchester', *EHR* 35 (1920), 382–400. [**34–5, 45**]

Galbraith 1961   V. H. Galbraith, *The Making of Domesday Book* (Oxford, 1961). [**142**]

Galbraith 1974   V. H. Galbraith, *Domesday Book: Its Place in Administrative History* (Oxford, 1974). [**4, 9, 142**]

Garnett 1986a   George Garnett, 'Coronation and Propaganda: Some Implications of the Norman Claim to the Throne of England in 1066', *Transactions of the Royal Historical Society*, 5th ser., 36 (1986), 91–116. [**2, 4–5, 7–11, 14, 16, 18–19, 24**]

Garnett 1986b   G. Garnett, ' "Franci et Angli": The Legal Distinctions Between Peoples After the Conquest', *Anglo-Norman Studies* 7, Proceedings of the Battle Conference 1985, ed. R. Allen Brown (Woodbridge and Wolfboro, NH, 1986), pp. 109–137. [**145**]

Gatch 1977   Milton McC. Gatch, *Preaching and Theology in Anglo-Saxon England: Ælfric and Wulfstan* (Toronto and Buffalo, 1977). [**91**]

Gelling 1973   Margaret Gelling, *The Place-Names of Berkshire*, 3 vols., English Place-Name Society 49–51 (Cambridge, 1973–6). [**141**]

Gelling 1982   M. Gelling, 'Some Meanings of Stow' in *The Early Church in Western Britain and Ireland: Studies Presented to C. A. Ralegh Radford....*, ed. Susan M. Pearce, British Archaeological Reports, British Series 102 (Oxford, 1982), pp. 187–96. [**41**]

Gibbs 1939   *Early Charters of the Cathedral Church of St. Paul, London*, ed. Marion Gibbs, Camden Society, 3rd ser., 58 (London, 1939). [**27, 36–7, 39, 43**]

Gilbert 1838   Davies Gilbert, *The Parochial History of Cornwall, Founded on the Manuscript Histories of Mr Hals and Mr Tonkin*, 4 vols. (London, 1838). [**87–9**]

Giles 1845   *Scriptores Rerum Gestarum Willelmi Conquestoris*, ed. John A. Giles, Publications of the Caxton Society (London, 1845); rptd Burt Franklin: Research and Source Works Series 154 (New York, 1967). [**25**]

Goebel 1937   Julius Goebel, Jr., *Felony and Misdemeanor: A Study in the History of Criminal Law*, Vol. 1, Publications of the Foundation for Research in Legal History, Columbia University School of Law (New York, 1937). [8, 145]

Gomme 1907   George L. Gomme, *The Governance of London: Studies on the Place Occupied by London in English Institutions* (London, 1907). [8]

Gomme 1912   G. L. Gomme, *The Making of London* (Oxford, 1912). [8]

Goodwin 1855   C. W. Goodwin, 'On Two Ancient Charters, in the Possession of the Corporation of King's Lynn', *Norfolk Archaeology* 4 (1855), 93–117. [28]

Gough 1682   William Gough, *Londinum Triumphans, Or An Historical Account of the Grand Influence the Actions the City of London have had upon the Affairs of the Nation for Many Ages Past* (London, 1682). [8]

Gover *et al.* 1931   *The Place-Names of Devon*, ed. John E. B. Gover, Allen Mawer and Frank M. Stenton, 2 vols., English Place-Name Society 8–9 (Cambridge, 1931–2). [98–9]

Gransden 1982   Antonia Gransden, 'Baldwin, Abbot of Bury St Edmunds, 1065–1097', *Proceedings of the Battle Conference on Anglo-Norman Studies IV – 1981*, ed. R. Allen Brown (Woodbridge, 1982), pp. 65–76 and 187–95. [18, 20, 28]

Grant 1978   Raymond J. S. Grant, *Cambridge, Corpus Christi College 41: The Loricas and the Missal*, Costerus: Essays in English and American Language and Literature, New Series 17 (Amsterdam, 1978). [91–2]

Green 1863–4   John R. Green, 'Earl Harold and Bishop Giso', *PSANHS* 12 (1863–4), 148–57. [11]

Green 1883 (= 1884)   J. R. Green, *The Conquest of England*, ed. Alice S. Green (London, 1883); 2nd ed. (1884). [8]

Green 1983   Judith A. Green, 'The Sheriffs of William the Conqueror, *Anglo-Norman Studies* 5, Proceedings of the Battle Conference on Anglo-Norman Studies 1982, ed. R. Allen Brown (Woodbridge, 1983), pp. 129–45. [1, 3, 8, 10, 12–13, 21, 23–5, 33]

Green 1986   J. A. Green, *The Government of England under Henry I*, Cambridge Studies in Medieval Life and Thought, 4th ser., 3 (Cambridge, 1986). [58]

Greenway 1968   John Le Neve, *Fasti Ecclesiae Anglicanae 1066–1300 I. St Paul's London*, ed. Diana E. Greenway (London, 1968). [10]

Greenwell 1872   *Foedarium Prioratus Dunelmensis*, ed. William Greenwell, SS 58 (Durham, London and Edinburgh, 1872). [64]

Gross 1890   Charles Gross, *The Gild Merchant: A Contribution to British Municipal History*, 2 vols. (Oxford, 1890). [90]

Haddan & Stubbs 1869   *Councils and Ecclesiastical Documents Relating to Great Britain and Ireland*, ed. Arthur W. Haddan and William Stubbs, 3 vols. in 4 parts (Oxford, 1869–78). [87–9, 135–40]

Hale 1865   *Registrum sive Liber Irrotularius et Consuetudinarius Prioratus Beatae Mariae Wigorniensis*, ed. William H. Hale, Publications of the Camden Society 91 (London, 1865). [63]

Hall 1896   *The Red Book of the Exchequer*, ed. Hubert Hall, 3 vols., RS 99 (London 1896). [145]

Hall 1908   Hubert Hall, *Formula Book of Diplomatic Documents* (Cambridge, 1908). [29]

Hall 1920   *Selections from Early Middle English 1130–1250*, ed. Joseph Hall, 2 vols. (Oxford, 1920). [51]

Hamilton 1870   *Willelmi Malmesbiriensis Monachi De Gestis Pontificum Anglorum Libri Quinque*, ed. Nicolas E. S. A. Hamilton, RS 52 (London, 1870). [Introduction]

Hardwick 1856–67   C. Hardwick *et al.*, *A Catalogue of the Manuscripts Preserved in the Library of the University of Cambridge*, 5 vols. and Index (Cambridge 1856–67). [5, 18–20, 27–8, 92, 102]

Hardwick 1858   Thomas of Elmham, *Historia Monasterii S. Augustini Cantuarensis*, ed. Charles Hardwick, RS 8 (London, 1858). [6]

Hardy 1837   *Rotuli Chartarum in Turri Londinensi Asservati*, ed. Thomas D. Hardy, Vol. I, Part 1, RCP 25, HMSO (London, 1837). [51]

Hardy 1840   *Willelmi Malmesbiriensis Monachi Gesta Regum Anglorum, atque Historia Novella*, ed. Thomas D. Hardy, 2 vols., English Historical Society (London, 1840). [145]

Harmer 1936   Florence E. Harmer, 'Three Westminster Writs of King Edward the Confessor', *EHR* 51 (1936), 97–103. [12, 15]

Harmer 1952   *Anglo-Saxon Writs*, ed. F. E. Harmer (Manchester, 1952). [Introduction, 4, 9, 11, 19, 22, 26, 28, 33, 44, 46–8, 51, 54, 57]

Hart 1863   *Historia et Cartularium Monasterii Sancti Petri Gloucestriae*, ed. William H. Hart, 3 vols., RS 33 (London, 1863–7). [78]

Hart 1868   W. H. Hart, 'Calendar of Royal Charters, Which Occur in Letters of Inspeximus, Exemplification, or Confirmation, and in Cartularies, in the Public Record Office. Part I: From Æthilberht of Kent to William II', Appendix 5, *The Twenty-Ninth Annual Report of the Deputy Keeper of the Public Records (25 February 1868)*, HMSO (London, 1868), pp. 7–48. [Introduction, 6, 8, 10, 14, 19, 22–3, 26–7, 42]

Hart 1869   W. H. Hart, 'Calendar of Royal Charters Which Occur in Letters of Inspeximus, Exemplification, or Confirmation, and in Cartularies, in the Public Record Office. Part II: Henry I', Appendix 5, *The Thirtieth Annual Report of the Deputy Keeper of the Public Records (25 February 1869)*, HMSO (London, 1869), pp. 197–211. [Introduction, 46–9]

Hart 1970   Cyril Hart, *The Hidation of Northamptonshire*, University of Leicester, Department of English Local History Occasional Papers, 2nd ser., no. 3 (Leicester, 1970). [142]

Harvey 1970   Sally Harvey, 'The Knight and the Knight's Fee in England', *Past and Present* no. 49 (1970), 1–43. [143]

Harvey 1971   S. Harvey, 'Domesday Book and Its Predecessors', *EHR* 86 (1971), 753–73. **[Introduction]**

Hasted 1778   Edward Hasted, *The History and Topographical Survey of the County of Kent...*, 3 vols. in 4 parts (Canterbury, 1778–90). **[62]**

Hayward 1613   I. H[ayward], *The Lives of the III. Normans, Kings of England: William the first. William the second. Henrie the first* (London, 1613). **[8]**

Healey & Venezky 1980   Antonette diPaolo Healey and Richard L. Venezky, *A Microfiche Concordance to Old English: The List of Texts and Index of Editions*, Publications of the Dictionary of Old English 1 (Toronto, 1980); rptd with revisions (1985). **[Introduction, 1–31, 33–6, 38–9, 41–8, 50–1, 54, 57, 61–4, 67–8, 70–89, 91-142, 144–6, 148]**

Hearne 1720   *Textus Roffensis*, ed. Thomas Hearne, 2 vols. (Oxford, 1720). **[25, 145]**

Hearne 1723   *Hemingi Chartularium Ecclesiae Wigorniensis*, ed. T. Hearne, 2 vols. (Oxford, 1723). **[3, 63, 67, 146–7]**

Hearne 1727   *Adami de Domerham Historia de rebus gestis Glastoniensibus*, ed. T. Hearne, 2 vols. (Oxford, 1727). **[58]**

Heslop 1980   T. A. Heslop, 'English Seals from the Mid Ninth Century to 1100', *JBAA* 133 (1980), 1–16. **[62–3]**

Hickes 1703   George Hickes, *Antiquæ Literaturæ Septentrionalis Libri Duo*, 2 vols. (Oxford, 1703–5). [Published in separately paginated sections (see Hickes 1703 and Wanley 1705 below).]

Hickes 1703, I   G. Hickes, *Ad Reverendum Virum Adamum Ottley S.T.P....Auctoris de opere suo Præfatio*, in Antiq. Lit. Sept., Vol. I, pp. I–XLVIII (Oxford, 1705). **[6, 33, 46, 51]**

Hickes 1703, II   G. Hickes, *Institutiones Grammaticæ Anglo-Saxonicæ, & Moeso-Gothicæ*, in Antiq. Lit. Sept., Vol. I, Part 1, pp. 1–235 (Oxford, 1703). **[57, 64, 147]**

Hickes 1703, V   G. Hickes, *Dissertatio Epistolaris ad Bartholomæum Showere*, in Antiq. Lit. Sept., Vol. I, [Part 4], pp. 1–159 (Oxford, 1703). **[17, 78, 93–103, 105, 109, 120–2, 124–40]**

Hist. MSS Comm. 1885   Historical Manuscripts Commission, *Tenth Report, Appendix III, Report on the Manuscripts of Wells Cathedral*, HMSO (London, 1885). **[11, 29, 56–7]**

Hist. MSS Comm. 1907   *Calendar of the Manuscripts of the Dean and Chapter of Wells*, Vol. I, Historical Manuscripts Commission, HMSO (London, 1907). **[11, 29, 56–7]**

Hoad 1975   Terence F. Hoad, Review of *A Plan for the Dictionary of Old English*, ed. Roberta Frank and Angus Cameron, *Review of English Studies*, n.s. 26 (1975), 322–4. **[1–2, 4–20, 22–30, 33–7, 39, 62, 141–2, 144]**

Holinshed 1577 (= 1807)   Raphaell Holinshed, *Chronicles...*, 2 vols. (London 1577). Vol. I, imprinted for George Bishop, is entitled *The Firste Volume of the Chronicles of England, Scotlande, and Irelande*; Vol. II, imprinted for Lucas Harison [sic], is entitled *The Laste Volume of the Chronicles of England,*

Scotlande, and Irelande, with Their Descriptions; rptd apparently from the edition of 1586 as Raphael Holinshed, *Chronicles of England, Scotland, and Ireland*, 6 vols. (London, 1807–8). [8]

Holmes 1911   T. Scott Holmes, 'Ecclesiastical History' in *The Victoria History of the County of Somerset*, Vol. II, ed. William Page, VCH (London, 1911), pp. 1–63. [11, 56]

Holt & Mortimer 1986   Acta *of Henry II and Richard I*, ed. James C. Holt and Richard Mortimer, List & Index Society, Special Series 21, ([Cambridge], 1986). [51, 54]

Home 1927   Gordon Home in collaboration with Edward Foord, *Mediaeval London* (London, 1927). [8]

Honeybourne 1932–3   Marjorie B. Honeybourne, 'The Sanctuary Boundaries and Environs of Westminster Abbey and the College of St. Martin-le-Grand', *JBAA*, n.s. 38 (1932–3), 316–32 + 3 pls. [65–6]

Hooper 1876   John H. Hooper, 'On Some of the Documents Lately Restored to the Dean and Chapter of Worcester', *JBAA* 32 (1876), 210–14. [63]

Howlett 1976   David R. Howlett, 'Two Old English Encomia', *English Studies* 57 (1976), 294–309. [Introduction]

Hughson 1816   See under Pugh 1816.

Hume 1762 (= 1763)   David Hume, *The History of England, From the Invasion of Julius Caesar to the Accession of Henry VII*, 2 vols. (London, 1762); new ed., corrected, entitled *The History of England, from the Invasion of Julius Caesar to the Revolution in 1688*, 8 vols. (1763). [8]

Hunt 1893   *Two Chartularies of the Priory of St. Peter at Bath*, ed. William Hunt, Somerset Record Society 7 (London, 1893). [1, 30, 70–8]

Hunter 1811   Henry Hunter, *The History of London and Its Environs....*, 2 vols. (London, 1811). [8]

Hurnard 1949   Naomi D. Hurnard, 'The Anglo-Norman Franchises', *EHR* 64 (1949), 289–323 and 433–60. [Introduction]

Hutchins 1774 (= 1796 = 1861)   John Hutchins, *The History and Antiquities of the County of Dorset*, 2 vols. (London, 1774); 2nd ed., ed. Richard Gough and John B. Nichols, 4 vols. (1796–1815); 3rd ed., ed. William Shipp and James W. Hodson, 4 vols. (1861–73). [26, 143]

Insley 1982   John Insley, 'Some Scandinavian Personal Names from South-West England', *Namn och Bygd* 70 (1982), 77–93. [Introduction, 87, 93, 95–6, 100, 103, 106, 111–2, 114, 119, 136, Index A]

Insley 1985   J. Insley, 'Some Scandinavian Personal Names in South-West England from Post-Conquest Records', *Studia Anthroponymica Scandinavica* 3 (1985), 23–58. [Introduction, 83, Index A]

Ivimey 1936   Alan Ivimey, *A History of London* (London, [1936]). [8]

James 1900–2   Montague R. James, *The Western Manuscripts in the Library of Trinity College, Cambridge: A Descriptive Catalogue*, 3 vols. (Cambridge, 1900–2). [58, 92]

James 1905   M. R. James, A *Descriptive Catalogue of the Manuscripts in the Library of Pembroke College, Cambridge* (Cambridge, 1905). [27]

James 1907   M. R. James, A *Descriptive Catalogue of the Manuscripts in the Library of Trinity Hall* (Cambridge, 1907). [6]

James 1909–12   M. R. James, A *Descriptive Catalogue of the Manuscripts in the Library of Corpus Christ College, Cambridge*, Vol. I (Cambridge, 1909–12). [1, 30, 61, 70–86, 91–2, 145]

James & Jenkins 1930–2   M. R. James and Claude Jenkins, *Descriptive Catalogue of the Manuscripts in the Library of Lambeth Palace* (Cambridge, 1930–2). [33, 44, 46, 50–1, 54]

J. E. 1738 (= 1745)   *The Charters of the City of London....*, trans. J. E. (London, 1738); 2nd ed. (1745). [8]

Johnson & Jenkinson 1915   Charles Johnson and [Charles] Hilary Jenkinson, *English Court Hand A.D. 1066 to 1500 Illustrated Chiefly from the Public Records*, 2 vols. (Oxford, 1915). [46, 48, 50, 54]

J. S. F. 1827   [J. S. F.], *The Citizen's Pocket Chronicle: Containing a Digested View of the History, Antiquity, and Temporal Government of the City of London* (London, 1827). [8]

Keller 1906   Wolfgang Keller, *Angelsächsische Palaeographie: Die Schrift der Angelsachsen mit besonderer Rücksicht auf die Denkmäler in der Volksprache*, Teil II, Palaestra 43.2 (Berlin, 1906). [51, 147]

Kemble 1839   *Codex Diplomaticus Ævi Saxonici*, ed. John M. Kemble, 6 vols. (London, 1839–48). [57, 68, 73–7, 79–89, 91, 144]

Kemble 1849 (= 1876)   J. M. Kemble, *The Saxons in England: A History of the English Commonwealth till the Period of the Norman Conquest*, 2 vols. (London, 1849); new ed., rev. Walter de G. Birch, 2 vols. (1876). [73–7, 79–85, 87–9]

Kempe 1825   Alfred J. Kempe, *Historical Notices of the Collegiate Church or Royal Free Chapel and Sanctuary of St. Martin-le-Grand, London....* (London, 1825). [8, 10]

Ker 1948 (= 1985)   Neil R. Ker, 'Hemming's Cartulary: A Description of the Two Worcester Cartularies in Cotton Tiberius A. xiii', *Studies in Medieval History Presented to Frederick Maurice Powicke*, ed. Richard W. Hunt, William A. Pantin and Richard W. Southern (Oxford, 1948), pp. 49–75; rptd in N. R. Ker, *Books, Collectors and Libraries: Studies in the Medieval Heritage*, ed. Andrew G. Watson (London and Ronceverte, WV, 1985), pp. 31–59. [63, 67, 146–7]

Ker 1954 (= 1985)   N. R. Ker, 'Liber Custumarum, and Other Manuscripts Formerly at the Guildhall', *The Guildhall Miscellany*, no. 3 (February 1954) [= Vol. 1 (1952–9)], 37–45; rptd in N. R. Ker, *Books, Collectors and Libraries*, ed. Andrew G. Watson (London and Ronceverte, WV, 1985), pp. 135–42. [8]

Ker 1957   N. R. Ker, *Catalogue of Manuscripts Containing Anglo-Saxon* (Oxford, 1957). [Introduction, 22, 61, 70–89, 91–140, 145–7]

Ker 1960   N. R. Ker, *English Manuscripts in the Century After the Norman Conquest*, The Lyell Lectures 1952–3 (Oxford, 1960). [17, 22, 28, 46–8, 51, 54]

Ker 1969   N. R. Ker, *Medieval Manuscripts in British Libraries. I. London* (Oxford, 1969). [8]

Kershaw 1922   *Anglo-Saxon and Norse Poems*, ed. and trans. Nora Kershaw (Cambridge, 1922). [91]

Keynes 1988   Simon Keynes, 'Regenbald the Chancellor (*sic*)', *Anglo-Norman Studies* 10, Proceedings of the Battle Conference 1987, ed. R. Allen Brown (Woodbridge and Wolfboro, NH, 1988), pp. 185–222. [1–2, 4–39, 41, 43–4, 46–8, 62]

Keynes 1989   S. Keynes, 'The Lost Cartulary of Abbotsbury', *Anglo-Saxon England* 18 (1989), 207–43. [26]

Kingsford 1908   *A Survey of London by John Stow Reprinted from the Text of 1603*, with intro. and notes by Charles L. Kingsford, 2 vols. (Oxford, 1908); rptd (1971). (See also Stow 1603 and Strype 1720.) [8, 10, 27, 39]

Klipstein 1849   Louis F. Klipstein, *Analecta Anglo-Saxonica: Selections, in Prose and Verse, From the Anglo-Saxon Literature....*, Vol. 1 (New York, 1849). [145]

Kluge 1904   Friedrich Kluge, *Mittelenglisches Lesebuch* (Halle a S., 1904). [51]

Lambert 1806   B. Lambert, *The History and Survey of London and Its Environs. From the Earliest Period to the Present Time*, 4 vols. (London, 1806). [8, 23]

Landon 1939   *The Cartae Antiquae Rolls 1–10: Printed from the Original MSS. in the Custody of the Right Honourable the Master of the Rolls*, ed. Lionel Landon, PRS 55 (n.s. 17) (London, 1939). [6, 27, 51]

Lapidge 1983   Michael Lapidge, 'Ealdred of York and MS. Cotton Vitellius E.XII', *Yorkshire Archaeological Journal* 55 (1983), 11–25. [92]

Lapidge 1985   M. Lapidge, 'Surviving Booklists from Anglo-Saxon England' in *Learning and Literature in Anglo-Saxon England: Studies Presented to Peter Clemoes on the Occasion of His Sixty-Fifth Birthday*, ed. M. Lapidge and Helmut Gneuss (Cambridge, 1985), pp. 33–89. [91]

Leach 1897   *Memorials of Beverley Minster: The Chapter Act Book of the Collegiate Church of S. John of Beverley A.D. 1286–1347, With Illustrative Documents and Introduction*, ed. Arthur F. Leach, Vol. 1, SS 98 (Durham, London and Edinburgh, 1897). [14]

Leland 1715 (= 1774)   *Joannis Lelandi Antiquarii De Rebus Britannicis Collectanea*, ed. Thomas Hearne, 5 vols. in 6 parts (Oxford, 1715) [only 156 copies printed according to the Bodleian copy of 1774]; editio altera, superintended by Joseph Ayloffe, 6 vols. (London, 1774). [39]

Le Patourel 1944   John Le Patourel, 'Geoffrey of Montbray, Bishop of Coutances, 1049–1093', *EHR* 59 (1944), 129–61. [10, 111]

Lethaby 1902   William R. Lethaby, *London Before the Conquest* (London, 1902). [8, 10]

Levin 1969   Jennifer Levin, *The Charter Controversy in the City of London 1660–1688, and Its Consequences*, University of London Legal Series 9 (London, 1969). [**Introduction**]

Liebermann 1892   Felix Liebermann, *Quadripartitus, ein englisches Rechtsbuch von 1114* (Halle, 1892). [**145**]

Liebermann 1893   F. Liebermann, 'A Bilingual Ordinance of William I', *The Athenaeum* no. 3436 (2 September 1893), 322. [**145**]

Liebermann 1903a   F. Liebermann, 'Drei nordhumbrische Urkunden um 1100', *Archiv für das Studium der neueren Sprachen und Litteraturen* 111 (1903), 275–84. [**64, 148**]

Liebermann 1903b   F. Liebermann, *Die Gesetze der Angelsachsen*, 3 vols. (Halle, 1903–16). [**8, 145**]

Lloyd 1956 (= 1967)   Leslie J. Lloyd, *The Library of Exeter Cathedral*, with a description of the archives by Audrey M. Woodcock [now Erskine], [Exeter, 1956]; rptd [1967]. [**92**]

Lloyd 1972   L. J. Lloyd, 'Leofric as Bibliophile' in *Leofric of Exeter: Essays in Commemoration of the Foundation of Exeter Cathedral Library in A.D. 1072*, ed. Frank Barlow *et al.* (Exeter, 1972). [**91–2**]

Loftie 1883 (= 1884)   William J. Loftie, *A History of London*, 2 vols. (London, 1883), Supplement to the First Edition (1884); 2nd ed., 2 vols. (1884). [**8, 23**]

Loftie 1887   W. J. Loftie, *London*, Historic Towns (London, 1887). [**8, 23**]

Loyd 1949   Lewis C. Loyd, 'The Date of the Creation of the Earldom of Shrewsbury', in G[eorge] E. C[okayne], *The Complete Peerage*, ed. Geoffrey H. White, Vol. XI (London, 1949), Appendix K, pp. 155–8. [**10**]

Loyd & Stenton 1950   *Sir Christopher Hatton's Book of Seals*, ed. L. C. Loyd and Doris M. Stenton, Publications of the Northamptonshire Record Society 15 (Oxford, 1950 for 1941–2). [**62**]

Loyd 1951   L. C. Loyd, *The Origins of Some Anglo-Norman Families*, ed. Charles T. Clay and David C. Douglas, Publications of the Harleian Society 103 (Leeds, 1951). [**Index B**]

Luffman 1793   *The Charters of London Complete; Also Magna Carta, and the Bill of Rights*, with explanatory notes and remarks by John Luffmann (London, 1793). [**8, 23**]

Lye 1772   Edward Lye, *Dictionarium Saxonico et Gothico-Latinum*, ed. Owen Manning, 2 vols. (London, 1772). [**48, 79–86**]

Macdonald 1926 (= 1944)   Allan J. Macdonald, *Lanfranc: A Study of His Life, Work & Writing* (Oxford, 1926); 2nd ed. [with same pagination] (1944). [**25**]

Macray 1868 (= 1890)   William D. Macray, *Annals of the Bodleian Library, Oxford, A.D. 1598 – A.D. 1867; With a Preliminary Notice of the Earlier Library Founded in the Fourteenth Century* (London, Oxford and Cambridge, 1868); *Annals of the Bodleian Library, Oxford; With a Notice of the Earlier Library of the University*, 2nd ed. enlarged, and continued from 1868 to 1880 (Oxford, 1890); rptd (1984). [**91–2**]

Madan & Craster 1922   Falconer Madan and Herbert H. E. Craster, *A Summary Catalogue of Western Manuscripts in the Bodleian Library at Oxford*, Vol. II, Part 1 (Oxford, 1922). [92]

Madox 1702   *Formulare Anglicanum: Or, A Collection of Ancient Charters and Instruments of Divers Kinds....*, ed. Thomas Madox (London, 1702). [79–81]

Maitland 1739 (= 1756)   William Maitland, *The History of London, From Its Foundation by the Romans to the Present Time....* (London, 1739); 2nd ed., 2 vols (1756). [8, 23]

Maitland 1897 (= 1960)   Frederic W. Maitland, *Domesday Book and Beyond: Three Essays in the Early History of England* (Cambridge, 1897); rptd with intro. by Edward Miller (London, 1960). [90, 142]

Mason 1988   *Westminster Abbey Charters 1066–c.1214*, ed. Emma Mason, London Record Society 25 (London, 1988). [2, 12–13, 15, 21, 24, 38, 65–6]

McIntosh 1976   Angus McIntosh, 'The Language of the Extant Versions of *Havelok the Dane*', *Medium Ævum* 45 (1976), 36–49. [Introduction]

Meiklejohn 1908   Max J. C. Meiklejohn, *London: A Short History*, new and rev. ed. (London, [1908]). [8]

Merewether & Stephens 1835   Henry A. Merewether and Archibald J. Stephens, *The History of the Boroughs and Municipal Corporations of the United Kingdom; From the Earliest to the Present Time*, 3 vols. (London, 1835); rptd (Brighton, 1972). [8, 23]

Migne 1844   *Patrologiae Cursus Completus, Series Latina*, ed. Jacques P. Migne, 221 vols. (Paris, 1844–64). [101, 145]

Miller 1890   *The Old English Version of Bede's Ecclesiastical History of the English People*, Vol. I, ed. with trans. and intro. by Thomas Miller, Early English Text Society, OS 95 (London, 1890). [92]

Monasticon   William Dugdale, *Monasticon Anglicanum*, ed. John Caley, Henry Ellis and Bulkeley Bandinel, 6 vols. in 8 (London, 1846). [2, 7, 10, 12–13, 15, 17, 21, 24, 26, 28, 33, 38, 46, 51, 55, 57–8, 63, 65, 91, 143, 147]

Morlet 1968–85   Marie-Thérèse Morlet, *Les Noms de Personne sur le Territoire de l'Ancienne Gaule du VI ᵉ au XII ᵉ Siècle*, 3 vols. (Paris, 1968–85). [Introduction]

Morris 1927   William A. Morris, *The Medieval English Sheriff to 1300*, Publications of the University of Manchester 176, Historical Series 46 (Manchester, 1927). [1, 3, 8, 11–13, 19, 21, 23–4, 29, 31, 65–6]

Neufeldt 1907   Ernst Neufeldt, *Zur Sprache des Urkundenbuches von Westminster. (Cotton Faustina A III.)*, Rostock Ph.D. diss. (Berlin, 1907). [2, 12–13, 15, 21, 24, 38]

Newcourt 1708   Richard Newcourt, *Repertorium Ecclesiasticum Parochiale Londinense: An Ecclesiastical Parochial History of the Diocese of London*, 2 vols. (London, 1708–10). [8, 10]

Nicholson 1913   Edward W. B. Nicholson, *Introduction to the Study of Some of the Oldest Latin Musical Manuscripts in the Bodleian Library, Oxford*, Early Bodleian Music 3 (Oxford, 1913). [92]

Nightingale 1982   Pamela Nightingale, 'Some London Moneyers and Reflections on the Organization of English Mints in the Eleventh and Twelfth Centuries', *Numismatic Chronicle* 142 (1982), 34–50. [23]

Noorthouck 1773   John Noorthouck, *A New History of London, Including Westminster and Southwark* (London, 1773). [8, 23]

Norton 1829 (= 1869)   George Norton, *Commentaries on the History, Constitution, and Chartered Franchises of the City of London* (London, 1829); 3rd ed., revised (1869). [8, 23]

NPS I   New Palaeographical Society, *Facsimiles of Ancient Manuscripts, Etc.*, ed. Edward M. Thompson, George F. Warner, Frederic G. Kenyon and Julius P. Gilson, 1st ser., Vol. I (London, 1903–12). [64, 93–6]

Oakley 1970   Anne Oakley, *The Archives of the Dean and Chapter of Rochester c. 1100–1907. Part I: The Archives of Rochester Priory, etc.*, Vols. 1–2, Typescript in Maidstone, Kent County Archives Office, and Canterbury, Cathedral Archives (1970). [Vol. 1 contains the series DRc/T, vol. 2 the series DRc/R.] [Introduction, 40, 42, 49, 52–3, 55, 60, 145]

Offler 1968   *Durham Episcopal Charters 1071–1152*, ed. Hilary S. Offler, SS 179 (Gateshead, 1968 for 1964). [61, 64]

Oliver 1846   George Oliver, *Monasticon Dioecesis Exoniensis…and Additional Supplement* (Exeter, 1846–54). [87–9, 101]

Oliver 1861   G. Oliver, *Lives of the Bishops of Exeter, and A History of the Cathedral* (Exeter, 1861). [17, 91]

Olson 1989   Lynette Olson, *Early Monasteries in Cornwall*, Studies in Celtic History 11 (Woodbridge, Suffolk, and Wolfeboro, N.H., 1989). [87–9]

Owen 1968   Dorothy M. Owen, *A Catalogue of Lambeth Manuscripts 889 to 901 (Carte Antique et Miscellanee)* (London, 1968). [46, 48, 50–1, 54]

Page 1923   William Page, *London: Its Origin and Early Development* (London, 1923). [8]

Palgrave 1832 (= 1919)   Francis Palgrave, *The Rise and Progress of the English Commonwealth: Anglo-Saxon Period*, 2 vols. (London, 1832); rptd in *The Collected Historical Works of Sir Francis Palgrave*, ed. R. H. I. Palgrave, 10 vols. (Cambridge, 1919–22), in vol. 7 (1921). [143]

Parker ?1567   Matthew Parker, *A Testimonie of Antiquitie, shewing the auncient fayth in the Church of England touching the sacrament of the body and bloude of the Lord here publikely preached, and also receaued in the Saxons tyme, aboue 600* (London, ?1567) [91]

Parker 1572   M. Parker, *De Antiquitate Britannicae Ecclesiae & Priuilegiis Ecclesiae Cantuariensis, cum Archiepiscopis Eiusdem 70* (London, 1572). [44]

Parker 1885   James Parker, *The Early History of Oxford 727–1100*, Oxford Historical Society 3 (Oxford, 1885). [12]

Pedler 1856   Edward H. Pedler, *Anglo-Saxon Episcopate of Cornwall: With Some Account of the Bishops of Crediton* (London, 1856). [91]

Pegge 1770   Samuel Pegge, 'A Copy of a Deed in Latin and Saxon, of Odo, Bishop of Baieux, Half Brother of William the Conqueror; with Some Observations Thereon', *Archaeologia* 1 (1770), 335–46 + 1 Plate. [62]

Pelteret 1978   David A. E. Pelteret, 'Expanding the Word Hoard: Opportunities for Fresh Discoveries in Early English Vocabulary', *Indiana Social Studies Quarterly* 31 (1978), 56–65. [Introduction]

Pelteret 1986   D. A. E. Pelteret, 'Two Old English Lists of Serfs', *Mediaeval Studies* 48 (1986), 470–513. [Introduction]

Phillips 1834   Thomas Phillipps, 'List of Charters in the Cartulary of St. Nicholas, at Exeter', *Collectanea Topographica et Genealogia* 1 (1834), 60–5, 184–9, 250–4 and 374–88. [101]

Phillipps 1836   T. Phillipps, 'Three Inedited Saxon Charters, from the Cartulary of Cirencester Abbey', *Archaeologia* 26 (1836), 255–6. [4, 9]

Plucknett 1929 (= 1956)   Theodore F. T. Plucknett, *A Concise History of the Common Law* (New York, 1929); 5th ed. (London, 1956). [8]

Pole 1791   *Collections towards a Description of the County of Devon*, ed. Sir John-William De La Pole (London, 1791). [59]

Pollock & Maitland 1895 (= 1898)   Frederick Pollock and Frederic W. Maitland, *The History of English Law before the Time of Edward I*, 2 vols (Cambridge, 1895); 2nd ed. (1898); reissued with a new intro. and select bibliography by Stroud F. C. Milsom (1968). [145]

Poole 1908   Reginald L. Poole, 'The Dates of Henry II's Charters, *EHR* 23 (1908), 79–83. [54]

PRO 1895   *Calendar of the Patent Rolls Preserved in the Public Record Office. Richard II. A.D. 1377–1381*, [Vol. I], HMSO (London, 1895). [14, 46, 50, 54]

PRO 1897   *Calendar of the Patent Rolls Preserved in the Public Record Office. Edward IV. A.D. 1461–1467*, HMSO (London, 1897). [8, 23]

PRO 1900   *Calendar of the Patent Rolls Preserved in the Public Record Office. Edward IV. Henry VI. A.D. 1467–1477*, HMSO (London, 1900). [10, 49, 52, 55]

PRO 1901   *Calendar of the Patent Rolls, Preserved in the Public Record Office. Henry VI. [Vol. I] A.D. 1422–1429*, HMSO (London, 1901). [8, 10, 14, 23, 27, 42, 46, 49–50, 52, 54–5]

PRO 1903   *Calendar of the Patent Rolls Preserved in the Public Record Office. Henry IV. Vol. I. A.D. 1399–1401*, HMSO (London, 1903). [14, 27]

PRO 1906   *Calendar of the Charter Rolls Preserved in the Public Record Office. Vol. II. Henry III – Edward I. A.D. 1257–1300*, HMSO (London, 1906). [42, 49, 52, 55]

PRO 1907   *Calendar of the Patent Rolls, Preserved in the Public Record Office. Henry VI. Vol. II. A.D. 1429–1436*, HMSO (London, 1907). [22, 46–8, 51, 54]

PRO 1908a   *Calendar of the Charter Rolls Preserved in the Public Record Office. Vol. III. Edward I, Edward II. A.D. 1300–1326*, HMSO (London, 1908). [14, 26–7, 31]

PRO 1908b   *Calendar of the Patent Rolls, Preserved in the Public Record Office. Henry VI. Vol. IV. A.D. 1441–1446*, HMSO (London, 1908). [14]

PRO 1910   *Calendar of the Patent Rolls, Preserved in the Public Record Office. Henry V. Vol. I. A.D. 1413–1416*, HMSO (London, 1910). [27]

PRO 1912   *Calendar of the Charter Rolls, Preserved in the Public Record Office. Vol. IV. 1–14 Edward III. A.D. 1327–1341*, HMSO (London, 1912). [14, 27, 31, 42, 46, 49–50, 52, 54–5]

PRO 1914   *Calendar of the Patent Rolls Preserved in the Public Record Office. Henry VII. Vol. I. A.D. 1485–1494*, HMSO (London, 1914). [10]

PRO 1916   *Calendar of the Charter Rolls Preserved in the Public Record Office. Vol. V. 15 Edward III – 5 Henry V. A.D. 1341–1417*, HMSO (London, 1916). [8, 10, 14, 23, 27, 31, 46, 50, 54]

PRO 1927   *Calendar of the Charter Rolls Preserved in the Public Record Office. Vol. VI. 5 Henry VI – 8 Henry VIII. A.D. 1427–1516*, HMSO (London, 1927). [10]

Pugh 1816   *An Epitome of the Privileges of London, Including Southwark....*, digested and arranged by David Hughson [pseud. of Edward Pugh] (London, 1816). [8]

Pulling 1842   Alexander Pulling, *A Practical Treatise on the Laws, Customs, and Regulations of the City and Port of London, as Settled by Charter, Usage, By-Law, or Statute* (London, 1842). [8]

Raine 1839   *Historiae Dunelmensis Scriptores Tres, Gaufridus de Coldingham, Robertus de Graystanes, et Willielmus de Chambre*, ed. James Raine, SS 9 (London, 1839). [64]

Raine 1852   J. Raine, *The History and Antiquities of North Durham, as Subdivided into the Shires of Norham, Island, and Bedlington....* (London, 1852). [64]

Ramsay 1985   Nigel L. Ramsay, 'Provisional Guide to the Principal Categories of Material in the Archives of the Dean and Chapter of Canterbury', Cyclostyled [Canterbury, 1985]. Explains the classification of Bunce 1804–6. [Introduction]

Reddan 1909   M. Reddan, 'Religious Houses: Collegiate Church of St. Martin le Grand' in *The Victoria History of London: Including London Within the Bar, Westminster & Southwark*, Vol. I, ed. William Page, VCH (London, 1909), pp. 555–66. [10]

Redin 1919   Mats A. Redin, *Studies on Uncompounded Personal Names in Old English*, Inaugural Dissertation, Uppsala Universitets Årsskrift 1919 (Uppsala, 1919). [Introduction, Index A]

Regesta I – III   *Regesta Regum Anglo-Normannorum 1066–1154*, ed. Henry W. C. Davis *et al.*, 3 vols. (Oxford, 1913–68). [Introduction, 1–39, 41–50, 145]

Riley 1860   *Munimenta Gildhallae Londoniensis*, ed. Henry T. Riley, Vol. II, Parts 1 and 2: *Liber Custumarum*, RS 12 (London, 1860). [8]

Robertson 1925   *The Laws of the Kings of England from Edmund to Henry I*, ed. and trans. Agnes J. Robertson (Cambridge, 1925). [8, 145]

Robertson 1939 (= 1956)   *Anglo-Saxon Charters*, ed. with trans. and notes by A. J. Robertson, Cambridge Studies in English Legal History (Cambridge, 1939); 2nd ed. [with same pagination] (1956). [Introduction, 61, 91, 141–2, 144, 146]

Robinson 1911   J. Armitage Robinson, *Gilbert Crispin Abbot of Westminster: A Study of the Abbey under Norman Rule*, Notes and Documents Relating to Westminster Abbey 3 (Cambridge, 1911). [66]

Rose-Troup 1914–15   Frances B. Rose-Troup, 'Exeter Cathedral Library', *DCNQ* 8 (1914–15), 208, no. 170. [91]

Rose-Troup 1926–7   F. B. Rose-Troup, 'The First Dedication of the Church of Exeter', *DCNQ* 14 (1926–7), 97 and 304. [103]

Rose-Troup 1928–9   F. B. Rose-Troup, 'Bishop Leofric's Burial Places', *DCNQ* 15 (1928–9), 107–8. [103]

Rose-Troup & Watkin 1930–1   F. B. Rose Troup and Hugh R. Watkin, 'Pedigree of the Family of Baldwin the Sheriff', *DCNQ* 16 (1930–1), 370–3 [96, 113]

Rose-Troup 1932   F. B. Rose-Troup, 'The Hereditary Sheriffs of Devon', *RTDA* 64 (1932), 397–413. [96]

Rose-Troup 1933   F. B. Rose-Troup, *The Consecration of the Norman Minster at Exeter* (n.p., n.d. [1933]). [94–5, 97–8, 100, 103]

Rose-Troup 1937   F. B. Rose-Troup, 'Exeter Manumissions and Quittances of the Eleventh and Twelfth Centuries', *RTDA* 69 (1937), 417–45. [93–140]

Ross 1964   *The Cartulary of Cirencester Abbey Gloucestershire*, ed. Charles D. Ross, 2 vols. (London, 1964). [4, 9]

Round 1892   John H. Round, *Geoffrey de Mandeville: A Study of the Anarchy* (London, 1892); rptd Burt Franklin: Research & Source Works Series 11 (New York, 1972). [8, 28]

Round 1894   J. H. Round, 'Londoners and the Chase', *The Athenaeum* no. 3479 (30 June 1894), 838. [1, 8, 23, 33, 145]

Round 1895 (= 1964)   J. H. Round, *Feudal England: Historical Studies on the Eleventh and Twelfth Centuries* (London, 1895); reset with new foreword by Frank M. Stenton (1964). [4, 9, 19, 142]

Round 1897   J. H. Round, 'An Old English Charter of William the Conqueror, 1068 (?)', *EHR* 12 (1897), 105–107. Cf. Stevenson 1897 below. [10]

Round 1899   J. H. Round, *The Commune of London and Other Studies* (London, 1899). [10]

Round 1900   J. H. Round, 'The Hidation of Northamptonshire', *EHR* 15 (1900), 78–86. [142]

Round 1901   J. H. Round, 'Domesday Survey', A *History of Worcestershire*, Vol. I, ed. John W. Willis-Bund and Herbert A. Doubleday, VCH (London, 1901), pp. 235–340. [15]

Round 1902   J. H. Round, 'Introduction to the Northamptonshire Domesday', *A History of the County of Northampton*, Vol. I, ed. William R. D. Adkins and Robert M. Serjeantson, VCH (London, 1902), pp. 257–98. [142]

Round 1904   J. H. Round, 'The Officers of Edward the Confessor', *EHR* 19 (1904), 90–2. [4, 9]

Round 1907   J. H. Round, 'The Chronology of Henry II.'s Charters', *Archaeological Journal* 64 (1907), 63–79. [54]

Rumble 1980   Alexander R. Rumble, 'The Structure and Reliability of the *Codex Wintoniensis* (British Museum Add. MS. 15350; the Cartulary of Winchester Cathedral Priory)', London Ph.D diss., 1980. [32]

Rumble 1982   Alexander R. Rumble, 'The Purposes of the Codex Wintoniensis', *Proceedings of the Battle Conference IV – 1981*, ed. R. Allen Brown (Woodbridge, 1982), pp. 153–66 and 224–32. [32]

Salter 1907   *Eynsham Cartulary*, ed. Herbert E. Salter, 2 vols., Oxford Historical Society 49 and 51 (Oxford, 1907–8). [41]

Sanders 1865   *Facsimiles of National Manuscripts from William the Conqueror to Queen Anne....*, Part I, ed. with trans. and notes [by William B. Sanders], Ordnance Survey (Southampton, 1865). [8, 23, 42, 54]

Sanders 1878   *Facsimiles of Anglo-Saxon Manuscripts*, photozincographed by A. C. Cooke with trans. by W. B. Sanders, 3 parts, Ordnance Survey (Southampton, 1878–84). [17, 48, 54]

Savage 1911   Ernest A. Savage, *Old English Libraries: The Making, Collection, and Use of Books During the Middle Ages* (London, 1911). [92]

Sawyer 1957   *Textus Roffensis: Rochester Cathedral Library Manuscript A.3.5*, ed. Peter H. Sawyer, 2 vols., Early English Manuscripts in Facsimile 7 and 11 (London, 1957–62). [Introduction, 25, 145]

Sawyer 1968   P. H. Sawyer, *Anglo-Saxon Charters: An Annotated List and Bibliography*, Royal Historical Society Guides and Handbooks 8 (London, 1968). [Introduction, 57]

Schipper 1897   *König Alfreds Uebersetzung von Bedas Kirchengeschichte*, ed. Jacob M. Schipper, Bibliothek der angelsächsischen Prosa 4 (Leipzig, 1897–9). [92]

Schlemilch 1914   Willy Schlemilch, *Beiträge zur Sprache und Orthographie Spätaltenglischer Sprachdenkmäler der Uebergangszeit (1000–1150)*, Studien zur Englischen Philologie, Heft 34 (Halle, 1914). [Introduction]

Schmid 1832 (= 1858)   *Die Gesetze der Angelsachsen*, ed. Reinhold Schmid, 2 vols. (Leipzig, 1832); 2nd ed. (1858). [145]

Schmitt 1938   *S. Anselmi Cantuariensis Archiepiscopi Opera Omnia*, ed. Francis S. Schmitt, 6 vols. (Edinburgh, 1938–61). [101]

Selden 1623   *Eadmeri Monachi Cantuariensis Historiæ Novorum Sive Sui Saeculi libri VI*, ed. John Selden (London, 1623). [145]

S. G. 1680   *The Royal Charter of Confirmation Granted by King Charles II. To the City of London*, trans. by S. G., Gent. (London, 1680). [8, 23]

Sharpe 1894   Reginald R. Sharpe, *London and the Kingdom: A History Derived Mainly from the Archives at Guildhall in the Custody of the Corporation of the City of London*, Vol. I (London, 1894). [8, 23]

Shelly 1921   Percy Van Dyke Shelly, *English and French in England 1066–1100* (Philadelphia, 1921). [1–2, **4**, **8**, 13–15, 18–21, 23–5, 29–31, 33, 39, 41, 78]

Simpson 1873   *Registrum Statutorum et Consuetudinum Ecclesiae Cathedralis Sancti Pauli Londinensis*, ed. William Sparrow Simpson (London, 1873). [27]

Somner 1640   William Somner, *The Antiquities of Canterbury. Or a Survey of That Ancient Citie, with the Suburbs, and Cathedrall....* (London, 1640); reissued under the title, *The Most Accurate History of the Ancient City, and Famous Cathedral of Canterbury* (1661); 2nd ed. reissued under the original title, rev. and enlarged by N. Battely (1703) = Battely 1703. [90]

Somner 1660 (= 1726)   William Somner, *A Treatise of Gavelkind* (London, 1660); 2nd ed. (1726). [47]

Stenton 1908   Frank M. Stenton, *William the Conqueror and the Rule of the Normans*, Heroes of the Nations (New York and London, 1908). [1, **4**, **8**, 10–13, 15, 17, 21, 24, 27, 38]

Stenton 1932 (= 1961)   M. Stenton, *The First Century of English Feudalism 1066–1166* (Oxford, 1932); 2nd ed. (1961). [16, **90**]

Stenton 1934   F. M. Stenton, *Norman London: An Essay*, Historical Association Leaflets 93–4 (London, 1934). [8]

Stenton 1943 (= 1947 = 1971)   F. M. Stenton, *Anglo-Saxon England*, The Oxford History of England 2 (Oxford, 1943); 2nd ed. (1947); 3rd ed. (1971). [142]

Stevenson 1896   William H. Stevenson, 'An Old-English Charter of William the Conqueror in Favour of St. Martin's-le-Grand, London, A.D. 1068', *EHR* 11 (1896), 731–44. [9–10, 47, 51, 64–5]

Stevenson 1897   Reply to J. H. Round, 'An Old English Charter of William the Conqueror, 1068 (?)', *EHR* 12 (1897), 107–10. [10]

Stokes 1870–72   Whitley Stokes, 'The Manumissions in the Bodmin Gospels', *Revue Celtique* 1 (1870–2), 332–45. [87–9]

Stoneman 1987   William P. Stoneman, 'Another Old English Note Signed "Coleman" ', *Medium Ævum* 56 (1987), 78–82. [Introduction]

Stow 1598 (= 1603)   John Stow, *A Svrvay of London. Contayning the Originall, Antiquity, Increase, Moderne estate, and description of that Citie, written in the yeare 1598*, imprinted by Iohn Wolfe (London, [1598]); imprinted by Iohn Windet (1603) = Kingsford 1908. [See also Strype 1720.] [8, 10, 27, 39]

Stratmann 1884   Franz H. Stratmann, 'Eine englische Urkunde von 1155', *Anglia* 7 (1884) 220–1. [51]

Strype 1720   John Stow, *A Survey of the Cities of London and Westminster:...Written at first in the Year MDXCVIII by John Stow....*, Now Lastly,

Corrected, Improved, and very much Enlarged...by John Strype, 2 vols. paginated in 6 books (London, 1720). [See also Stow 1598.] [8, 10, 27, 39]

Stubbs 1870 (= 1913)   *Select Charters and Other Illustrations of English Constitutional History from the Earliest Times to the Reign of Edward the First*, ed. William Stubbs (Oxford, 1870); 9th ed., rev. Henry W. C. Davis (1913). [8]

Stubbs 1874 (= 1897)   W. Stubbs, *The Constitutional History of England in Its Origin and Development*, 3 vols. (Oxford, 1874–8); Vol. I, 6th ed. (1897). [8]

Stubbs 1887   *Willelmi Malmesbiriensis Monachi de Gestis Regum Anglorum, libri quinque*, ed. W. Stubbs., 2 vols., RS 90 (London, 1887–9). [145]

Stubbs 1906   W. Stubbs, *Lectures on Early English History*, ed. Arthur Hassall (London, New York and Bombay, 1906). [145]

Surtees 1816   Robert Surtees, *The History and Antiquities of the County Palatine of Durham....*, 4 vols. (London, 1816–40). [64]

Tait 1928–9   J[ames] T[ait], Short Notice, *History* 13 (1928–9), 279–80. [Cf. Thomas 1927.] [8]

Tait 1929   J. Tait, 'The First Earl of Cornwall', *EHR* 44 (1929), 86. [17]

Tait 1936   J. Tait, *The Medieval English Borough: Studies on Its Origins and Constitutional History* (Manchester, 1936). [90]

Tanner 1695   Thomas Tanner, *Notitia Monastica or A Short History of the Religious Houses in England and Wales* (Oxford 1695). [10]

Tanner 1744 (= 1787)   T. Tanner, *Notitia Monastica; Or, An Account of All the Abbies, Priories, and Houses of Friers, Formerly in England and Wales....*, published by John Tanner (London, 1744); rptd with additions by James Nasmith (Cambridge, 1787). [58]

Tatton-Brown 1987   Timothy Tatton-Brown, *Canterbury in Domesday Book*, Canterbury Heritage Series 1 (Canterbury, 1987). [62]

Taylor 1905   C. S. Taylor, 'Banwell', *PSANHS* 51 (3rd ser., 11), pt 2 (1905), 31–76. [11]

Taylor 1925   John G. Taylor, *Our Lady of Batersey: The Story of Battersea Church and Parish Told from Original Sources* (London, 1925). [2]

Taylor 1931   J. G. Taylor, *The Parish Church of St. Mary the Virgin Battersea*, Notes on Churches and Abbeys 52 (London, 1931). [2]

Tengvik 1938   Gösta Tengvik, *Old English Bynames*, Nomina Germanica 4 (Uppsala, 1938). [Introduction, 56, 77, 94, 98, 106, 136, Index A and B]

Thomas 1736   William Thomas, A *Survey of the Cathedral-Church of Worcester; with an Account of the Bishops Thereof, from the Foundation of the See, to the Year 1660. Also an Appendix of Many Original Papers and Records, Never Before Printed* (London, 1736) [in three separately paginated sections]. [63, 78]

Thomas 1927   A. H. Thomas, Clerk to the Records, 'Report–Library Committee', London, Corporation of London, Common Council Papers 15 December 1927 [see *Minutes of the Proceedings of the Court of Common Council, 1927* (London, 1928), p. 416]. [8]

Thompson 1883   *Catalogue of a Selection from the Stowe Manuscripts Exhibited in the King's Library in the British Museum*, [ed. Edward Maunde Thompson] (London, 1883). [54]

Thorpe 1769   John Thorpe, *Registrum Roffense*…. (London, 1769). [25, 42, 49, 52, 55]

Thorpe 1840a   *Ancient Laws and Institutes of England*, ed. Benjamin Thorpe, RCP 28, Folio ed., HMSO (London, 1840). [145]

Thorpe 1840b   *Ibid.*, Octavo ed., 2 vols., HMSO (London, 1840). [145]

Thorpe 1865   Benjamin Thorpe, *Diplomatarium Anglicum Aevi Saxonici* (London, 1865). [14, 57, 68, 73–8, 86–9, 91, 93–114, 120–40, 144, 146–7]

Todd 1812   Henry J. Todd, *A Catalogue of the Archiepiscopal Manuscripts in the Library at Lambeth Palace: With an Account of the Archiepiscopal Register and Other Records There Preserved* (London, 1812); rptd (1965). [51, 54]

Traill & Mann 1901   Henry D. Traill and James S. Mann, *Social England*, Illustrated ed., 6 vols. (London, 1901–4). [8, 23]

Turner 1852   Sharon Turner, *The History of the Anglo-Saxons from the Earliest Period to the Norman Conquest*, 3 vols., 7th ed. (London, 1852). [The 1st ed. of 1799 does not contain relevant material.] [73–4, 79–82, 85, 94, 102, 135–7, 139–40]

Twysden 1652   Roger Twysden, *Historiae Anglicanae Scriptores X* (London, 1652). [145]

Urry 1955   William Urry, 'Early Rentals and Charters Relating to the Borough of Canterbury', London Ph.D. diss., 1955. [90]

Urry 1958 (= 1959)   W. Urry, 'The Normans in Canterbury', *Annales de Normandie* 8 (1958), 119–38 = *The Normans in Canterbury*, Canterbury Archaeological Society Occasional Papers 2 ([Canterbury], 1959). [90]

Urry 1967   W. Urry, *Canterbury under the Angevin Kings*, University of London Historical Studies 19 (London, 1967). [90]

Urry 1978   *City of Canterbury: The Chief Citizens of Canterbury; A List of Portreeves (Prefects, Prepositi) from A.D. 780 until c. 1100; of Prepositi (Bailiffs) from the 12th Century until 1448 and of Mayors from 1448 until 1978*, Compiled until the Close of the 14th Century by W. Urry…and Thereafter by Cyprian R. Bunce (Canterbury, n.d. [1978]). [90]

Von Feilitzen 1937   Olof von Feilitzen, *The Pre-Conquest Personal Names of Domesday Book*, Nomina Germanica 3 (Uppsala, 1937). [Introduction]

Wanley 1705   Humphrey Wanley, *Librorum Vett. Septentrionalium, qui in Angliae Bibliothecis extant, nec non multorum Vett. Codd. Septentrionalium alibi extantium Catalogus Historico-criticus*…. (*Antiquae Literaturae Septentrionalis Liber Alter*) (Oxford, 1705). [1, 3, 6, 17, 25, 29–30, 57, 63–4, 67, 70–86, 91–9, 101–15, 117, 120–34, 145–7]

Warner & Ellis 1903   *Facsimiles of Royal and Other Charters in the British Museum. Vol. 1. William I – Richard I*, ed. George F. Warner and Henry J. Ellis (London, 1903). [46, 48, 51]

Warner & Gilson 1921   George F. Warner & Julius P. Gilson, *Catalogue of Western Manuscripts in the Old Royal and King's Collections*, 4 vols. (London, 1921). [145]

Warren 1883   *The Leofric Missal*, ed. Frederick E. Warren (Oxford, 1883). [91–2, 135–40]

Weinbaum 1929   Martin Weinbaum, *Verfassungsgeschichte Londons 1066–1268*, Beihefte zur Vierteljahrschrift für Sozial- und Wirtschaftsgeschichte 15 (Stuttgart, 1929). [8, 10, 33]

West 1959   F. J. West, 'An Early Justiciar's Writ', *Speculum* 34 (1959), 631–5. [1]

Westlake 1919   Herbert F. Westlake, *The Parish Gilds of Mediaeval England* (London, 1919). [78, 90, 120–2, 124–34]

Wharton 1691   Henry Wharton, *Anglia Sacra sive Collectio Historiarum, partim antiquitus, partim recenter scriptarum, de Archiepiscopis et Episcopis Angliae a prima Fidei Christianae Susceptione ad Annum MDXL*, 2 vols. (London, 1691); rptd (Farnborough, 1969). [25, 147]

Whitelock 1930   *Anglo-Saxon Wills*, ed. and trans. Dorothy Whitelock, Cambridge Studies in English Legal History (Cambridge, 1930). [68]

Wightman 1962   W. E. Wightman, 'The Palatine Earldom of William fitz Osbern in Gloucestershire and Worcestershire (1066–1071)', *EHR* 77 (1962), 6–17. [15]

Wilkins 1721   *Leges Anglo-Saxonicae Ecclesiasticae & Civiles....*, ed. David Wilkins (London, 1721). [8, 145]

Williams 1986   Ann Williams, 'The Knights of Shaftesbury Abbey' *Anglo-Norman Studies* 8, Proceedings of the Battle Conference 1985, ed. R. Allen Brown (Woodbridge and Wolfboro, NH, 1986), pp. 214–37 + 5 tables. [143]

Witney 1976   K. P. Witney, *The Jutish Forest: A Study of the Weald of Kent from 450 to 1380 A.D.* (London, 1976). [62]

Woodbine 1943   George E. Woodbine, 'The Language of English Law', *Speculum* 18 (1943), 395–436. [8, 29]

Wright 1842   Thomas Wright, *Biographia Britannica Literaria; or Biography of Literary Characters of Great Britain and Ireland, Arranged in Chronological Order, Vol. 1: Anglo-Saxon Period* (London, 1842). [91]

Wright 1862   T. Wright, 'On Bishop Leofric's Library', *JBAA* 18 (1862), 220–4. [91]

Wrottesley 1898–1903 (= 1903)   George Wrottesley, 'A History of the Family of Wrottesley of Wrottesley, co. Stafford', Annual supplements to *The Genealogist*, n.s. 15–19 (1898–1903); rptd in *Collections for a History of Staffordshire Edited by The William Salt Archaeological Society*, n.s. 6, Part 2 (London, 1903). [69]

Wyon & Wyon 1887   Alfred B. Wyon, *The Great Seals of England: From the Earliest Period to the Present Time....*, completed and carried through the press by Allan Wyon (London, 1887). [46]

MANUSCRIPTS, SEALS AND PRINTED SOURCES

ABBREVIATIONS

Add.	Additional MS
Auct.	Auctarium MS
BL	British Library
Bodl.	Bodley MS
CCC	Corpus Christi College
D & C	Dean and Chapter Library
Harl.	Harleian MS
PRO	Public Record Office
Univ. Lib.	University Library

A. MANUSCRIPTS

Citations of Oxford MSS are followed by the relevant *Summary Catalogue* (Madan & Craster 1923) reference in parentheses.

Cambridge, CCC, 41 [s. xi^2] [92]

Cambridge, CCC, 96 [s. xv] [145]

Cambridge, CCC, 101 [s. xvi transcript of Oxford, Bodleian, Auct. D. 2. 16 (2719)] [91]

Cambridge, CCC, 111 [s. xi^2] (Davis 1958, 5, no. 23) [1, 30, 70–8]

Cambridge, CCC, 140 [s. xi^2–xii^1] [79–86]

Cambridge, CCC, 173 [s. xi^2] [22]

Cambridge, CCC, 183 [s. xi^2] [61]

Cambridge, Pembroke College, 299 [s. xviii transcript of London, PRO, Cartae Antiquae Rolls, 25–37] [27]

Cambridge, Trinity College, B. 11. 2 (241) [s. xi^2] [92]

Cambridge, Trinity College, R. 5. 33 (724) [s. xiii; printed in Hearne 1727, I, 1–122]. S. xiv version in B.M. Add. 22934 and s. xviii version in Oxford, Bodleian, Rawlinson B. 201. [58]

Cambridge, Trinity Hall, 1 [s. xv¹; printed in Hardwick 1858] (Davis 1958, no. 198). S. xviii transcript in B.M. Harl. 686. [6]

Cambridge, Univ. Lib., Ee. 5. 21, 'Liber Statutorum' [s. xv] (Davis 1958, 68, no. 605) [27]

Cambridge, Univ. Lib., Ff. 2. 33 [s. xiii²] (Davis 1958, 16, no. 117) [5, 18–20, 28]

Cambridge, Univ. Lib., Gg. 4. 4 [s. xv] (Davis 1958, 15, no. 109) [19, 28]

Cambridge, Univ. Lib., Ii. 2. 11 [s. xi²–xii¹] [92, 102]

Cambridge, Univ. Lib., Mm. 4. 19, 'Nigrum Registrum' [s. xii²] (Davis 1958, 16, no. 118) [19, 28]

Canterbury, D & C, Blore Collection 88 [s. xx] [46–8]

Canterbury, D & C, Blore Collection 90 [s. xx] [47, 51, 54]

Canterbury, D & C, Ch. Ant. C. 4 [22]

Canterbury, D & C, Ch. Ant. C. 7 + C. 48 (formerly separated) [47]

Canterbury, D & C, Ch. Ant. C. 9 [47]

Canterbury, D & C, Ch. Ant. C. 14 [54]

Canterbury, D & C, Ch. Ant. C. 17 [51]

Canterbury, D.& C, Ch. Ant. C. 18 [51]

Canterbury, D & C, Ch. Ant. C. 18A [54]

Canterbury, D & C, Ch. Ant. C. 20 [51]

Canterbury, D & C, Ch. Ant. C. 46 (*inspeximus* of Robert of Battle [*de Bello*], abbot of St Augustine's Abbey, Canterbury [A.D. 1224–53]) [50, 51]

Canterbury, D & C, Ch. Ant. C. 200 [54]

Canterbury, D & C, Ch. Ant. C. 204 [22, 51]

Canterbury, D & C, Ch. Ant. C. 1310 (Roll) [46, 50, 51]

Canterbury, D & C, Register A [s. xiii²] (Davis 1958, 21, no. 169) [22, 46, 48, 51, 54]

Canterbury, D & C, Register E [s. xiii ex.] (Davis 1958, 21, no. 168) [22, 48, 54]

Canterbury, D & C, Register I [s. xiii²] (Davis 1958, 21, no. 165) [22, 46–8, 54]

?Cheltenham, Phillipps 26641 (*olim* 2777) (present location untraced) [s. xiii] [Introduction, 145]

Durham, Prior's Kitchen, D & C Muniments, 2.1, Pontificalium no. 9 [s.xi/xii] [64]

Durham, Prior's Kitchen, D & C Muniments, 'Cartuarium Vetus' of the monastery of Durham [s. xiii¹] [64]

Durham, Prior's Kitchen, D & C Muniments, 'Cartuarium Secundum' of the monastery of Durham [s. xv¹] [64]

Durham, Prior's Kitchen, D & C Muniments, 'Cartuarium Quartum' of the monastery of Durham [s. xvi in.] [64]

Exeter, Cathedral, 2528 [17]

Exeter, Cathedral, 2570 [s. xv transcript of a lost s. xiii MS] [91]

Exeter, Cathedral, 3501 [s. xi²/xii¹] [Introduction, 91, 93–134]

Exeter, Devon Record Office, W 1258/D 84/3, 'Russell Cartulary' (formerly

Woburn Abbey, Duke of Bedford's Muniments, Table 3, Drawer A. 3) [s. xiii] (Davis 1958, 108, no. 947) [59]

London, BL, Add. 6159 [s. xiv] (Davis 1958, no. 167) [22, 51]

London, BL, Add. 9067 [transcript of Exeter, Cathedral, 3501 made in A.D. 1831 by Robert Chambers] [91, 93–134]

London, BL, Add. 9381, 'Bodmin Gospels' [s. xi/xii] [87–9]

London, BL, Add. 14847 (Davis 1958, 14, no. 96) [s. xiii ex.] [5, 18–20, 28]

London, BL, Add. 15350, 'Codex Wintoniensis' [s. xii med.] (Davis 1958, 120, no. 1042) [Introduction, 32, 144]

London, BL, Add. 29436 [s. xiii med.] (Davis 1958, 120, no. 1043) [31, 34–5, 45]

London, BL, Add. 29437 [s. xvii notes from cartularies of Kentish houses: fols. 6–29r Rochester, 29v–87v Christ Church, Canterbury, and 88–172 St Augustine's, Canterbury] [25, 49]

London, BL, Add. 38131 [s. xiv in.] [8]

London, BL, Add. 47680, 'Quadripartitus MS' (formerly Holkham, Earl of Leicester, MS 228) [c. A.D. 1230] [145]

London, BL, Add. 61901 (formerly Bradfer-Lawrence, H.L., MS 3) [s. xiv] (Davis 1958, 8, no. 49). Source of London, BL, Harley 560 and Cotton Otho C. xvi. [14]

London, BL, Campbell Charter VII. 1 [42]

London, BL, Campbell Charter XXI. 6 [47–8]

London, BL, Campbell Charter XXIX. 5 [46]

London, BL, Cotton Charter VII. 1 [46]

London, BL, Cotton Charter VIII. 15 [s. xiv^1] [32]

London, BL, Cotton Charter XI. 51 [63]

London, BL, Cotton Charter XVI. 31 [62]

London, BL, Cotton Augustus II [28]

London, BL, Cotton Claudius C. ix [s. xiii] [145]

London, BL, Cotton Claudius D. ii [s. xvi] [145]

London, BL, Cotton Claudius D. x [s. xiii/xiv, *temp.* Edw I] (Davis 1958, 23, no. 193) [6]

London, BL, Cotton Domitian x (Refoliated 26.6.85) [s. xiii] (Davis 1958, 93, no. 818) [25, 42, 49, 52, 55]

London, BL, Cotton Faustina A. iii [s. xiii/xiv, *temp.* Edw I] (Davis 1958, 116, no. 1011) [2, 12–13, 15, 21, 24, 38, 65]

London, BL, Cotton Faustina B. v [s. xiv^2] [25]

London, BL, Cotton Julius C. ii [A.D. 1586; transcript of Maidstone, Kent Archives Office, DRc/R1] [25, 145]

London, BL, Cotton Otho C. xvi [s. xvi/xvii incomplete transcript on fols. 65–102r of London, BL, Harl. 560] [14]

London, BL, Cotton Tiberius A. xiii, 'Heming's Cartulary' [s. xi ex. – xii med.; ed. Hearne 1723] (Davis 1958, 123, no. 1068). S. xvii transcript in Oxford,

Bodleian, Rawlinson B. 445; partial transcript (A.D. 1583 x) in Oxford, Bodleian, Dugdale 39. [3, 63, 67, 146–7]

London, BL, Cotton Tiberius C. xiii [s. xiii] [145]

London, BL, Cotton Titus A. xxvii [s. xiii in.] [145]

London, BL, Cotton Vespasian A. xxii [s. xiii] (Davis 1958, 93, no. 821) [25]

London, BL, Cotton Vespasian B. xv [s. xvi] [27, 41]

London, BL, Cotton Vespasian D. xvi [s. xvi] [8]

London, BL, Cotton Vitellius A. xiii [s. xiii] (Davis 1958, 26–7, no. 222) [7, 145]

London, BL, Cotton Vitellius D. vii [s. xvi] [22]

London, BL, Cotton Vitellius D. ix [s. xiii] (Davis 1958, 45, no. 392) [101]

London, BL, Hargrave 313 [s. xiii] [145]

London, BL, Harl. Charter, 111 B. 49 [51]

London, BL, Harl. 61 [xv in.] (Davis 1958, 100, no. 885) [143]

London, BL, Harl. 76 [s. xii] (Davis 1958, 16, no. 122) [28]

London, BL, Harl. 84 [s. xvii transcript of London, PRO, Cartae Antiquae Rolls 1–24] [27]

London, BL, Harl. 85 [c. A.D. 1644 x 1645; transcript of London, PRO, Cartae Antiquae Rolls 25–41] [27]

London, BL, Harl. 258 [s. xvii transcript of Cambridge, CCC 101] [91]

London, BL, Harl. 261 [s. xiii] [145]

London, BL, Harl. 311 [s. xvii partial transcript by Simon D'Ewes of London, PRO, 'Liber Rubeus Scaccarii'] [145]

London, BL, Harl. 560 [s. xvi/xvii incomplete copy apparently derived from London, BL, Add. 61901] [14]

London, BL, Harl. 596 [s. xvii partial transcript of Maidstone, Kent County Archives Office, DRc/R1] [145]

London, BL, Harl. 686 [s. ?xviii transcript of Cambridge, Trinity Hall, 1] [6]

London, BL, Harl. 743 [s. xiv; temp. Edw III] (Davis 1958, 14, no. 97) [19]

London, BL, Harl. 2058 [s. xvi] [8, 23]

London, BL, Harl. 2961 [92]

London, BL, Harl. 4660 [s. xvii] [147]

London, BL, Harl. 6523 [s. xviii partial transcript of Maidstone, Kent County Archives Office, DRc/R1] [145]

London, BL, Harl. 6968 [incomplete s. xvii transcript of Wells, D & C, 'Liber Albus, pt I'] [57]

London, BL, Lansdowne 170 [s. xvii transcript of London, Corporation of London Records Office, 'Liber Fleetwood'] [10]

London, BL, Lansdowne 966 [s. xvii] [17]

London, BL, Royal 11 B. II [s. xii/xiii] [145]

London, BL, Royal 13 A. XVIII [s. xiv^1] [145]

London, BL, Sloane 754 [s. xvi] [8, 23]

London, BL, Stowe Charter 43 [48]

London, BL, Stowe Charter 44 [54]

London, BL, Stowe 940 [A.D. 1712; transcript of Maidstone, Kent Archives Office, DRc/R1] [25]

London, College of Arms, Young 72 [s. xv² version of London, Westminster Abbey, 'Liber Niger Quaternus', with some slight rearrangement] (Davis 1958, 117, no. 1016) [12]

London, Corporation of London, Records Office, 128.12 [s. xvi¹, *temp.* Hen VIII] [8, 23]

London, Corporation of London, Records Office, Ch 1a [Introduction, 8]

London, Corporation of London, Records Office, Ch 1b [s. xiv¹] [8]

London, Corporation of London, Records Office, Ch 2 [23]

London, Corporation of London, Records Office, Ch. 50 [*inspeximus* of 25 May 1400]. Chancery enrolment is London, PRO, Charter Rolls, 1 Hen IV, pt 3. [8, 23]

London, Corporation of London, Records Office, Ch 51 [*inspeximus* of 12 July 1414]. Chancery enrolment is London, PRO, Charter Rolls, 2 Hen V, pt 2. [8, 23]

London, Corporation of London, Records Office, Ch 53 [*inspeximus* of 7 October 1428]. Chancery enrolment is London, PRO, Charter Rolls, 5–20 Hen VI. [8, 23]

London, Corporation of London, Records Office, Ch 58 [*inspeximus* of 25 March 1462]. Chancery enrolment is London, PRO, Patent Rolls, 2 Edw IV, pt 5. [8, 23]

London, Corporation of London, Records Office, Ch 68 [*inspeximus* of 23 July 1505]. Chancery enrolment is London, PRO, Confirmation Rolls, 20 Hen VII. [8, 23]

London, Corporation of London, Records Office, Ch 70 [*inspeximus* of 5 Hen VIII, 12 July 1513] [8, 23]

London, Corporation of London, Records Office, Ch 76 [*inspeximus* of 21 February 1548]. Chancery enrolment is London, PRO, Confirmation Rolls, 2 Edw VI, pt 3. [8, 23]

London, Corporation of London, Records Office, Ch 80 [*inspeximus* of 1 Mary, 1 March 1554] [8, 23]

London, Corporation of London, Records Office, Ch 82 [*inspeximus* of 9 May 1562]. Chancery enrolment is London, PRO, Confirmation Rolls, 4 Eliz I, pt 2. [8, 23]

London, Corporation of London, Records Office, Ch 90 [*inspeximus* of 14 Chas I, 18 October 1638] [8, 23]

London, Corporation of London, Records Office, Ch 96 [*inspeximus* of 15 Chas II, 24 June 1663] [8, 23]

London, Corporation of London, Records Office, ChT 1 [Charters in English Wm I – Edw VI (1067–1552), compiled by Robert Smith in 1582] [8, 23]

London, Corporation of London, Records Office, ChT 2 [s. xvii transcript of charters in English Wm I – Edw VI (1067–1552) and copy of docket of

charter 14 Chas I; apparently transcript of London, Corporation of London,
Records Office ChT 1] [8, 23]

London, Corporation of London, Records Office, ChT 3 [s. xvii transcript of
charters Wm I – 50 Edw III] [8, 23]

London, Corporation of London, Records Office, ChT 4 [s. xvii translation of
London, Corporation of London, Records Office, Ch 90] [8, 23]

London, Corporation of London, Records Office, ChT 5 [s. xvii transcript of
London, Corporation of London, Records Office, Ch 90] [8, 23]

London, Corporation of London, Records Office, ChT 6 [s. xvii transcript of
London, Corporation of London, Records Office, Ch 90] [8, 23]

London, Corporation of London, Records Office, ChT 10 ['Cartularium Londinense Willielmus I – Edwardus III' compiled by T. D. Hardy in 1833–4]
[Introduction, 8, 23]

London, Corporation of London, Records Office, ChT 11 ['The Charters of
London William I – Edward III', transcribed by T. D. Hardy in 1833–4]
[Introduction, 8, 23]

London, Corporation of London, Records Office, ChT 12 ['The Charters of
London William I – Edward III', transcribed by T. D. Hardy in 1833–4]
[Introduction, 8, 23]

London, Corporation of London, Records Office, 'Liber Custumarum' (Cust 6)
[c. A.D. 1324] [8]

London, Corporation of London, 'Liber Fleetwood' (Cust 11) [A.D. 1576; transcript of London, Westminster Abbey, Muniment Book 5]. S. xvii transcript
in London, BL, Lansdowne 170. [10]

London, Corporation of London, Records Office, 'Liber Horn' (Cust 2) [A.D.
1311] [8]

London, Corporation of London, Records Office, 'Liber Memorandorum'
(Cust 3) [A.D. 1298] [8]

London, Guildhall Library, MS 25, 272, 'Carte Libertatum Ecclesie Sci. Pauli'
(formerly London, St Paul's, A/69) [s. xiii^2] (Davis 1958, 67–8, no. 598) [27,
36–7, 39, 43]

London, Guildhall Library, MS 25, 501, 'Liber A sive Pilosus' (*olim* London, St
Paul's, W.D. 1) [ff. 1–75 written A.D. 1241; ff. 76–144 written 1298x1340]
(Davis 1958, 67, no. 597) [27, 36–7, 39, 43]

London, Guildhall Library, MS 25, 504, 'Liber L' (*olim* London, St Paul's, W.D.
4) (Davis 1968, 67, no. 596) [s. xiii] [27]

London, Guildhall Library, MS 25, 516, 'Liber I' (*olim* London, St Paul's, W.D.
16) [A.D. ?1299] [141]

London, Guildhall Library, MS 25, 520, 'Statuta Minora' (*olim* London, St
Paul's, W.D. 20) [s. xv] [27]

London, Lambeth Palace, Cart. Misc. X/109 [48]

London, Lambeth Palace, Cart. Misc. XI/1 [46]

London, Lambeth Palace, Cart. Misc. XI/2 [54]

London, Lambeth Palace, Cart. Misc. XI/3 [51]

London, Lambeth Palace, Cart. Misc. XII/32 [*inspeximus* of Hen VI] [46, 54]

London, Lambeth Palace, Cart. Misc. XII/33 [*inspeximus* of Edw IV, 15 April 1463] [46, 50, 54]

London, Lambeth Palace, Cart. Misc. XII/34 [*inspeximus* of Hen VIII, 24 Feb 1510] [46, 50, 54]

London, Lambeth Palace, 873 [51]

London, Lambeth Palace, 1212 [xiii/xiv] [33, 44, 46, 50, 51, 54]

London, PRO, C 52 (Cartae Antiquae Rolls) [s. xiii]

London, PRO, Cartae Antiquae, Roll 1 (*olim* A. 3) [partially printed in Landon 1939] [27]

London, PRO, Cartae Antiquae, Roll 6 (*olim* F) [partially printed in Landon 1939] [51]

London, PRO, Cartae Antiquae, Roll 9 (*olim* I) [partially printed in Landon 1939] [6]

London, PRO, Cartae Antiquae, Roll 15 (*olim* P) [19]

London, PRO, Cartae Antiquae, Roll 19 (*olim* T) [51]

London, PRO, Cartae Antiquae, Roll 26 (*olim* BB. 9) [27]

London, PRO, Cartae Antiquae, Roll 27 (*olim* CC. 14) [27]

London, PRO, C 53 (Charter Rolls)

London, PRO, Charter Rolls, 50 Hen III (damaged) (C 53/55) [42]

London, PRO, Charter Rolls, 3 Edw I (C 53/63) [42, 49, 52, 55]

London, PRO, Charter Rolls, 2 Edw II (C 53/95) [10]

London, PRO, Charter Rolls, 4 Edw II (C 53/97) [14]

London, PRO, Charter Rolls, 8 Edw II (C 53/101) [26]

London, PRO, Charter Rolls, 9 Edw II (C 53/102) [27]

London, PRO, Charter Rolls, 10 Edw II (C 53/103) [31]

London, PRO, Charter Rolls, 4 Edw III (C 53/117) [14]

London, PRO, Charter Rolls, 9 Edw III (C 53/122) [31, 42, 46, 49–50, 52, 54–5]

London, PRO, Charter Rolls, 10 Edw III (C 53/123) [42, 49, 52, 55]

London, PRO, Charter Rolls, 12 Edw III (C 53/125) [27]

London, PRO, Charter Rolls, 17 Edw III (C 53/130) [10]

London, PRO, Charter Rolls, 1 Ric II (C 53/155) [10, 27]

London, PRO, Charter Rolls, 4 Ric II (C 53/158) [31]

London, PRO, Charter Rolls, 12 Ric II (C 53/162) [27]

London, PRO, Charter Rolls, 1 Hen IV, pt 1 (C 53/168) [46, 50, 54]

London, PRO, Charter Rolls, 1 Hen IV, pt 3 (C 53/170) [8, 23]

London, PRO, Charter Rolls, 1 Hen V, pt 1 (C 53/180) [14]

London, PRO, Charter Rolls, 1 Hen V, pt 3 (C 53/182) [27, 46, 50, 54]

London, PRO, Charter Rolls, 2 Hen V, pt 2 (C 53/184) [8, 23]

London, PRO, Charter Rolls, 5–20 Hen VI (C 53/187) [10, 27]

London, PRO, Charter Rolls, 2–4 Edw IV (C 53/193) [46, 50, 54]

London, PRO, C 56 (Confirmation Rolls)

London, PRO, Confirmation Rolls, 1 Ric III, pt 3 (C 56/3) [8, 23]

London, PRO, Confirmation Rolls, 2 Ric III, pt 2 (C 56/5) [27]
London, PRO, Confirmation Rolls, 2 Hen VII, pt 2 (C 56/11) [27]
London, PRO, Confirmation Rolls, 3 Hen VII, pt 3 (C 56/16) [27]
London, PRO, Confirmation Rolls, 4 Hen VII, pt 1 (C 56/19) [22, 46–8, 51, 54]
London, PRO, Confirmation Rolls, 5 Hen VII (C 56/22) [10]
London, PRO, Confirmation Rolls, 6–10 Hen VII (C 56/23) [26]
London, PRO, Confirmation Rolls, 20 Hen VII (C 56/24) [8, 23]
London, PRO, Confirmation Rolls, 1 Hen VIII, pt 2 (C 56/26) [14]
London, PRO, Confirmation Rolls, 1 Hen VIII, pt 3 (C 56/27) [22, 46–8, 51, 54]
London, PRO, Confirmation Rolls, 1 Hen VIII, pt 6 (C 56/30) [27]
London, PRO, Confirmation Rolls, 1 Hen VIII, pt 7 (C 56/31) [27]
London, PRO, Confirmation Rolls, 1 Hen VIII, pt 8 (C56/32) [42, 49]
London, PRO, Confirmation Rolls, 2 Edw VI, pt 3 (C 56/63) [8, 23]
London, PRO, Confirmation Rolls, 3 & 4 Phil & M, pt 1 (C 56/75) [14]
London, PRO, Confirmation Rolls, 2 Eliz I, pt 2 (C 56/84) [27]
London, PRO, Confirmation Rolls, 4 Eliz I, pt 2 (C 56/89) [8, 23]
London, PRO, Confirmation Rolls, 3 Jas I, pt 3 (C 56/106) [27]
London, PRO, Exchequer KR, Misc. Book 27 [6]
London, PRO, Exchequer Transcripts, no. 4 [untraced] [Introduction, 31]
London, PRO, Hilary recorda rotulet 28 (22 Hen VI) (E 368/216) [27]
London, PRO, 'Liber Rubeus Scaccarii' [s. xiii] [145]
London, PRO, C 66 (Patent Rolls).
London, PRO, Patent Rolls, 1 Ric II, pt 2 (C 66/298) [46, 50, 54]
London, PRO, Patent Rolls, 1 Ric II, pt 3 (C 66/299) [14]
London, PRO, Patent Rolls, 2 Hen IV, pt 2 (C 66/363) [14, 27]
London, PRO, Patent Rolls, 1 Hen V, pt 4 (C 66/392) [27]
London, PRO, Patent Rolls, 1 Hen VI, pt 3 (C 66/409) [10]
London, PRO, Patent Rolls, 2 Hen VI, pt 2 (C 66/413) [42, 49, 51–2, 55]
London, PRO, Patent Rolls, 2 Hen VI, pt 3 (C 66/414) [27, 46, 50, 54]
London, PRO, Patent Rolls, 6 Hen VI, pt 2 (C 66/423) [14]
London, PRO, Patent Rolls, 7 Hen VI, pt 2 (C 66/425) [8, 23]
London, PRO, Patent Rolls, 12 Hen VI, pt 2 (C 66/436) [22, 46–8, 51, 54]
London, PRO, Patent Rolls, 20 Hen VI, pt 4 (C 66/454) [14]
London, PRO, Patent Rolls, 2 Edw IV, pt 5 (C 66/503) [8, 23]
London, PRO, Patent Rolls, 8 Edw IV, pt 1 (C 66/521) [10]
London, PRO, Patent Rolls, 12 Edw IV, pt 2 (C 66/530) [42, 49, 52, 55]
London, PRO, Patent Rolls, 2 Hen VII, pt 2 (C 66/566) [10]
London, Society of Antiquaries, 60, 'Liber Niger' [s. xii med.] (Davis 1958, 86, no. 754). S. xviii transcript in London, Society of Antiquaries, 131. [68, 142]
London, Society of Antiquaries, 131 [s. xviii transcript of London, Society of Antiquaries, 60] [68, 142]
London, Society of Antiquaries, 177 [s. xviii transcript of Maidstone, Kent Archives Office, DRc/R1, 119–234r] [25, 145]

London, Westminster Abbey, Muniment Book 5, 'Cartulary of St Martin's-le-Grand' [s. xv, *temp.* Hen VI] (Davis 1958, 69, no. 615). Transcript (A.D. 1576) in London, Corporation of London, Records Office, 'Liber Fleetwood' and s. xvii transcript in London, BL, Lansdowne 170. [10]

London, Westminster Abbey, Muniment Book 11, 'Westminster Domesday' [s. xiv, after A.D. 1308] (Davis 1958, 116, no. 1013) [12–13, 15, 21, 24, 38, 66]

Maidstone, Kent County Archives Office, DRb/Ar 1/17 (*olim* DRc/R9), 'Registrum Spiritualium' [s. xvii] [55]

Maidstone, Kent County Archives Office, DRb/Ar 2 (*olim* DRc/R3), 'Registrum Temporalium' [s. xiv] (Davis 1958, 93, no. 820) [25, 42, 49, 52, 55]

Maidstone, Kent County Archives Office, DRc/R1, 'Textus Roffensis' [s. xii^1] (Davis 1958, 92–3, no. 817; Ker 1957, 443–7, no. 373; facsimile Sawyer 1957; partially printed in Hearne 1720). MS transcripts in London, BL, Cotton Julius ii (A.D. 1586), Harl. 596 (s. xviii) and Harl. 6523 (s. xvii), London, BL, Stowe 940 (A.D. 1712), London, Society of Antiquaries, 177, 1–110r (s. xviii) and Oxford, Bodleian, Gough Kent 1 (17947) (A.D. 1632). [Introduction, 25, 42, 145]

Maidstone, Kent County Archives Office, DRc/T51 [49]

Maidstone, Kent County Archives Office, DRc/T53 [*inspeximus* of Hen III, *c.* A.D. 1265] [52]

Maidstone, Kent County Archives Office, DRc/T58 [*c.* A.D. 1265] [40, 53, 60]

Maidstone, Kent County Archives Office, DRc/T60 [*inspeximus* of Hen III, *c.* A.D. 1265] [42, 49, 52, 55]

Maidstone, Kent County Archives Office, DRc/T65 [*inspeximus* of Edw IV, A.D. 1475] [42, 49, 52, 55]

Maidstone, Kent County Archives Office, DRc/T66 [*inspeximus* of Hen VII, A.D. 1486] [42, 49, 52, 55]

Manchester, John Rylands, 420 [s. xii] [145]

Northampton, Northamptonshire Record Office, F[inch] H[atton] 170, 'Sir Christopher Hatton's Book of Seals' [A.D. 1640 x 1641] [62]

Oxford, Bodleian, Auct. D. 2. 16 (2719) [s. xi^2] [91–2]

Oxford, Bodleian, Auct. F. 1. 15 (2455) [s. xi^2] [92]

Oxford, Bodleian, Auct. F. 3. 6 (2666) [s. xi^2] [92]

Oxford, Bodleian, Bodl. 297 (2468) [s. xii] [28]

Oxford, Bodleian, Bodl. 579 (2675), 'Leofric Missal' [s. xi^2] (Ker 1957, 378–9, no. 315; Drage 1978, 71–144) [92, 135–40]

Oxford, Bodleian, Bodl. 708 (2609) [s. xi/xii] [92]

Oxford, Bodleian, Dep. c. 392 (*olim* Northleach, Stowell Park, Lord Vestey, 'Registrum A'), 'Cirencester Cartulary' [s. xiii med.] (Davis 1958, 30, no. 255) [4, 9]

Oxford, Bodleian, Dugdale 39 (6527) [A.D. 1583 x ; partial transcript of London, Cotton Tiberius A. xiii] [3, 63]

Oxford, Bodleian, Gough Kent 1 (17947; *olim* 'Dering MS') [transcript made in

A.D. 1632 by Edward Dering of Maidstone, Kent County Archives Office, DRc/R1] [25, 145]

Oxford, Bodleian, Hatton 54 (4072) [s. xiv¹] [145]

Oxford, Bodleian, Rawlinson B. 445 (*olim* 443) (15474) [s. xvii copy of London, BL, Cotton Tiberius A. xiii] [3, 63, 67]

Oxford, Bodleian, Tanner 223 (10049) (Davis 1958, 20, no. 160) [s. xvi¹, *temp.* Hen VIII; appears to have been copied in revised sequence from London, Lambeth Palace, 1212] [46, 50, 54]

Oxford, Christ Church, Chapter Library, 'Eynsham Cartulary' [s. xii²] (Davis 1958, 46, no. 399; printed Salter 1910) [41]

Wells, D & C, 'Liber Albus I' (*olim* 'Registrum I') [s. xiii med.] (Davis 1958, 115, no. 1003). Partial transcript in London, BL, Harl. 6968. [29, 57]

Wells, D & C, 'Liber Albus II' (*olim* 'Registrum III') [s. xiv/xv] (Davis 1958, 115–6, no. 1006) [11, 56]

Worcester, Cathedral, Muniments, A. 2, 'Registrum Prioratus' [s. xiv¹] (Davis 1958, 124, no. 1077; printed in Hale 1865) [63]

Worcester Cathedral, Muniments, A. 4, 'Registrum I' [s. xiii med.] (Davis 1958, 123, no. 1070) [63]

Worcester, Cathedral, Muniments, B. 1680 [63]

York, Borthwick Institute, 'Magnum Registrum Album, pt I' [s. xiv, *temp.* Edw III] (Davis 1958, 126, no. 1087) [16, 148]

B. SEALS

London, British Museum, Seal LXXVII. 6 [63]

London, Society of Antiquaries, Seal Impression C. 31 (Wulfstan) [63]

C. PRINTED SOURCES

Eyton 1881 [69]

Hickes 1703 [33, 147]

Parker 1572 [44]

Pole 1791 [59]

Somner 1640 [90]

Wrottesley 1898–9 [69]

TEXTS

ROYAL CHARTERS

King William I

1

Christmas 1066 x March (possibly x December) 1067. Writ of King William (*Vuillelm*) I and William (*Willelm*), earl (identified as William [fitz Osbern, earl of Hereford,] by *Regesta* I but more probably the vernacular equivalent of *Willelmus dux Normannorum*; see West 1959), to Giso (*Gyso*), bishop (of Wells), Eadnoth (*Eadnoð*) the Staller, Tofi, sheriff (of Somerset), and all the thegns of Somerset (*on Sumerseatanscire*) declaring that he has granted to Wulfweald (*Wulfwolde*), abbot (of Bath and Chertsey), the land at Charlcombe (*Ceorlecumbæ*), (Somerset), for St Peter's Abbey (*mynstre*), Bath (*on Baðan*).
MS: Cambridge, CCC, 111, p. 94 (s. xii^2)
Printed: Hunt 1893, 36, no. 31; West 1959, 631.
Translated: EHD II, 461, no. 33.
References: Wanley 1705, 150; Round 1895, 430 n. 19 (= 1964, 329 n. 19); Stenton 1908, 415–16; James 1909–12, 230, no. 37; *Regesta* I, 3, no. 7; Shelly 1921, 82; Morris 1927, 43 (on Tofi) and 44 n. 25 (*contra Regesta* I, 3, no. 7); West 1959, 631–5; Hoad 1975, 323; Healey and Venezky 1980, 70, no. B15.1.166; Green 1983, 131; Keynes 1988, 211 and n. 149 and 217 n. 192.

2

A.D. 1066 x 1067. Writ of King William (*Willem*) I to Stigand (*Stigan*), archbishop (of Canterbury), Earl Eustace (*Eustacies*) (II, Count of Boulogne), and all his thegns in Surrey (*on Surreye*) declaring that he has granted Battersea (*at Batericheseye*), (Surrey), and Pyrford (*Piriforð*), (Surrey), to St Peter's (Abbey), Westminster (*into Westminstre*), as fully as Harold did on the day he was alive and dead.
MS: London, BL, Cotton Faustina A. iii, 112v (s. xiii/xiv, *temp.* Edw I)
Printed: *Monasticon* I, 301, no. XXXV; Freeman 1867, V, 793 *ex ?Monasticon*; Browning & Kirk 1890–1, 225; Neufeldt 1907, 38, no. 29.
References: Freeman 1867, V, 793; Browning & Kirk 1890–1, 225–35 (on the manor of Battersea); *Regesta* I, 13, no. 45; Shelly 1921, 83; Taylor 1925, 9–20 and map (bounds); Taylor 1931, 5; Hoad 1975, 322; Healey & Venezky 1980, 69, no. B15.1.184; Garnett 1986a, 99–100 and 101; Keynes 1988, 217 n. 192; Mason 1988, 27, no. 6.
Note: Both the reference to Harold and to Eustace, who led an uprising against William at Dover in 1067, make it likely that this was issued early in William's reign.

3

A.D. 1067. Diploma of King William I granting to Wulfstan, bishop of Worcester (*Wlstano, Uuigornensi episcopo*), two hides of land at *Cullaclife* (later Cookley Wood, near Kingsford in the manor of Wolverley, Worcs.) for the use of the monks of St Mary's Church (*ecclesie*), Worcester. Witnesses: Mathilda the queen; Ealdræd (*Aldredus*), archbishop (of York); Odo, bishop (of Bayeux); Wulfstan (*Wlstanus*), bishop (of Worcester); William (fitz Osbern), *dux* (earl of Hereford); Roger (*Rocgerus*) (of Montgomery), *dux* (earl of Shrewsbury); Richard (son of) Scrob; Urse (*Urs*) (d'Abbetot), *minister* (sheriff of Worcester); Osbern (*Osebeam*), *minister*; Robert d'Oyly (*Rodbeard Oli*) (Ouilly-le-Basset, Calvados). (All readings from MS 1.) *Latin charter with English bounds.*

MSS: 1.   London, BL, Cotton Tiberius A. xiii, 185 (*olim* 182) (bounds on
                  185v) (s. xi²)
            2.   Oxford, Bodleian, Dugdale 39 (6527), 119r (abstract of MS 1; no
                  English) (A.D. 1583 x)
            3.   Oxford, Bodleian, Rawlinson B. 445 (*olim* 443) (15474), 294r–295r
                  (s. xvii)

Printed: Hearne 1723, II, 413–5 *ex* MS 1.

References: Wanley 1705, 258, no. CXXXI *ex* MS 1; *Regesta* I, 3, no. 10 (for an addendum see *Regesta* II, 390); Morris 1927, 48 n. 40 (on Urse); Healey and Venezky 1980, 70, no. B15.8.645; Green 1983, 135.

4

A.D. 1067. Writ of King William (*Uyllelm*) I to Herman (*Hereman*), bishop (of Sherborne), Wulfstan (*Wulston*), bishop (of Worcester), Earl Eustace (II, Count of Boulogne), Eadric (*Eadrich*), Beorhtric (*Bristrich*), and all his thegns of Wiltshire (*Wylton'shyre*) and Gloucestershire (*Glouc'shyr'*) declaring that he has granted to his priest, Regenbald (*Reinbold*), land at Eisey (*æt Esi*) and Latton (*æt Latto'*), (Wilts.), with legal rights as fully as in King Harold's time (*Harald kinge…on dæge*).

MS: Oxford, Bodleian, Dep. c. 392, p. 26 (*olim* 6v; *recte* 13v) (s. xiii med.)

Printed: Phillipps 1836, 256; Round 1895, 422 (= 1964, 323) *ex* Phillipps; Ross 1964, I, 20, no. 26.

Translated: Baddeley 1924, 98 no. 2; EHD II, 461–2, no. 35.

References: Phillipps 1836, 255; Ellis 1879–80, 118–20 (on Regenbald); *DNB* XVI, 862, s.v. 'Regenbald'; Round 1895, 331 and 421–30 (= 1964, 257 and 323–9) (on Regenbald); Round 1904, 92 (on Regenbald); Stenton 1908, 228 and n. 1; *Regesta* I, v (on Regenbald) and 3, no. 9 (for a correction see *Regesta* II, 390); Shelly 1921, 82 and 83–4; Baddeley 1924, 89–90 and 97–8 (questions authenticity); Douglas 1932, xciii n. 1; Darlington 1933, 17 n. 6; Harmer 1952, 59–60, 212, 570 (on Regenbald); Douglas 1964, 292–3; Ross 1964, I, 20–1; Galbraith 1974, 176, 178–9 (on Regenbald); Hoad 1975, 322; Evans 1976, 46–59 (on Regenbald); Campbell 1979, 130–1 (= 1986, 149–50) (on Regenbald); Healey & Venezky 1980, 71, no. B15.1.167; Garnett 1986a, 99; Keynes 1988, 195–222, esp. p. 211 and n. 152, 217 n. 192 and 220 n. 216.

5

c. A.D. 1067 (*Regesta* I; Douglas 1932, 50: 1066 x 1087, 'probably early in the reign'). Writ of King William (*William*) I to his bishops, earls and thegns where

Baldwin (*Baldewyne*), abbot (of Bury St Edmunds), has land declaring that he is worthy of his abbacy and rights as granted by his kinsman, King Edward (1 *Eadward*; 2 *Eddward*).
MSS:　1.　Cambridge, Univ. Lib., Ff. 2. 33, 27v–28r (s. xiii^2)
　　　　2.　London, BL, Add. 14847, 38r (s. xiii)
Printed:　*Regesta* I, 118, no. I *ex* MS 2; Douglas 1932, 50, no. 6 *ex* MS 1.
References:　Hardwick 1856–67, II, 365, no. 147; *DNB* I, 950–1 (on Baldwin); *Regesta* I, 4, no. 12 (for addenda see *Regesta* II, 390); Douglas 1932, xxx and n. 1; Hoad 1975, 322; Healey & Venezky 1980, 68, no. B15.1.168; Garnett 1986a, 107 n. 116; Keynes 1988, 217 n. 192.

6

c. A.D. 1067. Writ of King William (1 *Willelm*, 4 *Williem*) I to his bishops, earls and thegns, French and English (1 *Frencisce 7 Englisce*), in those shires where St Augustine's (Abbey, Canterbury,) has land declaring that he has granted to St Augustine's and its congregation various rights just as his kinsman, King Edward (1 *Eadwowd*, 4 *Eadward*), did earlier. (All readings from MSS 1 and 4.)
Latin and English versions.
MSS:　1.　Cambridge, Trinity Hall, 1, 78r (*olim* 64r) (s. xv)
　　　　2.　London, BL, Cotton Claudius D. x, 57r (s. xiii/xiv, *temp.* Edw I; Latin version only)
　　　　3.　London, BL, Harl. 686, 207–208r (s. xvii; transcript of MS 1)
　　　　4.　London, PRO, Cartae Antiquae, Roll 9 (*olim* I), m. 1, no. 13 (English version only)
　　　　5.　London, PRO, Exch. KR, Misc. Book 27, 147 (*olim* 151) (Latin version only)
Printed:　Hickes 1703, I, XV *ex* MS 1; Hardwick 1858, 347 *ex* MS 1.
References:　Wanley 1705, 172 *ex* MS 1; Hart 1868, 32 *ex* MS 4; James 1907, 1–4 *ex* MS 1; Dale 1911, 265, 271 and 273–4 *ex* MS 1; *Regesta* I, 4, no. 13; Landon 1939, 131, no. 265 *ex* MS 4; Douglas 1964, 258 and n. 4; Hoad 1975, 322; Crawley 1976, 62 *ex* MS 1; Healey & Venezky 1980, 70, B15.1.169; Keynes 1988, 217 n. 192.

7

c. A.D. 1067. Writ of King William (*Willem*) I to his bishops, earls, sheriffs and thegns in the shires where Wulfweald (*Wlwold*), abbot (of Chertsey), has land and men, declaring he is worthy of his land as he formerly possessed it under King Edward (*on Eaduuardes daghe kinges*) and that he is to possess the rights he formerly had.
MS:　London, BL, Cotton Vitellius A. xiii, 53v (*olim* 52v) (s. xiii)
Printed:　*Monasticon* I, 431, no. X.
References:　*Regesta* I, 4, no. 14; Douglas 1964, 258 and n. 4; Hoad 1975, 322; Healey & Venezky 1980, 69, no. B15.1.170; Garnett 1986a, 101 n. 68; Keynes 1988, 217 n. 192.

8

A.D. 1067. Writ of King William (*Willelm*) I to William (*Willelm*), bishop (of London), Geoffrey (*Gosfregð*), the portreeve, and all the burghers of London (*burhwaru binnan Londone*), French and English (*Frencisce 7 Englisce*), declaring that all the laws should stand as they did in King Edward's day (*on Eadwerdes dæge kynges*). (All readings from MS 1.) *English and (later) Latin versions.*

MSS:
1. London, Corporation of London, Records Office, Ch 1a (English version) (original) (Sanders 1865, no. I; Sharpe 1894, Frontispiece; Trail & Mann 1901, I, 521 (1); Besant 1908, 252; Stenton 1908, pl. opp. 230; Bishop & Chaplais 1957, pl. XIV)

2. London, BL, Add. 38131, 85v (English with translation of A.D. 1314 into Middle English and Latin) (s. xiv)

3. London, BL, Cotton Vespasian D. xvi, 57r (English version) (s. ?xiv)

4. London, BL, Cotton Vespasian D. xvi, 57v (English and Latin versions) (s. xvi)

5. London, BL, Harl. 2058, 4r (incomplete) (s. xvi)

6. London, BL, Sloane 754, 1r (Mn Eng. transl.) (s. xvi)

7. London, Corporation of London, Records Office, 128.12, 1r (contemporary transcript of MS 14)

8. London, Corporation of London, Records Office, Ch 1b (Latin version; s. xiv[1]) (formerly stitched to MS 1)

9. London, Corporation of London, Records Office, Ch 50, [1v] (with seal) (English version only) (*inspeximus* of Hen IV, 25 May 1400: for Chancery copy, see MS 36; facsimile transcript of MS 1)

10. London, Corporation of London, Records Office, Ch 51, [1v] (with fragmentary seal) (English version only) (*inspeximus* of Hen V, 12 July 1414: for Chancery copy, see MS 37; transcript of MS ?9)

11. London, Corporation of London, Records Office, Ch 53, [1v] (English version only) (*inspeximus* of Hen VI, 7 October 1428: for Chancery copy, see MS 42; transcript of MS 10)

12. London, Corporation of London, Records Office, Ch 58, [1v] (with seal) (English version only) (*inspeximus* of Edw IV, 25 March 1462: for Chancery copy, see MS 43; transcript of MS 9 with attempt to reproduce its facsimile hand)

13. London, Corporation of London, Records Office, Ch 68, 1r (with fragmentary seal) (English version only) (*inspeximus* of Hen VII, 23 July 1505: for Chancery copy, see MS 39; transcript of MS 11)

14. London, Corporation of London, Records Office, Ch 70, [1v] (with fragmentary seal) (English version only) (*inspeximus* of Hen VIII, 12 July 1513: transcript of MS 13)

15. London, Corporation of London, Records Office, Ch 76, [1v] (with seal) (English version only) (*inspeximus* of Edw VI, 21 February 1548: for Chancery copy, see MS 40; transcript of MS 14)

16. London, Corporation of London, Records Office, Ch 80, [1v] (English version only) (*inspeximus* of Mary, 1 March 1554; transcript of MS 15)

17. London, Corporation of London, Records Office, Ch 82, 1v (English version only) (*inspeximus* of Eliz I, 9 May 1562: for Chancery copy, see MS 41; transcript of MS 16)

18. London, Corporation of London, Records Office, Ch 90, [1v] (English version only) (*inspeximus* of Chas I, 18 October 1638; transcript of MS 17)

19. London, Corporation of London, Records Office, Ch 96, 1v (with fragmentary seal) (English version only) (*inspeximus* of Chas II, 24 June 1663; facsimile transcript of MS 1)
20. London, Corporation of London, Records Office, Ch 96, 1v (with fragmentary seal) (English version only) (*inspeximus* of Chas II, 24 June 1663; transcript of MS 18)
21. London, Corporation of London, Records Office, ChT 1, 1r (Mn Eng. translation of A.D. 1582)
22. London, Corporation of London, Records Office, ChT 2, 1r (s. xvii Mn Eng. translation, apparently a transcript with variations of MS 21)
23. London, Corporation of London, Records Office, ChT 3, 1r (the preliminary unnumbered folios, [iii r] and [iv r], also contain partial copies of the text) (s. xvii)
24. London, Corporation of London, Records Office, ChT 4, p. 1 (s. xvii translation of MS 18)
25. London, Corporation of London, Records Office, ChT 5, 1 (s. xvii transcript of MS 18)
26. London, Corporation of London, Records Office, ChT 6, 1r (s. xvii transcript of MS 18)
27. London, Corporation of London, Records Office, ChT 10, 1r (facsimile transcription made in A.D. 1833 x 1834)
28. London, Corporation of London, Records Office, ChT 11, p. 1 (Mn Eng. translation of A.D. 1833 x 1834)
29. London, Corporation of London, Records Office, ChT 12, p. 1 (Mn Eng. translation of MS 19, employing the words of MS 28; A.D. 1833 x 1834)
30. London, Corporation of London, Records Office, ChT 12, p. 2 (Mn Eng. translation of MS 19, in turn drawn from MS 18, employing the words of MS 28; A.D. 1833 x 1834)
31. London, Corporation of London Records Office, 'Liber Custumarum', 13r (c. A.D. 1324) (English version)
32. London, Corporation of London Records Office, 'Liber Custumarum', 187r (c. A.D. 1324) (3 versions: 2 in English, 1 in Latin)
33. London, Corporation of London Records Office, 'Liber Horn', 205v (A.D. 1311) (3 versions as in MS 32)
34. London, Corporation of London Records Office, 'Liber Horn', 362r (A.D. 1311) (3 versions as in MS 33)
35. London, Corporation of London Records Office, 'Liber Memorandorum', 110v–111r (A.D. 1298) (3 versions as in MSS 32–4)
36. London, PRO, Charter Rolls, 1 Hen IV, pt 3, m. 38, no. 8(1) (English version; Chancery copy of MS 9)
37. London, PRO, Charter Rolls, 2 Hen V, pt 2, m. 49, no. 11 (English version; Chancery copy of MS 10)
38. London, PRO, Confirmation Rolls, 1 Ric III, pt 3, m. 1, no. 3(1) (English version)
39. London, PRO, Confirmation Rolls, 20 Hen VII, m. 1, no. 1 (English version; Chancery copy of MS 13)

40. London, PRO, Confirmation Rolls, 2 Edw VI, pt 3, m. 1, no. 2
      (English version; Chancery copy of MS 15)
41. London, PRO, Confirmation Rolls, 4 Eliz I, pt 2, m. 1, no. 4 (English
      version; Chancery copy of MS 17)
42. London, PRO, Patent Rolls, 7 Hen VI, pt 2, m. 24(1) (English
      version; Chancery copy of MS 11)
43. London, PRO, Patent Rolls, 2 Edw IV, pt 5, m. 23, no. 1 (English
      version; Chancery copy of MS 12)

Printed: Arnold ?1503 (= ?1521), fol. B iiiir (= 1811, 13); Holinshed 1577, II,
332 (*recte* 316) (= 1807, II, 25) *ex* MS ? (English and Latin versions); Anonymous 1680 (= 1682), [ii] *ex* MS ?; Brady 1690, 16 *ex* Holinshed (refers also to MS
43); Bohun 1702 (= 1723), x *ex* MSS 19–20; Strype 1720, II, bk 5, 347 *ex* MS 1;
Wilkins 1721, 290 *ex* MS ? (English and Latin version); Maitland 1739, 28 *ex*
MS 33 or 34 (= 1756, I, 37 *ex* MS 1); Noorthouck 1773, 773, no. I *ex* MS 1;
Allen 1827, I, 50 *ex* MS 1; Brayley 1829, I, 58 *ex* MS 1; Norton 1829, 324 (=
1869, 257) *ex* MS 1; Riley 1860, II.1, 25–6 *ex* MS 31, 246–7 *ex* MS 32 and II.2,
504 *ex* MS 1; Freeman 1867, IV, 29 n. 1 *ex* Riley 1860, II.2, 504; Ellis 1868–9,
134 *ex* Sanders; Stubbs 1870, 79 *ex* MS 32 (= 1913, 97 *ex* MS 1); Coote 1876–80,
282n. *ex* Noorthouck and MS ?1; Benham & Welch 1901, 4 *ex* MS 1; Liebermann 1903b, I, 486 *ex* MS 1 and Latin version *ex* MSS 32, 33 and 35; Ballard
1913, 4 *ex* Liebermann 1903b; Förster 1913 (= 1949), 34, no. I *ex* Liebermann
1903b collated with Sharpe 1894 and Traill & Mann 1901; Robertson 1925, 230
ex Sharpe 1894; Bishop & Chaplais 1957, no. 15 *ex* MS 1.

Translated: Stow 1603, 502 (omitted in 1598 ed.); Anonymous 1680 (= 1682),
[ii] and 1 (latter an epitome); S. G. 1680, 1–2 *ex* MSS 19–20; Brady 1690, 16;
Bohun 1702, 3 (= 1723, 1), abstract *ex* MSS 19–20; Strype 1720, II, bk 5, 347; J.
E. 1738 (= 1745), 2 *ex* MSS 19–20; Maitland 1739, 28 (= 1756, I, 37–8);
Anonymous 1765, 1 (abridged); Entick 1766, I, 79; Noorthouck 1773, 773, no. I;
Luffman 1793, 1; Lambert 1806, I, 43–4; Hunter 1811, I, 71; Hughson (pseudonym for Pugh) 1816, Introduction [i] and 1 (latter an epitome); Allen 1827, I,
50–1; J. S. F. 1827, 36–8 *ex* MS 33 or 34; Brayley 1829, I, 58; Norton 1829, 324
(= 1869, 257); Merewether & Stephens 1835, I, 287; Riley 1860, II.2, 594 *ex* MS
32; Sanders 1865, I, no. I; Ellis 1868–9, 134 n. 4; Stubbs 1870, 79–80 (= 1913,
97); Stubbs 1874, I, 404 (= 1897, I, 439) *ex* MS 1; Coote 1876–80, 282n; Loftie
1883 (= 1884), I, 78 *ex* Stubbs 1870; Birch 1887, 1, no. I *ex* MS 1; Loftie 1887,
25 *ex* Stubbs 1870; Sharpe 1894, 34 *ex* MS 1; Benham & Welch 1901, 5;
Liebermann 1903b, I, 486 (translation into German); Gomme 1907, 251; Besant
1908, 253–4 *ex* Stubbs 1874 or later ed.; Kingsford 1908, II, 148; Meiklejohn
1908, 34; Gomme 1912, 138; Ballard 1913, 4; Robertson 1925, 231; Home 1927,
70, 72; Plucknett 1929, 12 (= 1956, 13) *ex* Stubbs 1870; Ivimey 1936, 49; Brooke
1975, 29 *ex* Robertson 1925; EHD II, 1012, no. 269 *ex* MS 1; Brown 1984, 146,
no. 174 (*ex* Robertson).

References: Holinshed 1577, II, 332 (*recte* 316) (= 1807, II, 25); Stow 1598,
400, 416, 473 and 476 (= 1603, 483, 502, 553 and 556); Hayward 1613, 96–7;
Anonymous 1680 (= 1682), [ii–iii]; Gough 1682, 29; Brady 1690, 16–17; Bohun
1702 (= 1723), ix–x and 38; Newcourt 1708, I, 10; Strype 1720, II, bk 5, 3, 73 (*ex*
MS 32), 100 and 347; Wilkins 1721, 291; Maitland 1739, 28 (= 1756, I, 37–8);
Dalrymple 1757, 33 (= 1768, 35); Hume 1762, I, 169 and 408–9, Appendix II (=

1763, I, 254 and II, 120); Entick 1766, I, 79–80; Noorthouck 1773, 24 and note; Luffman 1793, 1–4 (quoting Brady 1690); Lambert 1806, I, 43–5 (quoting Brady 1690); Hunter 1811, I, 71–2; Hughson (pseudonym for Pugh) 1816, Introduction, ii; Kempe 1825, 15 n.[2] (reference to a drawing of the seal by Charles Alfred Stothard); Allen 1827, I, 50; J. S. F. 1827, 13–14 and 36; Brayley 1829, I, 57–8; Norton 1829, 22, 54, 104 and 325–36 (= 1869, 17, 41, 100 and 256–66); Merewether & Stephens 1835, I, 285–7; Pulling 1842, 6 and 131–2; Sanders 1865, I, Introductory Notes, no. I; Freeman 1867, IV, 29–30; Hart 1868, 43 *ex* MSS 36–41; Stubbs 1874, I, 404 (= 1897, I, 439); Green 1883 (= 1884), 573; Loftie 1883 (= 1884), I, 77–80; *DNB* XX, 350; Birch 1887, x–xii; Loftie 1887, 25–6; Round 1892, 347–57, esp. p. 354, and 439; Round 1894, 838; Sharpe 1894, 34–6; PRO 1897, 246 *ex* MS 43; PRO 1901, 556 *ex* MS 42; Traill & Mann 1901, I, 519; Lethaby 1902, 190–2; Liebermann 1903b, II, 391; Davis 1905 (= 1949), 10 and 42; Gomme 1907, 251–4; Besant 1908, 253–6; Kingsford 1908, II, 129, 148, 202, 205, 381 and 383; Meiklejohn 1908, 34–5; Stenton 1908, 240–1; Gomme 1912, 138; *Regesta* I, 4–5, no. 15; PRO 1916, 399 and 473 *ex* MSS 36 and 37 respectively; Shelly 1921, 68 and 82–3; Page 1923, 72–3 and nn. 24–6; Robertson 1925, 233 and 360; Home 1927, 70, 72; Morris 1927, 48 n. 50 and 52 n. 77 (on Geoffrey); Thomas 1927 (on date); Tait 1928–9, 279–80 (refutation of Thomas 1927); Weinbaum 1929, 11–12; Stenton 1934, 6–7; Ivimey 1936, 49; Goebel 1937, 385 and n. 167; Woodbine 1943, 405; Ker 1954, 38–9 (= 1985, 136–7) *ex* MS 32, 40, no. *e*(iv) and 42, no. 29 (= 1985, 138 and 140) *ex* MS 33; Bishop & Chaplais 1957, xx, 3(a)(iv) (on the seal) and no. 15; Douglas 1964, 258; Ker 1969, 21 *ex* MSS 31 and 32, 33, no. 78 *ex* MS 33, no. 80 *ex* MS 34; Brooke 1975, 28–9; Hoad 1975, 322; Healey & Venezky 1980, 71, no. B15.1.171; Green 1983, 131; Brown 1984, 146, no. 174; Garnett 1986a, 101; Keynes 1988, 217 nn. 192 and 194.

9

A.D. 1067. Writ of King William (*Uillelm*) I to all his officials (*holde*) declaring he has granted to his priest Regenbald all his land as fully as he possessed it under William's kinsman, Edward (*under Edweærde*).

MS: Oxford, Bodleian, Dep. c. 392, p. 26 (*olim* 6v; *recte* 13v) (s. xiii med.)

Printed: Phillipps 1836, 256; Round 1895, 422 (= Round 1964, 323) (extracts *ex* ?Phillipps 1836); Ross 1964, I, 21, no. 27.

Translated: Baddeley 1924, 98, no. 3; EHD II, 462, no. 36.

References: Phillipps 1836, 255; Ellis 1879–80, 118–20 (on Regenbald); *DNB* XVI, 862, s.v. 'Regenbald'; Round 1895, 331 and 421–30 (= 1964, 257 and 323–9) (on Regenbald); Stevenson 1896, 732 n. (on Regenbald); Round 1904, 92 (on Regenbald); *Regesta* I, xv (on Regenbald) and 5, no. 19 (for addenda see *Regesta* II, 390); Baddeley 1924, 89 and 97–8 (questions authenticity); Harmer 1952, 59–60, 212, 570 (on Regenbald); Douglas 1964, 292–3; Galbraith 1974, 178–9 (on Regenbald); Hoad 1975, 322; Evans 1976, 46–59 (on Regenbald); Campbell 1979, 130–1 (= 1986, 149–50) (on Regenbald); Healey & Venezky 1980, 71, no. B15.1.174; Garnett 1986a, 99 n. 52; Keynes 1988, 195–222, esp. 211 and 217 n. 192.

10

Whit-Sunday, 11 May 1068. Diploma of King William I at the request of Ingelric, his priest, to St Martin's(-le-Grand), London (*Lunden*), granting estates (in Essex) at Good Easter (*Estre in Eastsexa*), Mashbury (*æt Mæisbyrig*), ?Cold Norton (*Nortone*), Stanford Rivers (*Stanford*), Fobbing (*Fobbinge*), Bendysh (*Benedisc*) (in the parish of Radwinter), Chrishall (*Cristeshala*), Tolleshunt (*Tolesfunte*), Rivenhall (*Reuenhala*), Ongar (*Angra*), Benfleet (in *Benfleote*), Hoddesdon (in *Hoddesdone*) (later in Herts.) and Maldon (in *Mealdune*) as well as land outside Cripplegate (*wiðuten Crepelsgate*), and all churches, tithings, lands and houses granted to the church and canons before and after by others inside or outside London (*binnan Lunden oððe buten*). The Church of St Martin's (*Sanctes Martines mynster*) and canons are to be free of all royal, ecclesiastical and secular obligations (dative: *ðeowdome*). Witnesses (in Latin): William, king of the English and duke of the Normans; Mathilda (*Mathildis*) the queen; Richard (*Ricardus*), son of the king; Stigand, archbishop (of Canterbury); Ealdræd (*Aldredus*), archbishop (of York); William (*Willelmus*), bishop of London; Odo, bishop of Bayeux (*Baiocensis episcopus*); Hugh, bishop of Lisieux (*Hugo, Luxoviensis episcopus*); Geoffrey (*Goisfridus*), bishop (of Coutances); Herman (*Hermannus*), bishop (of Sherborne); Leofric (*Leovricus*), bishop (of Exeter); Giso, bishop (of Wells); Eadwine (*Eadwinus*), abbot (of Westminster); Wulfweald (*Wulwaldus*), abbot (of Bath and Chertsey); Baldwin, abbot (of Bury St Edmunds); Æthelsige (*Ægelsinus*), abbot (of St Augustine's, Canterbury); Thorsteinn (*Turstinus*), abbot (of Ely); Brandr (*Brand*), abbot (of Peterborough); Ælfwine (*Ælfwinus*), abbot (of Ramsey); Sigtryggr (*Sihtricus*), abbot (of Tavistock); William, son of Osbert, *comes*; Robert, brother of the king, *comes* (count of Mortain); Eadwine (*Eadwinus*), *comes* (earl of Mercia); Robert, *comes*; Morkar (*Marchere*), *comes* (earl of Northumbria); Waltheof (*Walðeof*), *comes* (earl of Huntingdon); Roger of Sainte-Foy de Montgommery (*de Montegomeri*), (Calvados), *comes* (earl of Shrewsbury); Richard, son of (Count) Gilbert (*Gislebertus*) (of Brionne), *princeps*; William Malet (*Willelmus malet*) (of Graville-Sainte-Honorine, near Le Havre), *princeps*; Herfast (*Arfastus*), chancellor (*cancellarius*) of the king; Michael, chaplain of the king; the chaplains Gilbert (*Gislebertus*), Osbern, William (*Willelmus*), Thomas, Bernard, Walter and Robert (*Rodbertus*); John, cardinal priest of the Holy Roman Church; and Peter, cardinal priest of the Holy Roman Church. (Readings from English version in Stevenson 1896, who lists variant forms.) *Latin and English versions.*

MSS:
1. London, BL, Lansdowne 170, 52 (Latin), 73v–74r (English) (s. xvii transcript of MS 2)
2. London, Corporation of London Records Office, 'Liber Fleetwood', 99–100r (Latin; witnesses omitted), 127–128r (English; witnesses omitted) (A.D. 1576; transcript of MS 12)
3. London, Corporation of London Records Office, 'Liber Fleetwood', 182–4v (English on 183) (A.D. 1576; transcript of MS 13)
4. London, PRO, Charter Rolls, 2 Edw II, m. 3, no. 4
5. London, PRO, Charter Rolls, 17 Edw III, m. 16, no. 21(1)
6. London, PRO, Charter Rolls, 1 Ric II, m. 11, no. 6(1)
7. London, PRO, Charter Rolls, 5–20 Hen VI, m. 27, no. 16
8. London, PRO, Confirmation Rolls, 5 Hen VII, m. 9, no. 16

   9. London, PRO, Patent Rolls, 1 Hen VI, pt 3, m. 4 (transcript of MS 4)
  10. London, PRO, Patent Rolls, 8 Edw IV, pt 1, m. 3
  11. London, PRO, Patent Rolls, 2 Hen VII, pt 2, m. 1(13)
  12. London, Westminster Abbey, Muniment Book 5, 9–10r (Latin), 29v–30r (English) (s. xv, *temp.* Hen VI)
  13. London, Westminster Abbey, Muniment Book 5, 75–77r (English on 76) (s. xv, *temp.* Hen VI)

Printed: Kempe 1825, 174–6 *ex* MS 1 (Latin version only); *Monasticon* VI, 1324–5, no. I *ex* MS 9 (Latin version only); Stevenson 1896, 739–44 *ex* MSS 4, 6–7 and 9.

Translated: Stow 1598, 11 and 28 (= 1603, 13 and 34) (partial translation); Kempe 1825, 11–14; Kingsford 1908, I, 12 and 33 (partial translation).

References: Stow 1598, 11–13, 28, 246 (= 1603, 12–14, 34, 309 and 311); Tanner 1695, 136 no. 3; Newcourt 1708, I, 424; Strype 1720, I, bk. 3, 106; Kempe 1825, 10–11, 14–16 and 176–8; Hart 1868, 41–2 *ex* MSS 4, 7–11; Freeman 1867, IV, 724; Stevenson 1896, 731–9; Round 1897, 105–7 (on authenticity); Stevenson 1897, 107–10 (on witnesses); Round 1899, 28–36; PRO 1900, 99 *ex* MS 10; PRO 1901, 89 *ex* MS 9; Lethaby 1902, 44–7 and 86–7; Kingsford 1908, I, 12–14, 33, 307 and 309, and II, 76, 270–1, 342 and 369; PRO 1908a, 129 *ex* MS 4; Stenton 1908, 260–1 (on witnesses); Reddan 1909, I, 555; *Regesta* I, 6, no. 22; PRO 1914, 167 *ex* MS 11; PRO 1916, 16 and 244 *ex* MSS 5 and 6 respectively; PRO 1927, 20 *ex* MS 7; Weinbaum 1929, 13–14; Douglas 1932, xxxi n. 5, lxiii n. 2 and xcix n. 1; Tengvik 1938, 350–1, s.v. Malet; Le Patourel 1944, 144 n. 1; Loyd 1949, Appendix K, 156–7; Greenway 1968, 89, s.v. 'Engelbric' (on Ingelric); Denton 1970, 29–31; Davis 1972, 9–10, 12 and 23–5; Hoad 1975, 322; Healey & Venezky 1980, 71, no. B15.1.175; Green 1983, 135; Garnett 1986a, 107, and 113 n. 159; Keynes 1988, 211 and n. 150, 218 n. 199 and 219.

Note: Stow 1598, 28 (= 1603, 34 = Kingsford 1908, I, 33) gives a brief partial translation of what appears to be a variant text from what he calls 'Lib. S. Bartholomew', which I have been unable to trace.

11

Whitsuntide, 1068. Diploma of King William I granting at the request of Giso (genitive: *Gisonis*), bishop (of Wells), thirty hides of land at Banwell (*Banawelle*), (Somerset), given by Duduc (ablative: *Dodoco*), bishop (of Wells), and despoiled by King (*Rex*) Harold, to augment the see and support the brothers (*fratrum*) of Wells. Witnesses: William, king of the English; Mathilda (*Mathyld*) the queen; Stigand, archbishop (of Canterbury); Ealdræd (*Aldrædus*), archbishop (of York); Odo, bishop (of Bayeux), brother of the king; Hugh (*Hugo*), bishop (of Lisieux); Geoffrey (*Goffrid*), bishop (of Coutances); Herman (*Heremannus*), bishop (of Sherborne); Leofric, bishop (of Exeter); Æthelmær (*Gilmær*), bishop (of Elmham); William (*Willhelmus*), bishop (of London); Æthelric (*Egelricus*), bishop (of Selsey); Walter, bishop (of Hereford); Wulfsige (*Wulfsig*) (i.e., ?Wulfstan), bishop (of Worcester); Remigius, bishop (of Dorchester up to A.D. 1072 and subsequently of Lincoln); Æthelnoth (*Æþelnoð*), abbot (of Glastonbury); Leofweard, abbot (of Muchelney); Wulfweald (*Wulfwold*), abbot (of Bath and Chertsey); Wulfgeat, abbot (of ?Athelney); William (*Willhelmus*) (fitz Osbern), *dux* (earl of Hereford); Waltheof (*Walþeof*), *dux* (earl of Huntingdon); Eadwine, *dux* (earl of Mercia); Robert (*Rotbertus*), (count of Mortain), brother of the king; Roger (*Rotgerus*) (?of Montgomery), *princeps* (?thegn); Walter Giffard (*Gefeheard*), (lord of Longueville); Hugh de Montfort (*Hugo de Muntforz*); William of Courseulles-sur-Mêr (*Willhelm de Curcello*); Serlo of Burcy (*de Burca*), (Calvados); Roger of Arundel (*Derundel*), (Sussex); Richard, son of the king; Walter the Fleming (*Waldtere Fleminc*); Rambriht the Fleming (*Flæminc*); Thurstan (*Purstan*); Baldwine (*Balduinus*) *de Warten Beige*; Æthelheard (*Othelheard*); Heimric (*Heimericus*); Tofi (*Toug*), *minister* (sheriff of Somerset); Dinni; Ælfgeard Thorn (*Ælfgearde Thorne*); William of Vauville (*Willhelm de Walvile*), (Manche); Bondi (*Bundi*) the Staller; Robert (*Rotbert*) (fitz Wymarc) the Staller; Robert d'Oyly (*Rotbert de Ylie*) (Ouilly-le-Basset, Calvados); Roger the butler (*pincerna*); Wulfweard; Hearding (*Herding*); Azur (*Adzor*); Beorhtsige (*Brixi*); and Beorhtric (*Brihtric*). *Latin with English rubric and bounds.*

MS: Wells, D & C, 'Liber Albus II', 246v (s. xiv/xv)

Printed: Dickinson 1877, 55–8; Hist. MSS Comm. 1885, 186 (rubric only); Earle 1888, 431–4 (from Dickinson but collated with the MS).

Translated: Taylor 1905, 48–52 (rubric excluded; only partial bounds); EHD II, 644–6, no. 77 (rubric and bounds excluded).

References: Green 1863–4, 148–57 (on Harold and Giso); Freeman 1867, II, 698–705 (on Harold and Giso); Freeman 1870, 28–31; Freeman 1876, 688–9; Dickinson 1877, 49–55 and 58–64; Taylor 1905, 50–3; Hist. MSS Comm. 1907, 431; Stenton 1908, 260–1 and 412–14 (on the witness list); Holmes 1911, II, 8; *Regesta* I, 7, no. 23 (for an addendum see *Regesta* II, 390); Morris 1927, 43 (on Tofi); Harmer 1952, 276; Douglas 1964, 258 and n. 4; Hoad 1975, 322; Healey & Venezky 1980, 69, no. B15.8.646; Garnett 1986a, 112 n. 151; Keynes 1988, 219–20.

12

A.D. 1066 x c. 1068. Writ of King William (*Willem*) I to Bondi (*Bundi*) the Staller, Sæweald (1 *Sawold*, 3 *Swawold*) the sheriff (of Oxon.) and all his thegns of Oxfordshire (1 *on Oxnefordesscire*, 3 *on Oxenfordesciwe*) declaring that the half hide at Marston (1 *at Mersttune*, 3 *at Mersctune*), (Oxon.), and all belonging to it is a possession of Westminster (Abbey) (*into Westminstre*) and that everything removed from it be returned within a week of the receipt of this document (1 *gewritt*, 3 *gewrit*). (All readings from MSS 1 and 3.)

MSS: 1.   London, BL, Cotton Faustina A. iii, 112v (s. xiii/xiv, *temp.* Edw I)
   2.   London, College of Arms, Young 72, lxxviiiv (memorandum in Latin) (s. xv^2)
   3.   London, Westminster Abbey, Muniment Bk 11, 273r (*olim* 295r) (s. xiv, after A.D. 1308)

Printed: *Monasticon* I, 301, no. XXXIV *ex* MS 1; Neufeldt 1907, 37–8, no. 28 *ex* MS 1.

References: Bentley 1836, 41, no. 284.17 *ex* MS 2; Parker 1885, 270–1 and 301; Stenton 1908, 229–30 and nos. **13, 15, 21, 24** and **38** below; *Regesta* I, 5, no. 18 (for addenda and a correction see *Regesta* II, 390); Morris 1927, 43 n. 20 (on Sæweald); Harmer 1936, 99 n. 3; Davis 1958, 116, no. 1011 *ex* MS 1 and no. 1013 *ex* MS 3; Douglas 1964, 258 and n. 4; Hoad 1975, 322; Healey & Venezky

1980, 69, no. B15.1.173; Green 1983, 131; Keynes 1988, 217 n. 192; Mason 1988, 27, no.7.

13

A.D. 1066 x 1068. Writ of King William (*Willem*) I to Leofwine, bishop (of Lichfield), Eadwine (1 *Edwine*, 2 *Eadwine*), earl (of Mercia), and all the thegns of Staffordshire (1 *on Staffordescire*, 2 *on Statfordescire*) declaring that all the land at Perton (1 *at Pertune*, 2 *at P'tune*), (Staffs.), belongs to St Peter's (Abbey), Westminster (*into Westminstre*), as fully as his kinsman, King Edward (1 *Edward*, 2 *Eadward*), granted it; he wishes Æthelwig (1 *Aglwi*, 2 *Ægelwi*), abbot (of Evesham), and Thorketill (*Purkill*), sheriff (of Staffs.), to have jurisdiction (*mund*) and guardianship (*weard*) over that holy place (1 *halagenstowe*, 2 *halganstowe*).

MSS: 1.   London, BL, Cotton Faustina A. iii, 113v (s. xiii/xiv, *temp.* Edw I)
      2.   London, Westminster Abbey, Muniment Bk 11, 648r (*olim* 679r) (s. xiv, after A.D. 1308)

Printed: Monasticon I, 301, no. XXXIX *ex* MS 1; Freeman 1867, V, 792 *ex ?Monasticon*; Neufeldt 1907, 39, no. 33 *ex* MS 1.

References: Freeman 1867, V, 792; Stenton 1908, 229–30: 'there is not sufficient reason for us to condemn the present writs as spurious' (229) and 'the personal names which occur in them suggest that they should be assigned to the very beginning of William's reign' (229 n. 2) and cf. no. 12 above and nos. 15, 21, 24 and 38 below; *Regesta* I, 7, no. 25; Shelly 1921, 82; Morris 1927, 43 n. 16 (on Thurkill); Darlington 1933, 12 and 17 n. 5; Cronne 1957–8, 26 and n. 39; Douglas 1964, 258 and n. 4; Hoad 1975, 322; Healey & Venezky 1980, 69, no. B15.1.176; Green 1983, 130; Keynes 1988, 217 n. 192; Mason 1988, 26–7, no. 5.

14

A.D. 1066 x 11 September 1069. Writ of King William (*Willelm*) I to all his thegns of Yorkshire (*on Eoferwicscire*), French and English (*Frencisce and Englisce*), declaring that he has granted to St John's Minster at Beverley (*æt Beuerlic*) the rights of sake and soke over the lands given in King Edward's time (*on Ædwærdes dieg cynges*) and acquired since by Ealdræd (*Ealdrad*), archbishop (of York), by testament (*on witword*) and in purchased land (*on caupland*); it is to be free except with respect to the bishop and the priests of the minster (*mynster*); and he wishes that the life of the minster (*mynsterlif*) and the assembly of canons (*canonica samnung*) should continue. (All readings from MS 4.) *English and Latin versions.*

MSS: 1.   London, BL, Add. 61901, 70v (Latin version only) (s. xiv)
      2.   London, BL, Cotton Otho C. xvi, 82 (s. xvi/xvii transcript of MS 3; damaged)
      3.   London, BL, Harl. 560, 23v (s. xvi/xvii transcript of MS 1)
      4.   London, PRO, Charter Rolls, 4 Edw II, m. 20, no. 52(2) (English version only)
      5.   London, PRO, Charter Rolls, 4 Edw III, m. 13, no. 25(2) (English version only)
      6.   London, PRO, Charter Rolls, 1 Hen V, pt 1, m. 11, no. 5(1[2])
      7.   London, PRO, Confirmation Rolls, 1 Hen VIII, pt 2, m. 2, no. 13 (English version only)

  8. London, PRO, Confirmation Rolls, 3 & 4 Phil & M, pt 1, m. 2, no.
      15 (English version only)
  9. London, PRO, Patent Rolls, 1 Ric II, pt 3, m. 8
 10. London, PRO, Patent Rolls, 2 Hen IV, pt 2, m. 6
 11. London, PRO, Patent Rolls, 6 Hen VI, pt 2, m. 6(1[2]) (English
      version only)
 12. London, PRO, Patent Rolls, 20 Hen VI, pt 4, m. 11 (English version
      only)

Printed: Thorpe 1865, 438–9 *ex* MS 4; Farrer 1914, I, 87, no. 89 *ex* MS 4.

Translated: Thorpe 1865, 438–9; Leach 1897, I, xxxi (partial translation);
Farrer 1914, I, 88, no. 89.

References: Hart 1868, 37 *ex* MSS 4–5, 7–8, 12; PRO 1895, 120 *ex* MS 9; Leach
1897, I, xxxi; PRO 1901, 490 *ex* MS 11; PRO 1903, 456 *ex* MS 10; PRO 1908a,
140 *ex* MS 4; PRO 1908b, 111, no. 1 *ex* MS 12; PRO 1912, 194 *ex* MS 5; *Regesta*
I, 9–10, no. 31 (for addenda see *Regesta* II, 391); PRO 1916, 456–7 *ex* MS 6;
Shelly 1921, 34 and 83; Hoad 1975, 322; Healey & Venezky 1980, 70,
B15.1.177; Garnett 1986a, 103 n. 84; Keynes 1988, 217 n. 192.

15

A.D. 1066 x 11 September 1069. Writ of King William (1 *Willem*, 2 *W*) I to
Ealdræd (1 *Elred*, 2 *Ealred*), archbishop (of York), Wulfstan (1 *Wlstan*, 2 *Wul-
stan*), bishop (of Worcester), William (1 *Willem*, 2 *Will'*) (fitz Osbern), earl (of
Hereford), and all the thegns of Gloucestershire (1 *on Gloucestresire*, 2 *on Glaw-
cæstrescire*) and Worcestershire (1 *on Wirecest'scire*, 2 *on Wigercestrescire*) and
Oxfordshire (*on Oxonfordescire* [only in MS 2]), declaring that the land at
Pershore (1 *Perssore*, 2 *Persora*), (Worcs.), and Deerhurst (1 *Dorhurst*, 2 *Deorhir-
sta*), (Gloucs.), granted by King Edward to St Peter's (Abbey), Westminster (*into
Westminstre*), remain under its control as fully as it did before.

MSS: 1.   London, BL, Cotton Faustina A. iii, 113v (s. xiii/xiv, *temp.* Edw I)
       2.   London, Westminster Abbey, Muniment Bk 11, 278v (*olim* 299v) (s.
            xiv, after A.D. 1308)

Printed: *Monasticon* I, 301, no. XL *ex* MS 1; Neufeldt 1907, 39–40, no. 34 *ex*
MS 1.

References: Round 1901, 240; Stenton 1908, 229–30 and 425–7 (on William's
earldom) and cf. nos. 12 and 13 above and nos. 21, 24 and 38 below; *Regesta* I,
10, no. 32 (for an addendum see *Regesta* II, 391); Shelly 1921, 83; Darlington
1933, 17 n. 6; Harmer 1936, 102 n. 1; Cronne 1957–8, 27 and n. 47; Wightman
1962, 12–13 and 16 n. 3; Douglas 1964, 258 and n. 4; Hoad 1975, 322; Healey &
Venezky 1980, 69, B15.1.178; Keynes 1988, 217 n. 192; Mason 1988, 26, no. 4.

16

A.D. 1066 x 11 September 1069. Writ of King William (*Willelm*) I to his earls
and thegns where Ealdræd, archbishop (of York), has land declaring that he is to
have his bishopric and his legal powers as fully as he did in the time of his
kinsman, King Edward (1 *on Eadwardes deges kynges*, 2 *on Eadwerdes dæge kinges*).
William will offer full compensation (*fulle bote*) to anyone wronged by any
person, French, Flemish or English (*Frencisc…Flemisc…Englisc*).

MSS: 1.   York, Borthwick Institute, 'Magnum Registrum Album, pt I', 62r
            (s. xiv, *temp.* Edw III)

2. York, Borthwick Institute, 'Magnum Registrum Album, pt I', 62v
    (s. xiv, *temp.* Edw III)
Printed: *Regesta* I, 118, no. II bis *ex* MS 2; Farrer 1914, I, 30, no. 12 *ex* MS 2.
Translated: Farrer 1914, I, 30, no. 12.
References: *Regesta* I, 10, no. 33; Stenton 1932, 24 (= 1961, 25); Douglas 1964,
267 and 268 and n. 4; Hoad 1975, 322; Healey & Venezky 1980, 70,
no. B15.1.179; Garnett 1986a, 107 n. 116; Keynes 1988, 217 n. 192.

17

A.D. 1069. Diploma of King William (*Wilhelmus*) I granting Leofric, bishop (of
Exeter), in Oxfordshire (*on Oxenafordscyre*) seven hides of land at Bampton (*æt
Bemtune*), Aston (*æt Esttune*), Chimney (*æt Ceommanige*), and in Devonshire
(*on Defnascyre*) Holcombe in Dawlish (*æt Holacumbe of Doflisclande*) for the
support of St Peter's (Cathedral), Exeter (*on Exancestre*), and of the canons.
Witnesses: William (*Wilhelmus*), king of the English; Mathilda (*Mahthilda*) the
queen; Stigand, archbishop (of Canterbury); Odo, bishop (of Bayeux); Herman
(*Hermannus*), bishop (of Sherborne); Leofric, bishop (of Exeter); Geoffrey (*Gos-
fredus*), bishop (of Coutances); Giso (*Gyso*), bishop (of Wells); William (*Wilhelmus*), bishop (of London); Baldwin (*Balduuinus*), abbot (of Bury St Edmunds);
Robert (*Rodbertus*), *comes* (count of Mortain); William (fitz Osbern), *comes* (earl
of Hereford); Brian (*Brient*), *comes* (possibly earl of Richmond or of Cornwall,
son of Eudo, count of Penthièvre); Eadwine (*Eduuinus*), *comes* (earl of Mercia);
Morkar (*Morkerin'*), *comes* (earl of Northumbria); Ralph (*Raulfus*), *comes* (earl of
East Anglia); Herfast (*Arfastus*) the chancellor (*cancellarius*); Ingelric the priest;
William the sheriff (*Wilhelmus uicecomes*); Robert (*Rodbertus*) (fitz Wymarc),
sheriff (*uicecomes*) (of Essex); Roger the sheriff (*Rocgerius uicecomes*); Leofnoth
(*Leofnoðus*) *minister*; Richard (*Ricardus*) *minister*; Fulko (*Folco*) *minister*; Hugh
(*Hugo*) *minister*; Ralph (*Raulfus*) *minister*. (All readings from MS 1 with place-
names taken from the endorsement.) *Latin charter with English bounds and endorse-
ment in Latin and English.*
MSS: 1.   Exeter, Cathedral Library, 2528 (original) (Sanders 1878, II, Exeter,
            pl. XVI (incorrectly numbered XV); Barlow *et al.* 1972, pl. I)
       2.   London, BL, Lansdowne 966, 70v–71v (incomplete) (s. xvii)
Printed: Hickes 1703, V, 77–8 *ex* MS 1; *Monasticon* II, 531, no. VI *ex* MS 2;
Oliver 1861, 10–11 *ex* MS 1 (Latin only); Sanders 1878, II, Exeter, no. XVI *ex*
MS 1; Davidson 1881, 121–3 *ex* Hickes; Davidson 1883, 299–301 *ex* MS 1.
Translated: Sanders 1878, II, Exeter, no. XVI *ex* MS 1; Davidson 1881, 123–4.
References: Wanley 1705, 281, no. 5; Oliver 1861, 6–7; Sanders 1878, II, xii;
Davidson 1881, 124–6; Davidson 1883, 298–9; Stenton 1908, 324 (on Brian);
Regesta I, 8–9, no. 28 (for corrections see *Regesta* II, 390–1); Tait 1929, 86 (on
Brian); Douglas 1932, xxxii and n. 3 ('authentic'); Ker 1960, 19 n. 4; Douglas
1964, 147 and 293; Chaplais 1966, 31–3; Blake 1970, 62; Barlow *et al.* 1972, 11;
Hoad 1975, 322; Drage 1978, 42 *ex* MS 1 and 172–3; Healey & Venezky 1980,
68, no. B15.8.647; Blair 1984, 47–8; Keynes 1988, 211 n. 150.

18

A.D. 1066 x April 1070. Writ of King William (*William*) I to Æthelmær
(*Aylmer*), bishop (of Elmham), Ralph (*Rauf*), earl (of East Anglia), and all his
thegns in Suffolk (1 *on Suff*, 2 *on Suthf*) and Norfolk (1 *on Norf*, 2 *on Northf*)

declaring that he wishes Baldwin (1 *Baldewine*, 2 *Baldewyne*), abbot (of Bury St Edmunds), to seize for him the lands of those men who belonged to St Edmund's jurisdiction (1 *into seynt Eadmundes sokne*, 2 *into Edmundes sokne*) and who were slain when they stood in revolt against him; he wishes those to be the men of the abbot just as their forebears earlier had been and whom his predecessor had had.

MSS: 1.   Cambridge, Univ. Lib., Ff. 2. 33, 28r (s. xiii²)
      2.   London, BL, Add. 14847, 38r (s. xiii)
Printed: *Regesta* I, 119, no. VI *ex* MS 2; Douglas 1932, 47, no. 1 *ex* MS 1.
Translated: *Regesta* I, 119, no. VI.
References: Hardwick 1856–67, II, 365, no. 148 *ex* MS 1; *Regesta* I, 12, no. 40 (for addenda see *Regesta* II, 391); Shelly 1921, 83 and 84; Douglas 1932 xxx and n. 1, lxv and xcvi–xcvii; Hoad 1975, 322; Healey & Venezky 1980, 68, no. B15.1.181; Gransden 1982, 67 and n. 42; Garnett 1986a, 104; Keynes 1988, 217 n. 192.

19

A.D. 1066 x April 1070. Writ of King William (1–2, 4–5 *William*, 3, 6 *Willelm*) I to Æthelmær (1 *Aylm'*, 2 *Ailmier*, 3 *Ailm'*, 4 *Aylmer*, 5 *Aegelmaer*, 6 *Æigelmer*), bishop (of Elmham), Ralph (1–4 *Rauf*, 5–6 *Raulf*), earl (of East Anglia), Northmann (1–2, 4 *Norman*, 3, 5–6 *Norðman*) and all the thegns of Suffolk (1, 4 *on Suff*, 2 *on Suffolk'*, 3 *on Suthfolk'*, 5 *on Sudfolke*, 6 *on Suðfolce*) declaring that the soke of the eight-and-a-half hundreds should remain with the minster at Bury St Edmunds (1 *minstre at Seynt Eadmundesbiri*, 2 *minstre at Seint Edmundesbyry*, 3 *minstre at Seint Eadmundesbyrig*, 4 *ministre at Seint Edmundes Biri*, 5 *mynstr' aet seynt Eadmundes birg*, 6 *mynstre æt Sc'e Ædmundes Byrig*) as fully as Ælfric, Wihtgar's son (1 *Alfrich Withgares sone*, 2 *Alfrich Wythgares sone*, 3 *Alfric Withgeres sune*, 4 *Alfrich Wythgares sone*, 5 *Aelfric Wythgares sone*, 6 *Ælfric Wichtgares sune*), and Ordgar (1–2, 4 *Org'*, 3 *Ordger*, 5 *Ordar*, 6 *Orðgar*) administered it after Queen Emma (1–4, 6 *Ymme*, 5 *Imme*), the mother of his kinsman, King Edward (genitive: 2, 4 *Edwardes*, 1, 3, 5 *Eadwardes*, 6 *Ædwardes*), granted it, viz., with certain powers that are listed. He forbids anyone, English, French or Danish (1 *eiþer Englissce or Freinsschissen or Denisscen*, 2 *eue' Englissce or Ffrenisschissen or Denisschen*, 3 *eyther Engliscen oþer Freinciscen oþer Denniscen*, 4 *oiþe Englissce or Frenschissen or Deinssen*, 6 *æðer ge Engliscan ge Frenskiskan ge Denniscan*), except St Edmunds and Abbot Baldwin (1 *Seynt Eadmund 7 þen abbote*, 2 *Seint Edmund and þen abbot*, 3 *Seint Eadmunde 7 þan abbote*, 4 *Seint Edmund 7 þen abbotte*, 5 *Seynt Edmunde and Baldewyne abbote*, 6 *Sance Ædmunde and þan abbode*) to control that soke.

MSS: 1.   Cambridge, Univ. Lib., Ff. 2. 33, 24r (s. xiii²)
      2.   Cambridge, Univ. Lib., Gg. 4. 4, 98r (*olim* 164r) (s. xv)
      3.   Cambridge, Univ. Lib., Mm. 4. 19, 93v (s. xii²)
      4.   London, BL, Add. 14847, 32v (*olim* 36v) (s. xiii)
      5.   London, BL, Harl. 743, 59v–60r (s. xiv)
      6.   London, PRO, Cartae Antiquae, Roll 15 (*olim* P), m. 1, no. 6
Printed: Round 1895, 427 (= 1964, 327) *ex* MS 5 (partial); Davis 1909, 423, no. I, *ex* MSS 4–6; *Regesta* I, 119, no. VII *ex* MSS 4–6; Douglas 1932, 48, no. 3 *ex* MS 6; Conway Davies 1960, 89, no. 448 *ex* MS 6.
References: Hardwick 1856–67, II, 362, no. 84 *ex* MS 1, III, 105, no. 291 *ex* MS

2 and IV, 235, no. 165 *ex* MS 3; Hart 1868, 38 *ex* MS 6; Round 1895, 427–9 (=
1964, 327–9); Davis 1909, 421; *Regesta* I, 12, no. 41 (for addenda see *Regesta* II,
391); Shelly 1921, 83 and 84; Morris 1927, 43 n. 21 (on Northmann); Douglas
1932, xxx and nn. 1 and 3, cx and clv–clvi; Harmer 1952, 145; Douglas 1964,
251; Hoad 1975, 322; Healey & Venezky 1980, 68, no. B15.1.182; Garnett
1986a, 107 n. 116; Keynes 1988, 217 n. 192.

20

A.D. 1066 x April 1070. Writ of King William (*William*) I to Æthelmær
(*Aylmer*), bishop (of Elmham), Ralph (*Rauf*), earl (of East Anglia), and all his
thegns in Norfolk (1 *Norf* 2 *Northf*) and Suffolk (*Suff*) declaring that he has
granted to Baldwin (1 *Baldewine*, 2 *Baldewyne*), abbot (of Bury St Edmunds), to
have a moneyer attached to Bury St Edmunds (1 *withinnen seynt Eadmundesbiri*, 2
withinnen seint Edmundesbiri) as freely in all respects as granted earlier by King
Edward (1 *Eadward*, 2 *Edward*).
MSS: 1.   Cambridge, Univ. Lib., Ff. 2. 33, 28r (s. xiii²)
        2.   London, BL, Add. 14847, 38r (s. xiii)
Printed: Davis 1909, 424, no. III *ex* MS 2; *Regesta* I, 119, no. V *ex* MS 2; Douglas
1932, 50, no. 5 *ex* MS 1.
References: Hardwick 1856–67, II, 365, no. 149 *ex* MS 1; *DNB* I, 950; Cox
1907, II, 58 and n. 8; *Regesta* I, 12, no. 42 (for addenda see *Regesta* II, 391);
Shelly 1921, 83 and 84; Douglas 1932, xxx and nn. 1 and 3; Hoad 1975, 322;
Healey & Venezky 1980, 68, no. B15.1.183; Gransden 1982, 67 and n. 44;
Keynes 1988, 217 n. 192.

21

A.D. 1066 x c. 1070. Writ of King William (*Willem*) I to Eadmund (1 *Edmund*, 2
Ædmund), sheriff (of Herts.), Ælfwine Gottune (1 *Alfwine Gottune*, 2 *Ælfwine
Gottun*, possibly an error for *Gotsune* 'Good Son' or 'Godson') and Leofwine
?'Push' (1 *Scune*, probably an error for *Scuue*, 2 *Scufe*) declaring that St Peter's
(Abbey), Westminster (1 *into Westminstre*, 2 *inte Westmenstre*), be worthy of the
land at Watton-at-Stone (1 *at Wattone*, 2 *æt Watton'*), (Herts.), and Datchworth
(1 *att Dakkewrð*, 2 *æt Daccewurðe*), (Herts.), as fully as they were formerly.
MSS: 1.   London, BL, Cotton Faustina A. iii, 112v–113r (s. xiii/xiv; *temp.*
              Edw I)
        2.   London, Westminster Abbey, Muniment Bk 11, 227r (*olim* 238r)
              (s. xiv, after A.D. 1308)
Printed: *Monasticon* I, 301, no. XXXVI *ex* MS 1; Neufeldt 1907, 38, no. 30 *ex*
MS 1.
References: Stenton 1908, 229–30 and cf. nos. 12, 13, 15 above and nos. 24
and 38 below; *Regesta* I, 5, no. 16; Shelly 1921, 34 and 82; Morris 1927, 43 n. 20
and 52 n. 80 (on Eadmund); Davis 1958, 116, no. 1011 *ex* MS 1 and no. 1013 *ex*
MS 2; Douglas 1964, 258 and n. 4; Healey & Venezky 1980, 69, no. B15.1.172;
Green 1983, 131; Keynes 1988, 217 n. 192; Mason 1988, 27–8, no. 8.

22

A.D. ?1070. Writ of King William I to his bishops, earls, reeves and thegns in the
shires where Lanfranc (*Lanfram*), archbishop (of Canterbury), and the Community of Christ Church, Canterbury (*on Cantuareb'i*), have lands declaring that

they are to have their legal powers just as they did under his kinsman, King Edward (*Eadward*). (All readings from MS 1.)

MSS: 1. Canterbury, D & C, Ch. Ant. C. 4 (first line of the text original) (Bishop & Chaplais 1957, pl. IV [a])
2. Canterbury, D & C, Ch. Ant. C. 204 (no. 2)
3. Canterbury, D & C, Register A, 148v (*olim* 158v) (s. xiii[2])
4. Canterbury, D & C, Register E, 53v (*olim* 21v), no. 110 (s. xiii ex.)
5. Canterbury, D & C, Register I, 59v (*olim* 71v) (s. xiii[2])
6. London, BL, Add. 6159, 7r (s. xiv)
7. London, BL, Cotton Vitellius D. vii, 40r (s. xvi[2]) (damaged)
8. London, PRO, Confirmation Rolls, 4 Hen VII, pt 1, m. 14, no. 4
9. London, PRO, Confirmation Rolls, 1 Hen VIII, pt 3, m. 9, no. 6
10. London, PRO, Patent Rolls, 12 Hen VI, pt 2, m. 9, no. 3

Printed: PRO 1907, 416, no. 3 *ex* MS 10; Bishop & Chaplais 1957, no. 4 *ex* MS 1.

References: Hart 1868, 32 *ex* MSS 8 and 9; *Regesta* I, 11, no. 38; Harmer 1952, 173 and nn. 2 and 3, and 452; Bishop & Chaplais 1957, no. 4; Ker 1957, 472, no. 408 *ex* MS 7 and cf. Ker 1957, 57, no. 39; Ker 1960, 20 n. 3 *ex* MS 1; Cameron 1973, 190, no. B16.6.10; Hoad 1975, 322; Healey & Venezky 1980, 71, no. B15.1.180 and 166, no. B16.6.10; Keynes 1988, 218 n. 198.

Note: The missing first folio of Cambridge, Corpus Christi College, 173 may have been the source of MS 7: see Ker 1957, 57, no. 39 and 472, no. 408. The relationship of MS 7 to MS 1 is unclear: the former text, now incomplete, twice appears to employ the phrase 'French and English', which is omitted in MS 1; the two MSS differ in the spelling of various words; MS 7 uses *hæfde* where MS 1 employs *dyde* in the penultimate line; and MS 7 omits the concluding sentence, *God eow gehealde*.

23

A.D. 1066 x 1075. Writ of King William (*Willelm*) I to William (*Willelm*), bishop (of London), Sveinn (*Swegn*), sheriff (of Essex), and all his thegns of Essex (*on Eastseaxan*) declaring that he has granted to Deormann (*Deormanne*) the hide of land at Gaddesden (*Gyddesdune*), (Herts.), of which he had been deprived. (All readings from MS 1.)

MSS: 1. London, Corporation of London, Records Office, Charter 2 (original) (Sanders 1865, I, no. 2; Sharpe 1894, Frontispiece; Traill & Mann 1901, I, 521 (2); Bishop & Chaplais 1957, pl. XV)
2. London, BL, Harl. 2058, 4r (incomplete) (s. xvi)
3. London, BL, Sloan 754, 1r (incomplete Mn Eng. trans.)
4. London, Corporation of London, Records Office, 128.12, 1r (contemporary transcript of MS 10)
5. London, Corporation of London, Records Office, Ch 50, [1v] (with seal) (*inspeximus* of Hen IV, 25 May 1400: for Chancery copy, see MS 27; facsimile transcript of MS 1)
6. London, Corporation of London, Records Office, Ch 51, [1v] (with fragmentary seal) (*inspeximus* of Hen V, 12 July 1414: for Chancery copy, see MS 28; transcript of MS 5)

7. London, Corporation of London, Records Office, Ch 53, [1v] (*inspeximus* of Hen VI, 7 October 1428: for Chancery copy, see MS 33; transcript of MS 6)

8. London, Corporation of London, Records Office, Ch 58, [1v] (with seal) (*inspeximus* of Edw IV, 25 March 1462: for Chancery copy, see MS 34; transcript of MS 5)

9. London, Corporation of London, Records Office, Ch 68, 1r (with fragmentary seal) (*inspeximus* of Hen VII, 23 July 1505: for Chancery copy, see MS 30; transcript of MS 7)

10. London, Corporation of London, Records Office, Ch 70, [1v] (with fragmentary seal) (*inspeximus* of Hen VIII, 12 July 1513; transcript of MS 9)

11. London, Corporation of London, Records Office, Ch 76, [1v] (with seal) (*inspeximus* of Edw VI, 21 February 1548: for Chancery copy, see MS 31; transcript of MS 10)

12. London, Corporation of London, Records Office, Ch 80, [1v] (*inspeximus* of Mary, 1 March 1554; transcript of MS 11)

13. London, Corporation of London, Records Office, Ch 82, 1v (*inspeximus* of Eliz I, 9 May 1562: for Chancery copy, see MS 32; transcript of MS 1)

14. London, Corporation of London, Records Office, Ch 90, [1v] (*inspeximus* of Chas I, 18 October 1638; transcript of MS 13)

15. London, Corporation of London, Records Office, Ch 96, 1v (with fragmentary seal) (*inspeximus* of Chas II, 24 June 1663; facsimile transcript of MS 1)

16. London, Corporation of London, Records Office, Ch 96, 1v (with fragmentary seal) (*inspeximus* of Chas II, 24 June 1663; transcript of MS 14)

17. London, Corporation of London, Records Office, ChT 1, 1r (Mn Eng. translation of A.D. 1582 of only the initial words of the text)

18. London, Corporation of London, Records Office, ChT 2, 1r (Mn Eng. partial translation, apparently a transcript with variations, of MS 17)

19. London, Corporation of London, Records Office, ChT 3, 1r (s. xvii)

20. London, Corporation of London, Records Office, ChT 4, p. 1 (s. xvii translation of MS 14 with only the opening words of this text)

21. London, Corporation of London, Records Office, ChT 5, 1 (s. xvii translation of MS 14 with only the opening words of this text)

22. London, Corporation of London, Records Office, ChT 6, 1r (s. xvii transcription of MS 14)

23. London, Corporation of London, Records Office, ChT 10, 1r (facsimile transcription of MS 1 made in A.D. 1833 x 1834)

24. London, Corporation of London, Records Office, ChT 11, p. 1 (Mn Eng. translation of A.D. 1833 x 1834)

25. London, Corporation of London, Records Office, ChT 12, p. 1 (Mn Eng. translation of MS 16; A.D. 1833 x 1834)

26. London, Corporation of London, Records Office, ChT 12, p. 2 (Mn Eng. translation of MS 16, in turn drawn from MS 14, employing the words of MS 24; A.D. 1833 x 1834)
27. London, PRO, Charter Rolls, 1 Hen IV, pt 3, m. 38, no. 8(2)
28. London, PRO, Charter Rolls, 2 Hen V, pt 2, m. 49, no. 11
29. London, PRO, Confirmation Rolls, 1 Ric III, pt 3, m. 1, no. 3(2)
30. London, PRO, Confirmation Rolls, 20 Hen VII, m. 1, no. 1
31. London, PRO, Confirmation Rolls, 2 Edw VI, pt 3, m. 1, no. 2
32. London, PRO, Confirmation Rolls, 4 Eliz I, pt 2, m. 1, no. 4
33. London, PRO, Patent Rolls, 7 Hen VI, pt 2, m. 24(2)
34. London, PRO, Patent Rolls, 2 Edw IV, pt 5, m. 23, no. 2

Printed: Maitland 1739, 28 (= 1756, I, 38) *ex* MS 1; Noorthouck 1773, 773, no. II *ex* MS 1; Allen 1827, I, 51 *ex* MS 1; Coote 1865–9, 153; Freeman 1867, V, 791 *ex* MS 1; Ellis 1868–9, 135 *ex* Sanders; Birch 1887, xii *ex* MS 1; Förster 1913 (= 1949), 34, no. II *ex* Birch 1887 collated with Sharpe 1894 and Traill & Mann 1901; Bishop & Chaplais 1957, no. 16 *ex* MS 1.

Translated: S. G. 1680, 1–2 *ex* MS 1; Maitland 1739, 28–9 (=1756, I, 38) *ex* MS 1; Entick 1766, I, 80 (defective); Noorthouck 1773, 773, no. II *ex* MS 1; Luffman 1793, 4–5 (defective); Lambert 1806, I, 46 (defective); Allen 1827, I, 51; Merewether & Stephens 1835, I, 288; Sanders 1865, 1, no. 2 *ex* MS 1; Coote 1865–9, 153; Ellis 1868–9, 135 n. 2; Birch 1887, 2, no. II; Besant 1908, 260.

References: Maitland 1739, 28–9 (= 1756, 38); Entick 1766, I, 81; Noorthouck 1773, 25 *ex* MS 1; Luffman 1793, 4–5; Lambert 1806, I, 45–6; Allen 1827, I, 51; Norton 1829 324 n. 2 (= 1869, 257 n. 3); Merewether & Stephens 1835, I, 287–8; Sanders 1865, I, Introductory Notes, no. II; Freeman 1867, V, 791; Hart 1868, 43 *ex* MSS 27–32; Loftie 1883 (= 1884), I, 86–7; Birch 1887, xii–xiii; Loftie 1887, 130–3; Round 1894, 838; PRO 1897, 246 *ex* MS 34; PRO 1901, 556 *ex* MS 33; Besant 1908, 260; *Regesta* I, 22, no. 84; PRO 1916, 399 and 473 *ex* MSS 27 and 28 respectively; Shelly 1921, 34; Morris 1927, 43 n. 17 and 51 (on Sveinn); Allen 1935, 901 *ex* MS 1; Bishop & Chaplais 1957, no. 16; Brooke 1975, 218–9; Hoad 1975, 322; Healey & Venezky 1980, 71, no. B15.186; Nightingale 1982, 38–40 and 42–3 (on Deormann); Green 1983, 132; Keynes 1988, 217 n. 192.

24

A.D. 1066 x 1075. Writ of King William (*Willem*) I to William (1 *Willem*, 2 *Will'm*), bishop (of London), Sveinn (1 *Swein*, 2 *Sweing*), sheriff (of Essex), and all his thegns of Essex (1 *on Estsexen*, 2 *on Eastsexan*) declaring that the two estates (*twa land*) at Feering (*Feringe*), (Essex), and Ockendon (1 *Wokindon'*, 2 *Wokindun*), (Essex), be granted to Westminster (Abbey) (1 *into Westminstr'*, 2 *into Westmenstr'*) in return for Windsor (1 *for Windlesor'*, 2 *for Windlesore*), (Berks.), and that Swein (1 *Sweyn*, 2 *Sweing*) is to convey those lands to the Abbey.

MSS: 1.   London, BL, Cotton Faustina A. iii, 113r (s. xiii/xiv, *temp*. Edw I)
      2.   London, Westminster Abbey, Muniment Bk 11, 243r (*olim* 244r) (s. xiv, after A.D. 1308)

Printed: *Monasticon* I, 301, no. XXXVII *ex* MS 1; Neufeldt 1907, 38–9, no. 31 *ex* MS 1.

References: Stenton 1908, 229–30 and cf. nos. **12, 13, 15** and **21** above and no. **38** below; *Regesta* I, 22, no. 87; Shelly 1921, 34 and 83; Morris 1927, 61 and n. 166; Douglas 1964, 258 and n. 4; Hoad 1975, 322; Healey & Venezky 1980, 69, no. B15.1.187; Green 1983, 132; Garnett 1986a, 99–100; Keynes 1988, 217 n. 192; Mason 1988, 28, no. 9.

25

After A.D. 1077. (On the date, see Bates 1982, 4.) Writ of King William (Latin: *Willelmus*, English: *Will'm*) I to Herfast (Latin [dative]: *Erfasti* [sic], English: *Erfast*), bishop (of Thetford), Baldwin (Latin: *Balduino*, English: *Baldewine*), abbot (of Bury St Edmunds), Picot, sheriff (of Cambridge), and Robert (Latin: *Rotberto*, English: *Rodbært*) Malet, (lord of Eye), and all his thegns declaring that he has granted Lanfranc, archbishop (of Canterbury), the land at Freckenham (Latin: *Frachenham*, English: *æt Fracenham*), (Suffolk), as fully as Harold (Latin: *Heroldus*, English: *Harold*) held it and as Thorbjorn (Latin: *Turbertus*, English: *Þurbeam*) and Gauti (Latin: *Gotinus*, English: *Goti*) held it of Harold (Latin ablative: *Heroldo*, English: *of Harolde*). (All readings from MS 9.) *Latin and English versions.*

MSS: 1. London, BL, Add. 29437, 8r (*olim* 6r) (transcript of MS ?2) (s. xvii)
2. London, BL, Cotton Domitian x, 110v (*olim* 108v) no. xxi (Latin version) (s. xiii)
3. London, BL, Cotton Faustina B. v, 72r (*olim* 71r) (Latin version) (s. xiv²)
4. London, BL, Cotton Julius C. ii, 606 (A.D. 1586; transcript of MS 9)
5. London, BL, Cotton Vespasian A. xxii, 123v (*olim* 127v) (Latin version) (s. xiii²)
6. London, BL, Stowe 940, 73v–74r (Latin), 74r (English) (A.D. 1712; transcript of MS 9)
7. London, Society of Antiquaries, 177, 41r (s. xviii transcript of MS 9)
8. Maidstone, Kent County Archives Office, DRb/Ar 2, 15r (Latin variant version only) (A.D. 1251 x 1256)
9. Maidstone, Kent County Archives Office, DRc/R1, 170v–171r (Latin version), 171r (English version) (Sawyer 1957, II, 170v–171r) (s. xii¹)
10. Oxford, Bodleian, Gough Kent 1 (17947), p. 167 (A.D. 1632; transcript of MS 9)

Printed: Wharton 1691, I, 336 *ex* MS 9; Hearne 1720, I, 141 *ex* MS 9 (Latin version only); Thorpe 1769, 359 *ex* MS 2, 445–6 *ex* MS 3; Giles 1845, 178 *ex* MS 4.

References: Wanley 1705, 186, no. IX *ex* MS 4 and 270, no. LXXI *ex* MS 9; *Regesta* I, 13, no. 47; Shelly 1921, 84; Macdonald 1926 (= 1944), 130–1; Hoad 1975, 322; Healey & Venezky 1980, 71, no. B15.1.185; Bates 1982, 4 and 168 n. 25; Green 1983, 143; Keynes 1988, 218 n. 198.

Note: London, BL, Cotton Vespasian A. xii, 123–4 gives a history in Latin of the estate at Freckenham.

26

A.D. 1066 x 1078. Writ of King William I to Herman (*Hereman*), bishop (of Sherborne), Beorhtwig (1 *Brihtwi*, 2 *Brihty*), Scewine and all his thegns in Dorset

(1 *on Dorsæton*, 2 *on Dorsatun*), declaring that the abbot of Abbotsbury (1 *Abbodesbyrig*, 2 *Abbodesbirg*), (Dorset), and the brotherhood are to have all the lands, men and things belonging to St Peter's Abbey, Abbotsbury (1 *Abbodesbirig*, 2 *Abbodesbirg*), under his protection (*mund*) as fully as were bestowed on them by Urk(i) (*Orc*) in the time of his kinsman, King Edward (*on Eadwardes dæge kyncges*). *Latin and English versions.*

MSS: 1.   London, PRO, Charter Rolls, 8 Edw II, m. 3, no. 5(3) (English version only)
     2.   London, PRO, Confirmation Rolls, 6–10 Hen VII, m. 41, no. 1

Printed: Dodsworth & Dugdale 1655, I, 279 *ex* MS 1; Hutchins 1796, II, 288 *ex* Dodsworth & Dugdale (= 1861, II, 733 *ex Monasticon*); *Monasticon* III, 56–7 no. VI *ex* MS 1.

References: Hutchins 1774, I, 533 (= 1796, II, 275 = 1861, II, 716); Hart 1868, 38 *ex* MSS 1–2; Calthrop 1908, II, 49; PRO 1908a, 274 *ex* MS 1; *Regesta* I, 28, no. 108; Harmer 1952, 119–20 and 120 n. 1; Hoad 1975, 322; Healey & Venezky 1980, 68, B15.1.188; Keynes 1988, 217 n. 192; Keynes 1989, 210–11 and 219 n. 68 (reference to a s. xvii translation by Sir Henry Spelman of a lost *inspeximus* charter of 8 Hen VIII that appears to have preserved a better text).

27

A.D. 1072 x 1078. Writ of King William I to all his lieges, French and English, declaring that he grants to St Paul's Church, London (10–11 *de Lundonia*, 9, 12 *de London'*), and its *rectores* and *servitores* rights over all the lands it holds or will hold inside and outside the city. Witnesses (all in the ablative case): Osmund the chancellor (*cancellario*); Lanfranc, archbishop of Canterbury (*Cantuarensi*); Thomas (9–11 *Toma* 12 *Thoma*), archbishop of York (*Eboracensi*); Roger, earl of Shrewsbury (*comite* 9 *de Seropesbira*, 10–11 *de Seropesbiria*, 12 *de Saropesberia*), Alan, earl (*comite*) (of Richmond); Geoffrey de Mandeville (9–11 *Gaufrido de Magnauilla*, 12 *Ganfrido de Magnauilla*); and Ranulf Peverel (*Peuerel*). (All readings from MSS 9–12.) *Bilingual.*

MSS: 1.   Cambridge, Univ. Lib., Ee. 5. 21, 97r (*olim* 79r) (s. xv transcript of *inspeximus* of Edward III)
     2.   Cambridge, Univ. Lib., Ee. 5. 21, 128v (*olim* 110v) (s. xv transcript of *inspeximus* of Hen VI)
     3.   Cambridge, Pembroke College, 299, 25v (s. xviii transcript of MS 14)
     4.   Cambridge, Pembroke College, 299, 62v–63r (English on 63r) (s. xviii transcript of MS 15)
     5.   London, BL, Cotton Vespasian B. xv, 42v (*olim* 40v) (s. xvi transcript of MS 12)
     6.   London, BL, Harl. 84, 1r (s. xvii transcript of MS 13)
     7.   London, BL, Harl. 85, 18r (s. xvii transcript of MS 14)
     8.   London, BL, Harl. 85, 42 (s.xvii transcript of MS 15)
     9.   London, Guildhall, 25, 272, m. 2, no. 13 (s. xiii^2)
   10.   London, Guildhall, 25, 501, IIa, no. 9 (A.D. 1241)
   11.   London, Guildhall, 25, 504, 16v–17r (s. xiii)
   12.   London, Guildhall, 25, 520, 71v–72r (English on 71v) (s. xv)
   13.   London, PRO, Cartae Antiquae, Roll 1, m. 1, no. 1 (*olim* A. 3)

14. London, PRO, Cartae Antiquae, Roll 26, no. 9 (*olim* BB. 9)
15. London, PRO, Cartae Antiquae, Roll 27, no. 14 (*olim* CC. 14)
16. London, PRO, Charter Rolls, 9 Edw II, m. 12, no. 37(2)
17. London, PRO, Charter Rolls, 12 Edw III, m. 8, no. 13 (1[2])
18. London, PRO, Charter Rolls, 12 Ric II, m. 22, no. 22 (1[3])
19. London, PRO, Confirmation Rolls, 2 Ric III, pt 2, m. 14, no. 10
20. London, PRO, Confirmation Rolls, 2 Hen VII, pt 2, m. 24, no. 9
21. London, PRO, Confirmation Rolls, 3 Hen VII, pt 3, m. 8, no. 11
22. London, PRO, Confirmation Rolls, 1 Hen VIII, pt 6, m. 34, no. 1
23. London, PRO, Confirmation Rolls, 1 Hen VIII, pt 7, m. 12, no. 7
24. London, PRO, Confirmation Rolls, 2 Eliz I, pt 2, m. 4, no. 7
25. London, PRO, Confirmation Rolls, 3 Jas I, pt 3, m. 1, no. 10
26. London, PRO, Hilary recorda rotulet 28 (22 Hen VI)
27. London, PRO, Patent Rolls, 2 Hen IV, pt 2, m. 29
28. London, PRO, Patent Rolls, 1 Hen V, pt 4, m. 3
29. London, PRO, Patent Rolls, 2 Hen VI, pt 3, m. 15 (1[2])

Printed: Dugdale 1658, 190–1 (= 1818, 298, App. No. XVIII) *ex* MSS 16 and
28; Simpson 1873, 112–13 *ex* MSS 1, 2 and 12; PRO 1908a, 291, no. 37(2) *ex*
MS 16; Gibbs 1939, 13–14, no. 9 *ex* MSS 9–12.
Translated: Stow 1598, 262 (= 1603, 326); Strype 1720, I, bk. 3, 142; Kingsford
1908, I, 324.
References: Dugdale 1658, 5 (= 1818, 4); Hardwick 1856–67, II, 182, no. 13 *ex*
MSS 1 and 2; Hart 1868, 48 *ex* MSS 13 and 19–25 (recorded under William II);
PRO 1901, 209 *ex* MS 29; PRO 1903, 433 *ex* MS 27; James 1905, 263 *ex* MSS 3
and 4; Kingsford 1908, II, 345; PRO 1908a, 291 *ex* MS 16; Stenton 1908, 324
(on Alan); PRO 1910, 147 *ex* MS 28; PRO 1912, 451 *ex* MS 17; PRO 1916, 310
ex MS 18; *Regesta* I, 29, no. 111 (for addenda see *Regesta* II, 393); Landon 1939,
1, no. 1 *ex* MS 13; Doyle 1949, 32–5 (on MS 1/2); Hoad 1975, 322; Healey &
Venezky 1980, 71, B15.1.190 = 72, no. B15.1.203; Keynes 1988, 218 n. 198.

28

31 May 1081. Diploma of King William I to archbishops, bishops, abbots, earls
and all the faithful, supporting the rights of Baldwin (*Baldwine*), abbot of Bury St
Edmunds (*on Sc'e Eadmundes mynstre*), against the claims of Herfast (*Arfast*),
bishop (of Thetford). Witnesses (in Latinized form): William, king of the
English; Mathilda (*Mathildis*) the queen; Lanfranc (*Landfrancus*), archbishop of
Canterbury (*Cantuariensis*); Thomas, archbishop of York (*Eboracensis*); Odo,
bishop of Bayeux (*Baiocensis*); Geoffrey (*Goffridus*), bishop of Coutances (*Con-
stantiensis*); Hugh (*Hugo*), bishop of London (*Lundoniensis*); Walchelin (*Uual-
quelinus*), bishop of Winchester (*Uuintoniensis*); Wulfstan (*Uulfstanus*), bishop
(of Worcester); Remigius, (bishop of Lincoln); Stigand, (bishop of Chichester);
Osbert, (bishop of ?); Peter (*Petrus*), (bishop of Lichfield); Herfast (*Arfastus*),
(bishop of Thetford); Gundulf (bishop of Rochester); Osmund, (bishop of Salisbury); Robert (*Rodbertus*) (of Lorraine), (bishop of Hereford); Robert (*Rodbertus*), son of the king and count (*comes*) (of Maine); William, son of the king;
Henry (*Heinricus*), son of the king; Maurice, chancellor (*cancellarius*) of the
king; Bernard, chaplain (*cappellanus* [*sic*]) of the king; Scotland, abbot of St
Augustine's (Abbey, Canterbury); Wulfweald (*Uulfuuoldus*), abbot (of Bath and

Chertsey); Vitalis (*Uitalis*), abbot (of Westminster); Æthelnoth (*Ægelnodus*), abbot (of Glastonbury); Turold (*Toroldus*), abbot (of Peterborough); Riwallon (*Ruallonus*), abbot (of New Minster, Winchester); Roger (*Rocgerius*) (of Montgomery), *comes* (earl of Shrewsbury); Hugh (*Hugo*), *comes* (earl of Chester); Alan, *comes* (earl of Richmond); Aubrey (de Vere, probably ancestor of the earls of Oxford) (*Albericus comes*); Robert of Beaumont-le-Roger (*Rodbertus de Bello Monte*), (Eure); Hugh of Montfort-sur-Risle (*Hugo de Monteforti*), (Eure); Richard, son of Count Gilbert (genitive: *Gisleb'ti*) (of Brionne); Baldwin (*Balduuinus*), his brother; Henry of Ferrières-Saint-Hilaire (*Heinricus de Ferrariis*), (Eure); Hugh of Grandmesnil (*Hugo de Grentemaisnil*); Walter Giffard (*Uualterius Gifardus*); Edward (*Eduuardus*), sheriff (of Wiltshire); and Roger (*Rocgerius*) (Bigod), sheriff (of Norfolk and Suffolk). (All readings from MS 1; for variants, see Douglas 1932.) *Latin and English versions.*

MSS: 1.   London, BL, Cotton Augustus II, no. 25 (purported original)
       2.   London, BL, Add. 14847, 31v–32v (Latin version only; witnesses imperfect) (s. xiii)
       3.   London, BL, Harl. 76, 140–141r (Latin version only) (s. xii)
       4.   Cambridge, Univ. Lib., Ff. 2. 33, 23v (Latin version only) (s. xiii^2)
       5.   Cambridge, Univ. Lib., Gg. 4. 4, 97v–98r (*olim* 163v–164r; Latin version only) (s. xv)
       6.   Cambridge, Univ. Lib., Mm. 4. 19, 91v–93r (Latin version only) (s. xii^2)
       7.   Oxford, Bodleian, Bodl. 297 (2468), pp. 387–9 (Latin version only) (s. xii)

Printed: *Monasticon* III, 141, no. XII *ex* MS 7; Arnold 1890, I, 347–50, no. VI *ex* MS 7; Goodwin 1855, 99–101 *ex* MS ?1 (English version only); Douglas 1932, 50–5, no. 7 *ex* MS 1.

Translated: Goodwin 1855, 101–103.

References: Hardwick 1856–67, II, 362, no. 80 *ex* MS 4, III, 108, no. 289 *ex* MS 5 and IV, 235, no. 161 *ex* MS 6; *DNB* IX, 694; Round 1892, 388–9 (on Aubrey de Vere); Cox 1907, II, 58; *Regesta* I, 36, no. 137 ('The style bears all the marks of a forgery') (for addenda and a correction see *Regesta* II, 394); Douglas 1932, xxv n. 7 *ex* MS 3, xxxii–xxxiv ('the case for forgery is as yet not proven' [xxxiv]) and lxii–lxiii; Harmer 1952, 142–4; Bishop 1953, 434 *ex* MS 1; Ker 1960, 19–20 and 20 n. 1 *ex* MSS 1 and 3; Hoad 1975, 322; Healey & Venezky 1980, 68, no. B15.1.191; Gransden 1982, 70–2 and 191–2 nn. 85–98 ('forgery'); Keynes 1988, 220 n. 217 ('matter requires more detailed investigation').

29

A.D. 1076 x 1083. Writ of King William I to William of Courseulles-sur-Mêr (dative: *Willelme de Curcello*) ordering that he see that Peter's Pence (English: *Rom feoh*, Latin: *denarii Romani*) be paid by his men by Michaelmas and that he make this known at Montacute (English: *to Munt Acuht*, Latin: *aput Montem Acutum*), (Somerset), and Bristol (English: *to Bristoye*, Latin: *Bristoll'*), (Gloucs.); the bishop (of Wells) and William should investigate who does not pay; no one, furthermore, is to take possession of the land of Giso (English: *Gyse*, Latin: G.), bishop (of Wells), before he comes. *English and Latin versions.*

MS: Wells, D & C, 'Liber Albus I' ('Registrum I'), 18r (s. xiii med.)

Printed: Hist. MSS Comm. 1885, 10; Hist. MSS Comm. 1907, I, 17; Hall 1908, 52, no. 47.
References: Wanley 1705, 285, no. 9; Hall 1908, 16 and 51; *Regesta* I, 51, no. 187; Shelly 1921, 82; Morris 1927, 62 and n. 176; Woodbine 1943, 405 n. 3; Hoad 1975, 322; Healey & Venezky 1980, 70, no. B15.1.192; Keynes 1988, 218 n. 198.

30

A.D. 1066 x 1084. Writ of King William (*Uuillelm*) I to his bishops, earls and thegns, in those shires where Wulfweald (*Wulfwold*), abbot (of Bath and Chertsey), has lands and men, confirming his rights and that Charlcombe (*æt Ceorlecumbe*), (Somerset), remain in the possession of St Peter's (Abbey), Bath (*on Baðan*), as before. The bounds of Charlcombe (*æt Ceorlacumbe*) are appended.
MS: Cambridge, CCC, 111, pp. 94–5 (s. xii^2)
Printed: Hunt 1893, 37, no. 32 (incorrectly numbered 31).
References: Wanley 1705, 150; James 1909–12, 230, no. 39; *Regesta* I, 64, no. 241; Shelly 1921, 82; Hoad 1975, 322; Healey & Venezky 1980, 70, no. B15.1.194; Keynes 1988, 217 n. 192.

31

A.D. 1070 x 1087. Writ of King William (*Willelm*) I to Walchelin, bishop (of Winchester), Hugh of Port-en-Bessin (*Hugan de Port*), (Calvados), Edward (*Eadward*), sheriff (of Wilts.), Odo (1 *Oda*, 2 *Odan*), Æthelsige (*Ægelsi*), Sæwulf (*Saulf*), Ælfsige of Hatch (*Ælfsi æt Hæccan*), (?Hants.), Cola (*Cole*), Eadric and all his thegns in Hampshire (1 *Hamtunscyre*, 2 *Hamtunscire*) and Wiltshire (1 *Wiltunscyre*, 2 *Wiltunscire*) declaring that St Peter's (i.e. New Minster, later Hyde Abbey, Winchester) and Walchelin be entitled to all the rights (*beon ealra þære lagena weorðe*) which Ælfwine (1 *Ælwine*, 2 *Ælfine*), bishop (of Winchester), possessed in King Edward's day (1 *on Eadwerdes dage kynges*, 2 *on Eardwerdes dage kynges*). (All readings from MSS 1 and 2.)
MSS: 1.   London, BL, Add. 29436, 10v (s. xiii med.)
       2.   London, PRO, Charter Rolls, 10 Edw II, m. 6, no. 7(3)
       3.   London, PRO, Charter Rolls, 9 Edw III, m. 10, no. 40(3)
       4.   London, PRO, Charter Rolls, 4 Ric II, m. 13, no. 10(3)
       5.   London, PRO, Exchequer Transcripts, 31/16, no. 4 (untraced; see *Regesta* I, 70, no. 267)
Printed: PRO 1908a, 348, no. 3 *ex* MS 2.
References: *Regesta* I, 70, no. 267; PRO 1912, 340 *ex* MS 3; PRO 1916, 271 *ex* MS 4; Shelly 1921, 34; Morris 1927, 47 n. 47 (on Hugh de Port); Healey & Venezky 1980, 71, no. B15.1.189; Keynes 1988, 218 n. 198.

32

A.D. 1070 x 1087. Writ of King William (1 *Willælm*, 2 *Willæm*) I to Walchelin (*Wælcælin*), bishop (of Winchester), Hugh of Port-en-Bessin (accusative: *Hugæn dæ Port*), (Calvados), Edward (*Eadward*), sheriff (of Wilts.), and all his thegns in Hampshire and Wiltshire (1 *on Hampton' 7 Wiltonæ sciræ*, 2 *on Hæmpton' 7 on Wilton' sciræ*) declaring that he has granted the land at Buttermere (*æt Bwtærmæræ*), (Wilts.), to the (monastic) congregation of the Old Minster at Winchester (*on Wintanceastræ*) to have as freely as they had it in the time of Wulfwig (genitive: *Wlwiæ*), when he gave it to the Old Minster on becoming a monk in the time of King Cnut (1 *on Ciningæ Cænut dægæ*, 2 *on Cining Cænut dægæ*). Written at London (*æt London*) and witnessed by Walchelin (*Wælcælin*), bishop (of Winchester); Odo (*Odan*); Æthelsige (1 *Ælgælfsi*, 2 *Ælgælsi*); Sæwulf (1 *Saulf*, 2 *Sawlf*); Ælfsige (*Ælfsi*); and Eadric.

MSS: 1. London, BL, Add. 15350, 119v (s. xiv[1]) (Rumble 1980, pl. XXIII)

2. London, BL, Cotton Charter VIII. 15 (s. xiv[1])

Unprinted.

References: *Regesta* I, 70, no. 268 *ex* MS 2; Rumble 1980, 232–3, no. 242; Rumble 1982, 224 n. 4 (date of MS 1); Keynes 1988, 218 n. 198.

33

A.D. 1070 x 1087. Writ of King William (Eng.: *Willelm*, Lat.: Hickes *Willelmus*, MS *Willelmus*) I to Geoffrey (Eng.: *Gosfregð*, Lat. [dative]: Hickes *Goisfredo*, MS *Goisfrido*), sheriff (of London), and all the citizens of London (Eng.: *ealle þe burhwaru binnan Lundene*, Lat.: Hickes *ceteris Lundoniensibus*, MS *ceteris Lundoniensibus*) ordering them not to take wild animals nor hunt without permission on the land at Harrow on the Hill (Eng.: *into Hergan*, Lat.: Hickes *ad Hergam*, MS *ad Hergam*), (Middlesex), that belongs to Lanfranc, archbishop (of Canterbury). *English and Latin versions.*

Source: Hickes 1703, I, XVI *ex* apparently lost Cotton MS

MS: London, Lambeth Palace, 1212, 8v (p. 15), no. 3 (Latin version only; MS notes: 'Idem in anglico ibidem') (s. xiii/xiv)

Printed: *Monasticon* I, 111, no. XXXIX *ex* Hickes.

References: Round 1894, 838; *Regesta* I, 69, no. 265 (for an addendum see *Regesta* II, 397); Shelly 1921, 82; Weinbaum 1929, 12; James & Jenkins 1930–2, 831 *ex* MS; Harmer 1952, 179 and n. 2; Hoad 1975, 322; Healey & Venezky 1980, 69, no. B15.1.195; Green 1983, 131; Keynes 1988, 218 n. 198.

34

A.D. 1070 x 1087. Writ of King William (*Willelm*) I to his bishops, earls, sheriffs and all his thegns, French and English (*Frencisce 7 Englisce*), in the shires where Walchelin (*Walkelin*), bishop (of Winchester), has land, confirming him in his bishopric and the legal rights attached to it. Witness: Robert d'Oyly (*R de Oileio*) (Ouilly-le-Basset, Calvados).

MS: London, BL, Add. 29436, 11v (s. xiii med.)

Printed: Galbraith 1920, 386, no. II.

References: *Regesta* II, 398, no. 288f; Hoad 1975, 322; Healey & Venezky 1980, 70, no. B15.1.199; Keynes 1988, 218 n. 198.

35

A.D. 1070 x 1087. Writ of King William (*Willelm*) I to his bishops, earls, sheriffs, and all his thegns in Hampshire (*on Hamtescyram*) where Walchelin (*Walkelin*), bishop (of Winchester), has land confirming him in his bishopric and the legal rights attached to it.

MS: London, BL, Add. 29436, 11r (s. xiii med.)

Printed: Galbraith 1920, 386, no. III.

References: *Regesta* II, 398, no. 288g; Hoad 1975, 322; Healey & Venezky 1980, 70, no. B15.1.200; Keynes 1988, 218 n. 198.

36

A.D. 1071 x 1087 (Gibbs; *Regesta* II, 396: '1075 or 1085'). Writ of King William I to his bishops, earls and thegns where St Paul's Minster (*mynstre*), (London), has land declaring that it should possess the same rights as it had in the time of any former king.

MSS: 1.   London, Guildhall, 25, 272, m. 1, no. 1 (s. xiii^2)
         2.   London, Guildhall, 25, 501, I, no. 3 (A.D. 1241)
Printed: Gibbs 1939, 10, no. 3 *ex* MS 2.
References: Davis 1925, 51; *Regesta* II, 396, no. 208b; Hoad 1975, 322; Healey & Venezky 1980, 70, no. B15.1.193; Keynes 1988, 218 n. 198.

37

A.D. 1071 x 1087. Writ of King William (1 *Willeam*, 2 *W.*) I to his sheriffs and thegns in the shires, where the canons of St Paul's Minster (dative: *mynstre*), (London), have land, confirming their legal rights.

MSS: 1.   London, Guildhall, 25, 272, m. 1, no. 2 (s. xiii^2)
         2.   London, Guildhall, 25, 501, I, no. 2 (A.D. 1241)
Printed: Gibbs 1939, 9–10, no. 2 *ex* MS 2.
References: *Regesta* I, 116–7 no. 484 (for addenda see *Regesta* II, 408); Hoad 1975, 322; Keynes 1988, 218 n. 198.
Note: Gibbes 1939, 10 n. 1 states that this 'is perhaps an O.E. version of [Gibbs 1939, 12,] No. 6' dated by her as July 1099 x 1100 and accepted as such in *Regesta* II, 408. The later date is possible.

38

A.D. 1085 x 1087. Writ of King William (*Willem*) I to all his true friends where St Peter's (Abbey, Westminster), and Gilbert (*Gilleberd*) (Crispin), abbot (of Westminster), have land, granting the abbot legal rights.

MSS: 1.   London, BL, Cotton Faustina A. iii, 113 (s. xiii/xiv, *temp.* Edw I)
         2.   London, Westminster Abbey, Muniment Bk 11, 53r (*olim* 47r)
            (s. xiv, after 1308)
Printed: *Monasticon* I, 301, no. XXXVIII *ex* MS 1; Neufeldt 1907, 39, no. 32 *ex* MS 1.
References: Stenton 1908, 229–30 and cf. nos. **12, 13, 15, 21** and **24** above; *Regesta* I, 73, no. 279 ('spurious'); Healey & Venezky 1980, 69, no. B15.1.197; Keynes 1988, 218 n. 198; Mason 1988, 39, no. 42.

39

Christmas 1085 x 1087. Writ of King William I to Osmund, bishop of Salisbury (*Seorbyrig*), Robert of Ely (*Eli*), Peter of Valognes (1 *Piedres of Valoniis*, 2 *Aloynes*), (Manche), his sheriffs and officials (*holdas*), French and English (*Frencisce 7 Englisce*), declaring that he has given to Maurice, bishop of London (*Lundene*), the castle at Bishop's Stortford (*Estorteford*), (Herts.), and all the land formerly held by William (*Will'm*), bishop (of London), as well as the land held of him by William the deacon (*Will'm þe diacon*) and Ralph (*Raulf*) (his brother), together with the rights held by Bishop William (*Will's* [*sic*]).

MSS: 1.   London, Guildhall, 25, 272, m. 1, no. 4 (s. xiii^2)
         2.   London, Guildhall, 25, 501, I, no. 5 (A.D. 1241)

Printed: Dugdale 1658, 196 (= 1818, App. XXIII, p. 304) *ex* MS 2; Gibbs 1939, 12, no. 5 *ex* MS 2.
Translated: Dugdale 1658, 196–7 (= 1818, App. XXIII, p. 305 (translation into Latin); Leland 1715, I.2, 358 (= 1774, II.358) (abstract in Latin) *ex* MS 2.
References: Stow 1598, 261 (= 1603, 326); Dugdale 1658, 5 (= 1818, 4); Strype 1720, I, bk 3, 142; Kingsford 1908, I, 324 and II, 345; *Regesta* I, 72–3, no. 277 (for a correction and addenda see *Regesta* II, 398); Shelly 1921, 82; Hoad 1975, 322; Healey & Venezky 1980, 70, no. B15.1.196; Keynes 1988, 218 n. 198.

King William I or King William II

40

A.D. 1070 x 1087 or 1087 x 1089. Writ of King William to the archbishops, bishops, abbots, earls and other barons of England confirming to St Andrew's Church, Rochester (*ipsa ecclesia sancti Andrei Roffensis*) its manors, lands, possessions and rights. The document is confirmed by Lanfranc, archbishop of Canterbury. *Bilingual: Latin with English rights clause.*
MS: Maidstone, Kent County Archives Office, DRc/T58/1 (*c*. A.D. 1265)
Unprinted.
Reference: Oakley 1970, I.1, 154.

41

A.D. 1070 x May 1092. Writ of King William (*Will'm*) (I or II) to Thomas (*Þomas*), archbishop (of York), Thoraldr (*Þurold*), Earnwig, his sheriff(s) and all the thegns in Nottinghamshire (*on Snotingehamscyre*) and Lincolnshire (*on Lincolscyre*), French and English (*Frencisce 7 Englisce*), declaring that he grants to St Mary's (Abbey) at Stow (*æt Stowe*), (Lincs.), and the monks Newark (*Niweweorce*), (Notts.), Fledborough (*Fladburh*), (Notts.), Brampton (*Brantune*), (Lincs.), and Well Wapentake (*Wylle Wepentæc*), (Lincs.), with legal rights as fully as Godgifu (*Godgyfe*) had it in the time of King Edward (*on Eadweardes dæge kynges*). (All readings from MS 2.)
MSS: 1.   London, BL, Cotton Vespasian B. xv, 9v (*olim* 7v) (s. xvi)
      2.   Oxford, Christ Church, Chapter Library, 'Eynsham Cartulary', Kitchen's Catalogue, no. 341, 17v, no. XXVII (Brown 1904, I, 18) (s. xii[2])
Printed: Salter 1907, I, 48–50 *ex* MS 2.
Translated: W. H. Stevenson in Brown 1904, I, 18; Salter 1907, I, 50.
References: W. H. Stevenson in Brown 1904, I, 18; W. H. Stevenson in Salter 1907, I, 48 n. 2 (on date) and 50 nn. 1–3; *Regesta* I, 87, no. 333; Shelly 1921, 82 and 83; Healey & Venezky 1980, 71, no. B15.1.201; Gelling 1982, 191 (on the place-name Stow); Keynes 1988, 218 n. 198.

King William II

42

A.D. 1088. Diploma of King William II to the archbishops, bishops, abbots, earls and other barons of England granting to the Church of St Andrew the Apostle,

Rochester (*Roffensis*), the manor of Haddenham (*Hedrehan*), (Bucks.), at the request of Lanfranc, archbishop (of Canterbury), and also the Church of St Mary of Lambeth (*Lamhytha*), (Surrey), and its vill in reparation for damage caused the church by the king when acting against his enemies in the city. Witnesses (all in the genitive case): Lanfranc, archbishop of Canterbury (*Cantuariensis*); Thomas (*Thome*), archbishop of York (*Eboracensis*); Remigius, bishop of Lincoln (*Lincolniensis*); Walchelin (*Walcelini*), bishop of Winchester (*Wintoniensis*); Maurice, bishop of London (*Londoniensis*); Osmund, bishop of Salisbury (*Seresberiensis*); Robert (*Roberti*), bishop of Hereford (*Herefordensis*); Baldwin (*Baldewini*), abbot of Bury St Edmunds (*Sancti Eadmundi*); Henry, son of the king; Alan (the Red), *comitis* (lord of Richmond); Hugh (*Hugonis*) (of Montgomery), *comitis* (earl of Shrewsbury); Hugh of Montfort-sur-Risle (*de Monte Forti Hugonis*), (Eure); Gilbert (fitz Richard) of Tonbridge (*Gileberti de Tunebruge*), (Kent). (All readings from MS 1.) *Bilingual: Latin with English rights clause.*

MSS: 1. London, BL, Campbell Charter VII. 1. a (original) (Sanders 1865, no. 4)

   2. London, BL, Cotton Domitian x, 107r–108r (*olim* 105r–106r), no. xi (witness list incomplete) (s. xiii)

   3. London, PRO, Charter Rolls, 50 Hen III, m. 1A(1) (damaged)

   4. London, PRO, Charter Rolls, 3 Edw I, m. 2(4)

   5. London, PRO, Charter Rolls, 9 Edw III, m. 8, no. 36(1)

   6. London, PRO, Charter Rolls, 10 Edw III, m. 25, no. 51(1)

   7. London, PRO, Confirmation Rolls, 1 Hen VIII, pt 8, m. 1, no. 2

   8. London, PRO, Patent Rolls, 2 Hen VI, pt 2, m. 27(2[1])

   9. London, PRO, Patent Rolls, 12 Edw IV, pt 2, m. 14(2[4])

  10. London, PRO, Patent Rolls, 12 Edw IV, pt 2, m. 13(4[1])

  11. London, PRO, Patent Rolls, 12 Edw IV, pt 2, mm. 12–11(5[1])

  12. Maidstone, Kent County Archives Office, DRb/Ar 2, 11v

  13. Maidstone, Kent County Archives Office, DRb/Ar 2, 15v (transcript of MS 14)

  14. Maidstone, Kent County Archives Office, DRc/T60/1 (witness list incomplete) (*inspeximus* of Hen III, A.D. 1265)

  15. Maidstone, Kent County Archives Office, DRc/T65/1 (partial) (*inspeximus* of Edw IV, A.D. 1475)

  16. Maidstone, Kent County Archives Office, DRc/T66/B. 4 (*inspeximus* of Hen VII, A.D. 1486)

  17. Maidstone, Kent County Archives Office, DRc/T66/D. 1. a (*inspeximus* of Hen VII, A.D. 1486)

  18. Maidstone, Kent County Archives Office, DRc/T66/E. 1. a (*inspeximus* of Hen VII, A.D. 1486)

Printed: Thorpe 1769, 382–3 (without witnesses) *ex* MS ?14; Clarke *et al.* 1816, 5 *ex* MS 14; PRO 1906, 194–5 *ex* MS 4.

Translated: Sanders 1865, I, no. 4.

References: Sanders 1865, I, Introductory Notes, no. 4; Hart 1868, 44 *ex* MSS 3–6; PRO 1900, 370 *ex* MSS 9 and 10 and 371 *ex* MS 11; PRO 1901, 182 *ex* MS 8; PRO 1906, 59–60 *ex* MS 3; PRO 1912, 341 *ex* MS 5 and 354 *ex* MS 6; *Regesta* I, 78, no. 301 (for an addendum see *Regesta* II, 399); Davis 1958, 93, no. 818 *ex* MS 2; Oakley 1970, I.1, 157–9 *ex* MS 14, 172 *ex* MS 15, 176 *ex* MS 16, 183 *ex*

MS 17, 184 *ex* MS 18 and I.2, 1007 *ex* MS 12–13; Healey & Venezky 1980, 72, B15.1.202.
Note: A document in Maidstone, Kent County Archives Office, DRc/R1 ('Textus Roffensis'), 212r–213r employs the same wording as part of this document but omits reference to Lanfranc and has no rights clause.

King Henry I

43

25 December 1100. Writ of King Henry (1 *Henri*, 2 *Henric*) I to his sheriffs and thegns of London (1 *of Londen'*, 2 *of Lundene*) and in Essex, Hertfordshire and Middlesex (1 *on Essex' and on Middelsex' and on Herford*, 2 *on Essaxan 7 on Hortfordscire 7 on Middelsexan*) declaring that he has granted to Maurice (1 *Mauriz*, 2 *Maurice*) the bishopric of London (1 *of Londen*, 2 *on Lundone*) with its legal rights as his father and brother had done. Witness: Robert (1 *Roberth'*, 2 *Rob'*), bishop of Lincoln (1 deficient, 2 *of Lincolne*). Declared at Westminster (1 *on Westmenstre*, 2 *on Westminystre*) at Christmas.
MSS: 1.   London, Guildhall, 25, 272, m. 1, no. 3 (imperfect) (s. xiii^2)
          2.   London, Guildhall, 25, 501, IIb (= 2r), no. 19 (A.D. 1241)
Printed: Gibbs 1939, 20–1, no. 23 *ex* MS 2.
References: *Regesta* II, 5, no. 506; Healey & Venezky 1980, 67, B15.1.204; Keynes 1988, 218 n. 198.

44

September 1100 x 1 July 1101. Diploma of Henry (*H.*) I, king of England (*Ænglelandes kining*), to Hugh of Buckland (Lat.: *Huge de Bocland*, Eng.: *Huge de Boclande*), W(illiam), (son of) Beinhard (Lat.: *Baignardo*, Eng.: *Bainard*), and all his officials (Lat.: *ministris*, Eng.: *wicnæres*) in London declaring that all the men of Anselm, archbishop (genitive: *arcebiscpes*) (of Canterbury), in London (Lat.: *in Lundonia*, Eng.: *on Lundene*) and all his men who come and go in the city be immune from all customs as was the case for Archbishop Lanfranc (Lat.: *Lanfrancus*, Eng.: *Landfranc*) in the time of his father. Witness: Hugh (*Hug.*), earl of Chester (Lat.: *Huge comite de Cestra*, Eng.: *Huge comite de Cestra*). At Westminster (Lat.: *Apud Westmoster'*, Eng.: *Ap' Westmonst'*). *Latin and English versions.*
Source: Parker 1572, 103
MS: London, Lambeth Palace 1212, 14r (= p. 25), no. 7 (Latin version only; MS notes: 'Idem in Anglico ibidem) (s. xiii/xiv)
Printed: Clarke *et al.* 1816, I, 12 *ex* Parker (English) and *ex* MS ?1 (Latin).
References: James & Jenkins 1930–2, 831 *ex* MS; Harmer 1952, 174 n. 3; *Regesta* II, 10, no. 532; Healey & Venezky 1980, 67, no. B15.1.205; Keynes 1988, 218 n. 198.

45

A.D. 1103, c. ?Jan 13 (*Regesta* II, 29). Writ of King Henry (*Henri*) I to his bishops, earls, sheriffs, thegns and his officials (*wicneras*), French and English (*Frencisce 7 Englisce*), throughout England (*ouer eall Englaland*) declaring that he has granted to St Peter's (*Sancte Petre*) (Cathedral, Winchester), and to William, bishop of Winchester (*þan biscope on Winceastre Willelme*), and his monks the

same freedom and rights that the Minster had in the time of King Edward (*on Eadwardes kynges dæge*), of his father, and of his brother.
MS: London, BL, Add. 29436, 13v–14r (s. xiii med.)
Printed: Galbraith 1920, 389, no. XIII.
References: Regesta II, 29, no. 627; Healey & Venezky 1980, 67, no. B15.1.209.

46

A.D. ?1107 (Birch 1873, 243: 1103 x 1106; Wyon & Wyon 1887, 10: 1100 x 21 April 1109). Writ of King Henry (H.) I to his bishops, earls, sheriffs and thegns, French and English (*Fræncisce & Ænglisce*), in the shires where Anselm, archbishop (of Canterbury), and the congregation of Christ Church, Canterbury (*on Cantewareberig*), have land, confirming the legal rights over the land that they had in the time of his kinsman, King Edward (*on Eadwordes kynges dæge*), and his father, King William I. (All readings from the English version of MS 1.) *Latin and English versions.*
MSS: 1. London, BL, Campbell Charter XXIX. 5 (with seal) (original) (Clanchy 1979, pl. III)
2. London, BL, Cotton Charter VII. 1 (original) (damaged)
3. London, Lambeth Palace, Cart. Misc. XI/1 (original) (damaged)
4. Canterbury, D & C, Blore Collection 88 (s. xx transcript *ex* MS 6)
5. Canterbury, D & C, Ch. Ant. C. 1310(2) (Roll) (damaged)
6. Canterbury, D & C, Register A, 80v (*olim* 91v), no. 239 (Latin version only) (s. xiii^2)
7. Canterbury, D & C, Register I, 62 (*olim* 74) (Latin version only, containing English rights clause; MS notes on 62v 'Item idem tenor Anglice') (s. xiii^2)
8. London, Lambeth Palace, Cart. Misc. XII/32 (*inspeximus* of Hen VI)
9. London, Lambeth Palace, Cart. Misc. XII/33 (with fragmentary seal) (*inspeximus* of Edw IV, 15 April 1463)
10. London, Lambeth Palace, Cart. Misc. XII/34 (*inspeximus* of Hen VIII, 24 February 1510)
11. London, Lambeth Palace, 1212, 98v (= p.189) (s. xiii/xiv)
12. London, PRO, Charter Rolls, 9 Edw III, m. 4, no. 19(1) (Johnson & Jenkinson 1915, II, pl. XXXIV)
13. London, PRO, Charter Rolls, 1 Hen IV, pt 1, m. 51, no. 19(1[1])
14. London, PRO, Charter Rolls, 1 Hen V, pt 3, m. 5, no. 2
15. London, PRO, Charter Rolls, 2–4 Edw IV, m. 15, no. 8
16. London, PRO, Confirmation Rolls, 4 Hen VII, pt 1, mm. 14–15, no. 4
17. London, PRO, Confirmation Rolls, 1 Hen VIII, pt 3, mm. 9–10, no. 6
18. London, PRO, Patent Rolls, 1 Ric II, pt 2, m. 12
19. London, PRO, Patent Rolls, 2 Hen VI, pt 3, m. 28(1[1])
20. London, PRO, Patent Rolls, 12 Hen VI, pt 2, m. 9, nos. 13–14
21. Oxford, Bodleian, Tanner 223 (10049), 24v (*olim* p. 44) (Latin version only) (s. xvi^2)
Printed: Hickes 1703, I, XVI *ex* MS 2; *Monasticon* I, 109, no. XXXII *ex* MS 21;

Monasticon I, 111, no. XXXIX *ex* Hickes; Birch 1873, 242 *ex* MS 1; PRO 1912, 345 *ex* MS 12; Johnson & Jenkinson 1915, I, 217–220 at pp. 218–19 *ex* MS 12.
References: Birch 1873, 242–5; Wyon & Wyon 1887, 10, nos. 19 and 20 and pl. III (seal); Hart 1869, 197 *ex* MSS 12 and 15–19; PRO 1895, 77 *ex* MS 18; PRO 1901, 197 *ex* MS 19; Warner & Ellis 1903, I, [6]; PRO 1907, 418, nos. 13–14 *ex* MS 20; Johnson & Jenkinson 1915, I, 216–17; PRO 1916, 384 and 466 *ex* MSS 13 and 14 respectively; James & Jenkins 1930–2, 831 *ex* MS 11; Harmer 1952, 174 and n. 3 and 175; *Regesta* II, 72, no. 840; Bishop 1960, 52, no. 335 *ex* MS 1, 53, no. 344 *ex* MS 2 and 56, no. 400 *ex* MS 3; Ker 1960, 20 n. 3 *ex* MSS 1–3; Owen 1968, 124 *ex* MS 3 and 139 *ex* MSS 8–10; Bishop 1971, xix and n. 3 *ex* MSS 1–3; Clanchy 1979, p. opp. pl. III *ex* MS 1; Healey & Venezky 1980, 67, no. B15.1.206; Keynes 1988, 218 n. 198.

47

After 29 June 1114. Writ of King Henry (H.) I to his bishops, earls, sheriffs and thegns, French and English (1 *Francisce 7 Æn…* [damaged], 2 *Fræncisc 7 Ænglisc*, Somner *Fræncisce 7 Ænglisc*), in the shires where Ralph (*Raulf*), archbishop (of Canterbury), and the congregation of Christ Church, Canterbury (*on Cantwareberig*), have land confirming the legal rights which they possessed in the time of his kinsman, King Edward (1, 2 *on Eadwordes kynges dæge*, Somner *on Eadwardes kinges dæge*) and his father, King William I. (All readings from MSS 1 and 2 and Somner.) *Latin and English versions.*
MSS: 1.   Canterbury, D & C, Ch. Ant. C. 7 + C. 48 (formerly separated) (original)
      2.   Canterbury, D.& C, Ch. Ant. C. 9 (with fragmentary seal) (original)
      3.   Canterbury, D & C, Blore Collection 88 (s. xx transcript *ex* MS 1)
      4.   Canterbury, D & C, Register I, 62v (*olim* 74v) (Latin version only, containing English rights clause; MS notes 'Item idem tenor Anglice') (s. xiii^2)
      5.   London, PRO, Confirmation Rolls, 4 Hen VII, pt 1, m. 14, no. 4
      6.   London, PRO, Confirmation Rolls, 1 Hen VIII, pt 3, m. 9, no. 6
      7.   London, PRO, Patent Rolls, 12 Hen VI, pt 2, m. 9, nos. 11–12
Printed: Somner 1660, 205–6 (Eng. on p. 206) (= 1726, 204–6 [Eng. on pp. 205–6]) *ex* apparently lost MS.
References: Somner 1660, 123 (= 1726, 123); Hart 1869, 197 *ex* MSS 5–6; Stevenson 1896, 735 n. 11; PRO 1907, 418, nos. 11–12 *ex* MS 7; Harmer 1952, 174 and n. 3 and 175; *Regesta* II, 116, no. 1055; Bishop 1960, 41 nos. 95 and 97 *ex* MSS 1–2 respectively; Ker 1960, 20 n. 3 *ex* MS 1; Healey & Venezky 1980, 67, no. B15.1.207; Keynes 1988, 218 n. 198.
Note: Blore in Canterbury, D & C, Blore Collection 90 (MS notes *ex* MSS 1–2) observes that 'C. 9 is written in exactly the same hand as BM Campbell Charters XXI. 6'.

48

February(?), 1123 (Owen 1968, 119: 1123 x 1135). Writ of King Henry (H.) I to his bishops, earls, sheriffs and thegns, French and English (1, 2 *Frencisce 7 Ænglisce*, 3 *Fræncisce 7 Ænglisce*), in the shires where William, archbishop (of Canterbury), and the congregation of Christ Church in Canterbury (1, 2 *on*

Cantwaraberig, 3 on *Cantwareberig*) have land, declaring that they have the rights over their land that they had in the time of his kinsman, King Edward (1, 2 *on Eadwordes kynges dæge*, 3 *on Eodwordes kynge[s *]*) and King William, his father, with legal powers. (All readings from the English version of MSS 1–3.) *Latin and English versions.*

MSS: 1. London, BL, Campbell Charter XX1. 6 (original) (Warner & Ellis 1903, I, pl. V; Johnson & Jenkinson 1915, II, pl. I[c])

  2. London, BL, Stowe Charter 43 (original) (Sanders 1878, III, pl. XLIV)

  3. London, Lambeth Palace, Cart. Misc. X/109 (damaged) (original)

  4. Canterbury, D & C, Blore Collection 88 (s. xx transcript *ex* MSS 1–3)

  5. Canterbury, D & C, Register A, 149r (*olim* 159r) (s. xiii^2)

  6. Canterbury, D & C, Register E, 54r (*olim* 22r), no. 112 (s. xiii ex.)

  7. Canterbury, D & C, Register I, 61v (*olim* 73v) (Latin), 61v–62r (English) (s. xiii^2)

  8. London, PRO, Confirmation Rolls, 4 Hen VII, pt 1, m. 14, no. 4

  9. London, PRO, Confirmation Rolls, 4 Hen VII, pt 1, m. 15, no. 4

  10. London, PRO, Confirmation Rolls, 1 Hen VIII, pt 3, m. 9, no. 6

  11. London, PRO, Confirmation Rolls, 1 Hen VIII, pt 3, m. 10, no. 6

  12. London, PRO, Patent Rolls, 12 Hen VI, pt 2, m. 9, nos. 9–10

  13. London, PRO, Patent Rolls, 12 Hen VI, pt 2, mm. 9–8, nos. 15–16

Printed: Lye 1772, II, Appendix II, no. 6 *ex* MS ?; Sanders 1878, III, no. XLIV *ex* MS 2; Warner & Ellis 1903, I, [6] *ex* MS 1; PRO 1907, 417–18, nos. 9–10, 15–16 *ex* MSS 12–13; Johnson & Jenkinson 1915, I, 86–7 *ex* MS 1 (English version only).

Translated: Sanders 1878, III, no. XLIV.

References: Hart 1869, 197 *ex* MSS 8–11; Warner & Ellis 1903, I, [6]; Johnson & Jenkinson 1915, I, 86; Harmer 1952, 174 and n. 3 and 175; *Regesta* II, 184, no. 1388; Bishop 1960, 52, no. 332 *ex* MS 1, 55, no. 390 *ex* MS 2 and 56, no. 399 *ex* MS 3; Ker 1960, 20 n. 3 *ex* MSS 1–2; Owen 1968, 119 *ex* MS 3; Healey & Venezky 1980, 67, no. B15.1.208; Keynes 1988, 218 n. 198.

49

A.D. 1123 x 1135. Diploma of King Henry (H.) I to the monks of St Andrew's Church, Rochester (*Rouecestria*), confirming the lands and possessions that they had in the time of his father, King William, and his brother, King William, including jurisdictional rights over all men within boroughs and without; the fourth penny from the toll of land and water in Rochester and from the ferry when the bridge is broken; the toll from the two-day fair held on the feast of St Paulinus (10 October); warrens of the demesne manors of the bishop and monks of Rochester will be under the king's protection; Boxley Church (*Boxle*), (Kent), should be in free alms; the churches (all in Kent) at Aylesford (*Eilesford*), Sutton at Hone (*Suthune*), Chislehurst (*Chiselherste*), Dartford (*Darenteford*) and Woolwich (*Wlewic*) shall have the churches appurtenant to them and tithes from their vills; tithes from the royal mills in Dartford; royal tithes from Strood (*Strodes*), (Kent), and Chalk (*Chealces*), (Kent); and tithes from whales caught within the bishopric of Rochester. Witnesses: William, archbishop of Canterbury (*Cant'*);

William *in Cec'*; Hugh (genitive: *Hugonis*) Bigot, the king's steward; Ansfrid (genitive: *Ansfridi*), the archbishop's steward; and Humphrey of Bohon (*Hunf de Buun*), (Manche). At London (*aput Lundoniam*). (All readings from MS 1.) *Latin with English rights clause.*

MSS: 1. Maidstone, Kent County Archives Office, DRcT/T51 (purported original)
  2. London, BL, Add. 29437, 6 (s. xvii)
  3. London, BL, Cotton Domitian x, 103r–104r (*olim* 101r–102r), no. iii (s. xiii)
  4. London, PRO, Charter Rolls, 3 Edw I, m. 2, no. 2(7)
  5. London, PRO, Charter Rolls, 9 Edw III, m. 8, no. 36(3)
  6. London, PRO, Charter Rolls, 10 Edw III, m. 25, no. 51(3)
  7. London, PRO, Confirmation Rolls, 1 Hen VIII, pt 8, m. 1, no. 2
  8. London, PRO, Patent Rolls, 2 Hen VI, pt 2, m. 27(2[3])
  9. London, PRO, Patent Rolls, 12 Edw IV, pt 2, m. 14(2[7]
  10. London, PRO, Patent Rolls, 12 Edw IV, pt 2, mm. 13–12(4[3])
  11. London, PRO, Patent Rolls, 12 Edw IV, pt 2, m. 11(5[2])
  12. Maidstone, Kent County Archives Office, DRb/Ar 2, 13r (A.D. 1261 x 1256)
  13. Maidstone, Kent County Archives Office, DRc/T60/3 (*inspeximus* of Hen III, A.D. 1265)
  14. Maidstone, Kent County Archives Office, DRc/T65/5 (*inspeximus* of Edw IV, A.D. 1475)
  15. Maidstone, Kent County Archives Office, DRc/T66/B. 7 (*inspeximus* of Hen VII, A.D. 1486)
  16. Maidstone, Kent County Archives Office, DRc/T66/D. 1. b (*inspeximus* of Hen VII, 1486)
  17. Maidstone, Kent County Archives Office, DRc/T66/E. 1. b (*inspeximus* of Hen VII, A.D. 1486)

Printed: Thorpe 1769, 34–5 *ex* MSS 1 and 3.

References: Hart 1869, 199 *ex* MSS 4–7 and 9; PRO 1900, 370 *ex* MS 9 and 371 *ex* MSS 10 and 11; PRO 1901, 182 *ex* MS 8; PRO 1906, 195 *ex* MS 4; PRO 1912, 341 *ex* MS 5 and 354 *ex* MS 6; *Regesta* II, 282–3, no. 1867; Davis 1958, 93, no. 818 *ex* MS 3; Oakley 1970, I.1, 117–9 *ex* MS 1, 159 *ex* MS 13, 173 *ex* MS 14, 177 *ex* MS 15, 183 *ex* MS 16, 184 *ex* MS 17; 1.2, 1007 *ex* MS 12.

King Stephen

50

December 1138 x 1154. Writ of King Stephen (S.) to his bishops, earls, sheriffs and thegns, French and English (*Frencisce & Ænglisce*), in the shires where Theobald (*Deobalð*), archbishop (of Canterbury) and the congregation of Christ Church, Canterbury (*on Cantiarabiris*), have land, declaring that they have the rights over their land that they had in the time of King Edward (*on Eadwordes kynges dæges*), his kinsman, King William (*on Willelmes kanges* [sic] *dæge*), his grandfather, and King Henry (*on Henries kinges dæge*), his uncle, with legal powers. (All readings from the English version of MS 6.) *Latin and English versions.*

MSS: 1. Canterbury, D & C, Ch. Ant. C. 46 (*inspeximus* of Robert of Battle [*de Bello*], Abbot of St Augustine's Abbey, Canterbury [A.D. 1224–53])
   2. Canterbury, D & C, Ch. Ant. C. 1310(1) (Roll) (damaged)
   3. London, Lambeth Palace, Cart. Misc. XII/33 (with fragmentary seal) (*inspeximus* of Edw IV, 15 April 1463)
   4. London, Lambeth Palace, Cart. Misc. XII/34 (*inspeximus* of Hen VIII, 24 February 1510)
   5. London, Lambeth Palace, 1212, 13v (= p. 24), no. 1 (Latin version only; MS notes: 'Idem in Anglico *super eamdem* cartam) (s. xiii/xiv)
   6. London, PRO, Charter Rolls, 9 Edw III, m. 4, no. 19(2) (Johnson & Jenkinson 1915, II, pl. XXXIV)
   7. London, PRO, Charter Rolls, 1 Hen IV, pt 1, m. 51, no. 19(1[2])
   8. London, PRO, Charter Rolls, I Hen V, pt 3, m. 5, no. 2
   9. London, PRO, Charter Rolls, 2–4 Edw IV, m. 15, no. 8
   10. London, PRO, Patent Rolls, 1 Ric II, pt 2, m. 12
   11. London, PRO, Patent Rolls, 2 Hen VI, pt 3, m. 28(1[2])
   12. Oxford, Bodleian, Tanner 223 (10049), 25v (*olim* 46) (Latin version only) (s. xvi[2])

Printed: PRO 1912, IV, 345–6 *ex* MS 6; Johnson & Jenkinson 1915, I, 217–20 at pp. 219–20 *ex* MS 6; *Regesta* III, 53–4, no. 144 *ex* MS 6.

References: PRO 1895, 77 *ex* MS 10; PRO 1901, 197 *ex* MS 11; Johnson & Jenkinson 1915, I, 216–17; PRO 1916, 384 and 466 *ex* MSS 7 and 8 respectively; James & Jenkins 1930–2, 831 *ex* MS 5; Owen 1968, 139 *ex* MSS 3–4; *Regesta* III, 54, no. 144; Healey & Venezky 1980, 72, no. B15.1.210.

King Henry II

51

February 1155 x 1161. Writ of King Henry (H.) II to his bishops, earls, sheriffs and thegns, French and English (1, 3–4 *Frencisce 7 Englisce*, 2 *Frencise 7 Englisce*, 5 *Frenchisce 7 Englisce*), in the shires where Theobald (1–3, 5 *Teodbald*, 4 *Teobalt*), archbishop (of Canterbury), and the congregation of Christ Church, Canterbury (1 *on Cantwarabirig*, 2–3 *on Cantwarebirig*, 4 *on Cantuarabirg*, 5 *on Cantwarebiry*), have land, declaring that they have the rights over their land that they had in the time of King Edward (1–3 *on Eduardes kinges dege*, 4 *en Edwardes kinges dege*, 5 *on Eaduardes kynges dege*), King William, his great-grandfather, and King Henry (genitive: *Henrices*), his grandfather, with legal powers. Witnesses (Latin version only): Philip, bishop of Bayeux (1, 4 *Philippo episcopo Baiocensi*, 2–3, 5 *Philippo Baiocensi episcopo*); Arnulf, bishop of Lisieux (1 *Arnulfo episcopo Lexouiensi*, 4 *Arnulfo episcopo Lexoviensi*, 2–3, 5 *Arnulfo Lexoviensi episcopo*); Thomas the chancellor (1 *Toma cancellario*, 2–3, 5 *Thoma cancellario*, 4 *Thoma cancellario*); Reginald, earl of Cornwall (1 *Reginaldo Comite Cornubie*, 2–3 *Reginaldo Comite Cornubie*, 4 *Reginaldo Comite Cornubie*, 5 *Reginaldo Comite Cornubie*); Robert, earl of Leicester (1 *Roberto Comite Legrecestrie*, 2–3 *Roberto*

Comite Legrecestrie, 4 Roberto *Comite Legrecestrie*, 5 Roberto Comite *Legrecestrie*); Henry of Essex, the constable (1 Henrico *de Essexa constabulario*, 2–3 Henrico *de Essex constabulario*, 4–5 Henrico *de Essexia constabulario*). At York (1 *Apud Eboracum*, 2 *Apud Eboracum*, 3 *Apud Eboracum*, 4 *Apud Eboracum*, 5 *Apud Eboracum*). (All readings from the English version and Latin witness list of MSS 1–5.) *Latin and English versions.*

MSS: 1. Canterbury, D & C, Ch. Ant. C. 17 (with seal) (?original)
         2. Canterbury, D & C, Ch. Ant. C. 18 (with seal) (?original)
         3. Canterbury, D & C, Ch. Ant. C. 20 (?original)
         4. London, BL, Harley Charter 111 B. 49 (with seal) (original) (Keller 1906, pl. XIII; Denholm-Young 1954 [= 1964], pl. 9)
         5. London, Lambeth Palace, Cart. Misc. XI/3 (?original)
         6. Canterbury, Blore Collection 90 (transcript of MSS 1–3 and 7)
         7. Canterbury, D & C, Ch. Ant. C. 46 (Latin version only) (*inspeximus* of Robert of Battle [*de Bello*], abbot of St Augustine's Abbey, Canterbury [A.D. 1224–53])
         8. Canterbury, D & C, Ch. Ant. C. 204, (no. 4) (text as in MS 4) (Latin version only)
         9. Canterbury, D & C, Ch. Ant. C. 1310(3) (Roll) (damaged)
        10. Canterbury, D & C, Register A, 81r (*olim* 92r), no. 244 (Latin version only) (s. xiii^2)
        11. London, BL, Add. 6159, 7v (s. xiv)
        12. London, Lambeth Palace, 873 (s. xii)
        13. London, Lambeth Palace, 1212, 99r (= p. 190) (s. xiii/xiv)
        14. London, Lambeth Palace, 1212, 100 (= pp. 192–3) (s. xiii/xiv)
        15. London, PRO, Cartae Antiquae, Roll 6 (*olim* F), m. 1, no. 2
        16. London, PRO, Cartae Antiquae, Roll 19 (*olim* T), m. 1, col. b, no. 4
        17. London, PRO, Confirmation Rolls, 4 Hen VII, pt 1, m. 15, no. 4
        18. London, PRO, Confirmation Rolls, 1 Hen VIII, pt 3, mm. 10–11, no. 6
        19. London, PRO, Patent Rolls, 12 Hen VI, pt 2, m. 8, nos. 26–7

Printed: Hickes 1703, I, XVI *ex* MS 4; Hardy 1837, p. xxxvii n. 1 *ex* MS 4; *Monasticon* I, 111, no. XXXIX *ex* Hickes; Birch 1873, 245 *ex* MS ?2; Birch 1878, 312–3 *ex* MS 4; Stratmann 1884, 220 (English version only) *ex* MS 4; Earle 1888, 346–8 *ex* MS 4; Kluge 1904, 5 *ex* MS 4; Keller 1906, p. opp. pl. XIII *ex* Birch 1878 (Latin) and Stratmann 1884 and Kluge 1904 (English); Hall 1920, I, 11–12, no. IV *ex* MS 4; Landon 1939, 99, no. 202 *ex* MS 15 (Latin version only).

References: Todd 1812, 197 *ex* MS 12–14; Birch 1878, 309–10; Eyton 1878, 5, no. 1 (date); Stratmann 1884, 221; Stevenson 1896, 735 and nn. 11–12; Warner & Ellis 1903, I, [6] *ex* MS 4; Keller 1906, p. opp. pl. XIII; Delisle 1907a, 275, no. 1 *ex* MS 4; PRO 1907, 419 *ex* MS 19; Delisle 1908, 548, nos. 2–4 (76–8) *ex* MSS 1–3; Hall 1920, 264–9; James & Jenkins 1930–2, 812 *ex* MSS. 12–14; Harmer 1952, 174 and n. 4 and 175; Denholm-Young 1954 (= 1964), 17 and p. opp. pl. 9; Bishop 1960, 41 no. 104 and p. opp. pl. XXVI(*b*) *ex* MS 1, 105, 107 and p. opp. pl. XXVI(*a*) *ex* MSS. 2–3, 55 no. 387 *ex* MS 4, 56 no. 402 and p. opp. pl. XXVIII(*b*) *ex* MS 5, 406 and p. opp. pl. XXV(*b*) *ex* MS 12; Ker 1960, 20 n. 3 *ex* MSS. 4 and 12; Owen 1968, 124 *ex* MS 5; Healey & Venezky 1980, 68, no. B15.1.211; Holt & Mortimer 1986, 43–4, no. 41 *ex* MSS 2, 4, 5 and 11–12.

52

A.D. 1154 x 1189. Writ of King Henry (H.) II confirming (St Andrew's
Church,) Rochester (*Roff'*), in its lands and possessions, with jurisdictional rights
over all men within boroughs and without; the monks have free passage over
Rochester bridge (*per pontem Roffensem*) for their victuals and the first right after
the king and his ministers to buy food in the city of Rochester (*aput civitatem
Roffen'*). (All readings from MS 1.) *Bilingual: Latin with English rights clause.*

MSS: 1. London, BL, Cotton Domitian x, 108v (*olim* 106v), no. xv (s.xiii)
        2. London, PRO, Charter Rolls, 3 Edw I, m. 1(4)
        3. London, PRO, Charter Rolls, 9 Edw III, m. 8, no. 36(6)
        4. London, PRO, Charter Rolls, 10 Edw III, m. 25, no. 51(6)
        5. London, PRO, Patent Rolls, 2 Hen VI, pt 2, m. 27(2[6])
        6. London, PRO, Patent Rolls, 12 Edw IV, pt 2, m. 12(4[6])
        7. London, PRO, Patent Rolls, 12 Edw IV, pt 2, m. 11(5[4])
        8. Maidstone, Kent County Archives Office, DRb/Ar 2, 12v
        9. Maidstone, Kent County Archives Office, DRb/Ar 2, 14r
    10. Maidstone, Kent County Archives Office, DRc/T53 (*inspeximus* of
        Hen III, *c.* A.D. 1265)
    11. Maidstone, Kent County Archives Office, DRc/T60/6 (*inspeximus* of
        Hen III, *c.* A.D. 1265)
    12. Maidstone, Kent County Archives Office, DRc/T65/6 (*inspeximus* of
        Edw IV, A.D. 1475)
    13. Maidstone, Kent County Archives Office, DRc/T66/C. 4 (*inspeximus*
        of Hen VII, A.D. 1486)
    14. Maidstone, Kent County Archives Office, DRc/T66/E. 1. e (*inspeximus* of Hen VII, A.D. 1486)

Printed: Thorpe 1769, 43–4 *ex* MS 1.

References: PRO 1900, 371 *ex* MSS 6 and 7; PRO 1901, 182 *ex* MS 5; PRO
1906, 196 *ex* MS 2; PRO 1912, 342 *ex* MS 3 and 354 *ex* MS 4; Davis 1958, 93,
no. 818 *ex* MS 1; Oakley 1970, I.1, 122–4 *ex* MS 10, 162 *ex* MS 11, 173 *ex* MS
12, 182 *ex* MS 13, 185 *ex* MS 14 and I.2, 1007 *ex* MS 8/9.

Note: An endorsement to MS 10 explains that it was a copy made of the
original, which was damaged as a result of being taken off to Winchester after the
siege of Rochester (in 1264 by the barons under Simon de Montfort); John (de
Rainham), the prior of Rochester, subsequently secured at great personal labour
and expense copies of damaged royal charters from King Henry III. See further,
Oakley 1970, I.1, 122–3.

53

A.D. 1154 x 1189. Writ of King Henry (H.) II to archbishops, bishops, abbots,
earls, nobles, sheriffs and other faithful men of the English realm confirming (St
Andrew's Church, Rochester) in its lands and possessions, with jurisdictional
rights within boroughs and without; it is also to be exempt from all castle work,
military duties and fortification. *Bilingual: Latin with English rights clause.*

MS: Maidstone, Kent County Archives Office, DRc/T58/2 (*c.* A.D. 1265)
Unprinted.

Reference: Oakley 1970, I.1, 155.

Note: 'may have been made after the disastrous fire of 1264' (Oakley 1970, I.1, 156). Cf. nos. **52** above and **60** below.

54

A.D. 1154 x 1161/1172 x 1189. Writ of King Henry (*H.*) II to his bishops, earls, sheriffs and thegns, French and English (1 *Fræncisce 7 Ænglisce*, 3 *Fræncise and Ænglisce*, 4 *Fræncissce 7 Ænglissce*), in the shires where Theobald (*Teodbald*), archbishop (of Canterbury), and the congregation of Christ Church, Canterbury (1, 3 *on Cantwareberig*, 4 *on Cantorebeⁱ*), have land, declaring that they have the rights over their land that they had in the time of his kinsman, King Edward (1, 3 *on Eadwordes kynges dæge*, 4 *on Eadwordes kinges dæige*), King William, his great-grandfather, and King Henry (1, 3 *on Henri kynges dæge*, 4 *on Hænries kinges dæige*), his grandfather, with legal powers as fully as his own officials (1, 3 *wicnæres*, 4 *wicneres*) might seek them and over as many thegns as his great-grandfather, King William, and his grandfather, King Henry, had ordained (*geteiðet*). (All readings from the English version of MSS 1, 3 and 4.) *Latin and English versions.*

MSS: 1. Canterbury, D & C, Ch. Ant. 14 (purported original)
   2. Canterbury, D & C, Ch. Ant. 18A (damaged) (purported original)
   3. London, BL, Stowe Charter 44 (purported original) (Sanders 1878, III, pl. XLV)
   4. London, Lambeth Palace, Cart. Misc. XI/2 (purported original)
   5. Canterbury, D & C, Blore Collection 90 (s. xx transcript *ex* MSS 1 and 2)
   6. Canterbury, D & C, Ch. Ant. C. 200 (Latin version only)
   7. Canterbury, D & C, Register A, 149r (*olim* 159r) (Latin version only) (s. xiii²)
   8. Canterbury, D & C, Register E, 54r (*olim* 22r), no. 113 (s. xiii ex.)
   9. Canterbury, D & C, Register I, 65v (*olim* 77v) (Latin version only; contains English rights clause; MS notes: 'Item idem tenor Anglice) (s. xiii²)
   10. London, Lambeth Palace, 1212, 14r (= p. 25) (Latin version only) (s. xiii/xiv)
   11. London, Lambeth Palace, 1212, 99v (= p. 191) (s. xiii/xiv)
   12. London, Lambeth Palace, Cart. Misc. XII/32 (*inspeximus* of Hen VI)
   13. London, Lambeth Palace, Cart. Misc. XII/33 (with fragmentary seal) (*inspeximus* of Edw IV, 15 April 1463)
   14. London, Lambeth Palace, Cart. Misc. XII/34 (*inspeximus* of Hen VIII, 24 February 1510)
   15. London, PRO, Charter Rolls, 9 Edw III, m. 4, no. 19(3) (Latin version only) (Johnson & Jenkinson 1915, II, pl. XXXIV)
   16. London, PRO, Charter Rolls, 1 Hen IV, pt 1, m. 51, no. 19(1[3])
   17. London, PRO, Charter Rolls, 1 Hen V, pt 3, m. 5, no. 2
   18. London, PRO, Charter Rolls, 2–4 Edw IV, m. 15, no. 8
   19. London, PRO, Confirmation Rolls, 4 Hen VII, pt 1, m. 15, no. 4
   20. London, PRO, Confirmation Rolls, 1 Hen VIII, pt 3, m. 10, no. 6
   21. London, PRO, Patent Rolls, 1 Ric II, pt 2, m. 12
   22. London, PRO, Patent Rolls, 2 Hen VI, pt 3, m. 28(1[3])

23. London, PRO, Patent Rolls, 12 Hen VI, pt 2, m. 8, nos. 24–5

24. Oxford, Bodleian, Tanner 223 (10049), 26 (*olim* pp. 47–8) (s. xvi[1])

Printed: Sanders 1878, III, no. XLV *ex* MS 3; Thompson 1883, 9–10, no. 15 *ex* MS 3; PRO 1912, 346–7 *ex* MS 15; Johnson & Jenkinson 1915, I, 217–20 at p. 220 *ex* MS 15.

Translated: Sanders 1878, III, no. XLV.

References: Todd 1812, 197 *ex* MS 14; PRO 1895, 77 *ex* MS 21; PRO 1901, 197 *ex* MS 22; PRO 1907, 419 *ex* MS 23; PRO 1916, 384 and 466 *ex* MSS 16 and 17 respectively; James & Jenkins 1930–2, 828–34 at p. 831, no. I *ex* MS 10 and no. III *ex* MS 11; Harmer 1952, 174 and n. 4 and 175 *ex* MSS 1, 7 and 8; Bishop 1960, 41, no. 101 *ex* MS 1, 55, no. 391 *ex* MS 3 and 56, no. 401 *ex* MS 4; Ker 1960, 20 n. 3 *ex* MS 10/11; Owen 1968, 124 *ex* MS 4 and 139 *ex* MSS 12–14; Healey & Venezky 1980, 68, no. B15.1.211; Holt & Mortimer 1986, 44–5, no. 42 *ex* MSS 1–4 ('spurious').

Note: In the light of the *Dei gratia* formula used in the text, the document possibly is to be dated May 1172 x February 1173 x 1189: see Delisle 1907b, *Post-scriptum* and plate, and Poole 1908, 82. Since this is a product of an ecclesiastical foundation rather than the royal chancery, however, it could be much earlier; Bishop 1960 dates the document on palaeographical grounds to '1154–61'. On the debate over the chronology of the *Dei gratia* formula, see Delisle 1906, 374–401; Delisle 1907a, 272–4 and 296–314; Round 1907, 63–9; Delisle 1907b, 3–12 + *Post-scriptum* + 1 pl.; Delisle 1908, 545–7 and see also 572–80; and Poole 1908, 79–83.

55

A.D. 1174 x 1189. Diploma of King Henry II to archbishops, bishops, earls, nobles, sheriffs and other faithful men in the counties where the monks of St Andrew's Church, Rochester (*de Rofa*), have lands and possessions, confirming the Church in the lands, possessions, gifts and tithes made to the Church and the monks up to the present time by kings, archbishops, bishops, earls or other nobles of the realm; the manors (in Kent) (all in the accusative case) of Wouldham (*Wldeham*), Frindsbury (*Frendesberiam*), Stoke (*Stoches*), Southfleet (*Sufflete*), Denton (*Denintunam*) and Lambeth (*Lametham*), (Surrey), with their appurtenances, and Haddenham with Cuddington (*Hedenham cum...Cudintuna*), (Bucks.), and 40 hides of land belonging to it, and other small lands and rents; Boxley Church (*ecclesiam de Boxle*), (Kent), given in alms by his grandfather, Henry I, and the churches (all in Kent) of Aylesford (*de Eilesford*) and Sutton at Hone (*de Sutuna*) with the chapels of Wilmington and Kingsdown (*cum capellis Wilmintuna & Kingesduna*); the churches (all in Kent) of Dartford (*de Darenteford*), Chislehurst (*de Chiselherste*) and Woolwich (*de Wlewic*) with their appurtenances, rights and the tithes of their vills; the tithes from Strood (*de Strodes*), (Kent), and Chalk (*de Chealces*), (Kent), and from whales caught in the bishopric; the fourth penny from the toll of land and water in Rochester (*Rofen'*) and from the ferry when the bridge is broken; a fourth of the issues accruing to the constable of the city, except for the king's tax, and the toll from the two-day fair held on the feast of St Paulinus (10 October), all given and confirmed by his grandfather, Henry I; no-one, French or English (*nec Francus nec Anglus*), may enter there without the permission of the church or its officials; the churches of

Northfleet (*de Norfliete*), (Kent), given by Archbishop Anselm, Rotherfield with Frant Chapel (*de Rethrefeld cum capella de Farnet*), (Sussex), Stourmouth (*de Sturemuth*), (Kent), Norton (*de Nortune*), (Kent), Stiford (*de Stiford*), (Essex), one in London called *Berchingechirche* (All Hallows, Berkingchurch by the Tower), Lambeth (*de Lamhethe*), (Surrey), and Haddenham with the chapels of Cuddington and *Eie* (*de Hedenham cum capellis Cudintune et Eie*), (Bucks.), with all appurtenances, tithes, lands and rents; all are confirmed with jurisdictional rights; it (St Andrew's Church) and its men are exempt from castlework, military service and fortification. Witnessed at Nottingham (*apud Notingeham*) by Geoffrey, bishop of Ely (ablative: *Galfrido Eliensi episcopo*) (1174–1189). (All readings from MS 1.) *Bilingual: Latin with English rights clause.*

MSS:
1. London, BL, Cotton Domitian x, 112r–114r (*olim* 110r–112r), no. xxv (s. xiii)
2. London, PRO, Charter Rolls, 3 Edw I, m. 1(5)
3. London, PRO, Charter Rolls, 9 Edw III, m. 8, no. 36(5)
4. London, PRO, Charter Rolls, 10 Edw III, m. 25, no. 51(5)
5. London, PRO, Patent Rolls, 2 Hen VI, pt 2, m. 27(2[5])
6. London, PRO, Patent Rolls, 12 Edw IV, pt 2, m. 13(3[5])
7. London, PRO, Patent Rolls, 12 Edw IV, pt 2, m. 12(4[5])
8. London, PRO, Patent Rolls, 12 Edw IV, pt 2, m. 11(5[3])
9. Maidstone, Kent County Archives Office, DRb/Ar 1/17, 82v (*ex MS* 10) (s. xvii)
10. Maidstone, Kent County Archives Office, DRb/Ar 2, 13v–14r (A.D. 1251 x 1256)
11. Maidstone, Kent County Archives Office, DRc/T60/5 (*inspeximus* of Hen III, A.D. 1265)
12. Maidstone, Kent County Archives Office, DRc/T65/7 (*inspeximus* of Edw IV, A.D. 1475)
13. Maidstone, Kent County Archives Office, DRc/T66/D. 1. d (*inspeximus* of Hen VII, A.D. 1486)
14. Maidstone, Kent County Archives Office, DRc/T66/E. 1. d (*inspeximus* of Hen VII, A.D. 1486)

Printed: Thorpe 1769, 45–6 *ex MS* 1; *Monasticon* I, 176–7, no. 51 *ex MS* ?1.

References: PRO 1900, 370 *ex MS* 6 and 371 *ex MSS* 7 and 8; PRO 1901, 182 *ex MS* 5; PRO 1906, 196 *ex MS* 2; PRO 1912, 342 *ex MS* 3 and 354 *ex MS* 4; Davis 1958, 93, no. 818 *ex MS* 1; Oakley 1970, I.1, 160–2 *ex MS* 11, 173 *ex MS* 12, 183 *ex MS* 13, 184 *ex MS* 14 and I.2, 1007 *ex MS* 10, 1012 *ex MS* 9.

56

28 February 1072. Diploma recording the sale by Azur (*Adzor*), son of Thorthr (*Þuredes*), to Giso, bishop (of Wells), in the presence of Edith, widow of King Edward (*to foren Eadgyþe þere hlefðian Edweardes cyncges lafe*), of land at Combe St Nicholas (*æt Cume*), (Somerset), in return for a payment of six marks of gold, witnessed by the priests Seaxsige (*Sæxi*), Cypping (*Kyppingc*) and Beorhtmær (*Brihtmær*); the deacons Godric and Waldere; Sumerlida/-leda or Sumarlithi (*Sumorlæte*) the sub-deacon; Hearding (*Herdincg*); Wulfweard White (*Hwite*); Æthelsige the steward (*Ægelsig stiweard*); Ælfweald the chamberlain (*Alfwold burþen*); Vitalis or Vitel (*Vitela*); Ælfweald (*Alfwold*); Beorhtric, Dodda's son (*Brihtric Doddasunu*); Beorhtsige, Ceolsige's son (*Brixi Ceolsig sunu*); Godwine *Hos*; Leofwine, Godwine's son; Agamund; Ælfric Long (*lange*); Ælfric, Ælfheah's son (*Ælfheges sunu*); the goldsmiths Wiederic (possibly a misreading of a form derived from *Theodric*) and Æthelsige (*Ægelsig*); Northmann, John's son (*Norðmann Ioh's sunu*); Æthelric ?'Cook' (*Ægelric coc*); and Rabel ?'Cook' (*coc*). This was done on Wednesday in Lent in the sixth year when King William reigned and Mathilda his wife (*Mathyld his gebedde*) and Prince Robert (*Rotb' Æþeling*) and Archbishop Lanfranc (*Landfranc*); in that same year Archbishop Stigand and Leofric, bishop of Exeter (*of Exacestre*) died, 1072 years from the birth of Christ and in the eleventh year that Giso came to the (episcopal) throne (*feng to rice*).

MS: Wells, D & C, 'Liber Albus II', 254r (s. xiv/xv)

Printed: Dickinson 1876, 107.

Translated: Dickinson 1876, 108 (translation by J. Earle).

References: Freeman 1876, 688–9; Dickinson 1876, 106–13; Hist. MSS Comm. 1885, 188; *DNB* VI, 389; Hist. MSS Comm. 1907, 434; Holmes 1911, II, 8 and 10, Tengvik 1938, 361, s.v. 'Coc'.

57

6 January 1066 x 18 December 1075. Writ of the lady, Edith, widow of King Edward (*Eadgyþ seo hlauedi Eadwardes kynges lefe*), to the hundred at Wedmore (*at Wedmore*) (later part of Bempstone Hundred, Somerset) declaring that she has granted to Giso (*Gyso*), bishop (of Wells), the land at Mark (*at Merkerun*), (Somerset), for his canons at St Andrew's (Cathedral), Wells (*æt Wyllan*), with sake and soke; she requests a just judgment against Wudumann (*of Wudemann*) to whom she granted her horse and who has withheld her rent (*gauel*) both in honey and money for six years. (All readings from the English version of MS 2.)

English and (partial) Latin versions

MSS: 1.   London, BL, Harl. 6968, p. 9 (s. xvii transcript of MS 2)

   2.   Wells, D & C, 'Liber Albus I', 17v (s. xiii med.)

Printed: Hickes 1703, II, 162 *ex* MS 2; *Monasticon* II, 287, no. 7; Kemble 1839, IV, 257, no. 918; Thorpe 1865, 427 *ex* MS 1; Harmer 1952, 285–6, no. 72 *ex* MS 2.

Translated: Thorpe 1865, 427; Harmer 1952, 286.

References: Wanley 1705, 285, no. 5 *ex* MS 2; Hist. MSS Comm. 1885, 9 *ex* MS

1; Hist. MSS Comm. 1907, 16; Harmer 1952, 274–7 and 491; Sawyer 1968, no. 1241; Cameron 1973, 165, no. B15.2.22; Healey & Venezky 1980, 55, no. B15.2.22.

58

A.D. 1100 x 24 October 1118 (Cowley 1977, 270: A.D. 1116). Diploma of Robert of La Haye-du-Puits (*Robertus de Haia*), (Manche), and his wife Gundrada (*Gundrede*) granting, with the permission of his lord, Robert, son of Haimo (*Hamo*) (i.e., Robert fitz Haimon) and his wife, Sibilia, to St Mary's Church, Glastonbury (*Glaston'*), (Somerset), the church of Bassaleg (*Basselech*), (Mon.), with the tithes and alms attached to the parish, including the churches (all in Mon.) of Machen (*Mahhayn*), Bedwas (*Bedewas*), Mynyddislwyn (*Menedwiscleluyn*) and Manmoel (*Mapmoil*), and the chapels of Coedkernew (*Coittarnen*) and *Pulcrud*, the boundaries of the parish of Bassaleg being appended; rights to woodland for wood and pannage; a harbour and its fish with fishing rights where the River Ebbw (*Elboth*) flows; they may have a court and also the right of assarting within bounds that are defined; each year they grant twenty *solidi*, being the tithes of ?Gwynllwg (*Gunleonc*) (cantref in Monmouthshire) for the clothing of the monks living at Bassaleg; they also give one of their men, Wrghi, son of Wrgan (*hominum nostrum, nomine Wrghi, filium Wrgan*), with his land for their service; they grant permission for any of their men, French, English or Welsh, to grant or sell to the Church of Bassaleg their land or to enter the monastic life with their land; (granted) in the presence of the following witnesses: William, the sheriff of Cardiff (*vicecomite Kard'*), Robert le Sor, Roger de Sumer (*de Sumeri*), Roger, son of Joze, Herebert of St Quentin (ablative: *Hereberto de Sancto Quintino*), (Manche), and Laudomar (?son of) Atso (*Aze*); representing Abbot Herlewin (genitive: *Herlewini*), Wido the monk (*modus*, probably a misreading of *mo'chus*), Samuel the monk (*mo'*), Moyses the monk (*mo'*), Ælfræd, (son of) Nicholas (*Aluredus de Nichol*) and his son, Robert, Osmund the granary-keeper (*granetarius* [sic]), Walter the chamberlain, Ælfræd (*Alured*) the butler (*pincerna*) of the abbot, and many others. *Latin with English bounds of the parish of Bassaleg.*
MS: Cambridge, Trinity College, R. 5. 33, 106v (s. xiii)
Printed: Hearne 1727, II, 604–7 (English on p. 605); *Monasticon* IV, 633–4 *ex* Hearne; Clark 1910, I, 38, no. 35 *ex* Hearne (incomplete).
References: Tanner 1744, 330 (= 1787, *Monmouthshire* I); *Monasticon* IV, 633; James 1900–2, II, 201, no. 724; Davies 1953, 65; Cowley 1977, 270; Green 1986, 258 (on Robert de la Haye).

59

c. A.D. 1174 x 1184. Diploma of Richard Basket (*Cofin, Cophin*) addressed generally. The dispute between the abbot and convent of Tavistock (genitive: *Tauistoch'*), (Devon), and him over the boundaries of their estate at Abbotsham (*de Abbedesham*) and of his estates at Alwington and Cockington (*de Alwintone 7 Kokemetone*), (Devon), is laid to rest. The church has granted him and his heir, Perynn (dative: *P'ynno*), the right to receive the monastic habit there when it is wished and, whenever he goes there, to receive the provisions of a monk. Walter the abbot and Master (*magister*) William who holds the farm of Abbotsham (*de Abbedesham*) have given him two marks of silver for his proof of the boundaries sustained by twelve jurors from four neighbouring booklands (*de quatuor vicinis*

bocland'; see Finberg 1947, 363 n. 2). The boundaries are appended. His lord, Geoffrey, son of Baldwin (*Galfr' fil' Bald'*), and his heir, Nicholas (*Nich'*), confirm this. Confirmed with his seal (*sigilli mei apposicione confirmaui*) in the presence of the county court (*comitatu*) of Exeter and affirmed in the presence of B(aldwin) the abbot. Witnesses: William Dacus (later le Deneys or Dennis); Richard of Bocombe (ablative: *Ricardo de Boccumb*) (in Parham, Shebbear Hundred, Devon); Joel of Launcells (*Joel de Launcell*), (Cornwall); Henry de Alneto (later Daunay); Ralph of Leigh (*de Lega*) (probably Leigh Barton in Milton Abbot, Devon); Hamelin of Leigh (*de Legh*); and Fulko (*Fulk*) de Veteri Ponte. *Latin with English bounds.*
MS: Exeter, Devon Record Office, W 1258/D 84/3, 7r–8r (s. xiii)
Source: Pole 1791, 386 (for the final five names of the witnesses)
Printed: Finberg 1944, 201; Finberg 1947, 363–4, no. xxix *ex* MS and source.
Translated: Finberg 1943a, 257; Finberg 1944, 202 (bounds only).
References: Finberg 1943a, 245–57; Finberg 1943b, 175; Finberg 1944, 201–2 (place-names); Finberg 1947, 363–4; Finberg 1951 (= 1969), 13–14 (identification of the surnames) and 30; Davis 1958, 108, no. 947.

ALLEGED PAPAL DOCUMENT

60

A.D. 1159 x 1181. Diploma of Pope Alexander (III) confirming the Church (of St Andrew's, Rochester) in its customs and liberties. A proem, opening with the phrase 'The words of Pope Alexander' (*Verba Alexandri pape*), includes a rights clause which is largely in English. *Bilingual.*
MS: Maidstone, Kent County Archives Office, DRc/T58/3 (c. A.D. 1265) Unprinted.
Reference: Oakley 1970, I.1, 155–6.
Note: Oakley 1970 I.1, 156 observes that the document 'may have been made after the disastrous events of 1264'. Cf. No. **53** above.

EPISCOPAL DOCUMENTS

61

A.D. 1071 x 1080. Memorandum of a lease of lands at Thornley (*æt Đornhlawa*), (co. Durham), and Wingate (*æt Windegatum*), (co. Durham), to Ealdgyth (dative: *Ealgyðe*) by Walcher (*Walchear*), bishop (of Durham), and the community at St Cuthbert's (Cathedral, Durham).
MS: Cambridge, CCC, 183, 96v (s. xi^2)
Printed: James 1909–12, 441; Craster 1925, 194; Robertson 1939 (= 1956), 230, App. I, no. 2; Offler 1968, 1, no. 1.
Translated: Craster 1925, 194; Robertson 1939 (= 1956), 231.

References: Robertson 1939 (= 1956), 480–1; Ker 1957, 65, no. 42 c; Offler 1968, 1–3; Cameron 1973, 191, no. B16.8.2; Healey & Venezky 1980, 166, no. B16.8.2.

62

A.D. 1071 x 1082. Writ of Odo, bishop of Bayeux (*Baius*), to Lanfranc (accusative: *Landfranc*), archbishop (of Canterbury), Haimo (accusative: *Hæimonem*), sheriff (of Kent), and the king's thegns of Kent (*on Cænt*) declaring that he has granted to Christ Church, Canterbury (*on Cantwarebyrig*), four 'denns' of land, Losenham (in Newenden, Kent), *Athelardendenn* (*Aðalardændæne*) (later Wassall Farm in Rolvenden, Kent), *Blacecota* (accusative: *Blacecotan*) (later Bly Court in Staplehurst, Kent), and *Oakdenn* (*Acdæna*) (later Hexden in Rolvenden, Kent), in exchange for twenty-five acres of land within his park (*deor falde*) of Wickhambreux (*æt Wiccham*), (Kent). (All readings from MS 1.) *Latin and English versions.*

MSS: 1.   London, BL, Cotton Charter XVI. 31 (much damaged by fire) (original)
      2.   Northampton, Northamptonshire Record Office, F.H. 170, 92r, no. 431 (transcribed A.D. 1640 x 1641) (Pegge 1770, pl. opp. p. 336 [English version and seal]; Loyd & Stenton 1950, pl. VIII; Tatton-Brown 1987, 31, fig. 21 *ex* Loyd & Stenton)

Printed: Pegge 1770, 336 (Latin version only); Loyd & Stenton 1950, 301, no. 431 *ex* MS 1 supplemented by readings from MS 2.

References: Hasted 1778, III, 660 and note s; Hoad 1975, 323; Witney 1976, 246, 268 and 274 (place-name identifications); Clanchy 1979, 165–6; Healey & Venezky 1980, 72, no. B15.3.59; Heslop 1980, 10 and pl. IIE (on the seal); Tatton-Brown 1987, 30 and 32; Keynes 1988, 218 n. 198.

63

20 May 1089 (first day of Pentecost). Diploma of Wulfstan (1 *Wulfstanus*, 2 *Wlfstanus*), bishop of Worcester (*UUigorniensis*), who, having increased the monastic congregation from twelve to forty, gives fifteen hides of land at Alveston (2 *Alfestun*; bounds: 2 *into Ælfestune*), (Glos.), acquired through his own labour and a gift from King William I to St Mary's (Cathedral, Worcester). Witnesses (all from MS 1): Thomas the prior with all the congregation of Worcester; Æthelric (*Agelricus*) the archdeacon; Coleman (*Colemannus*) the monk and chancellor (*cancellarius*); Frideric (*Frithericus*) the chaplain with all the clerics of the bishop; Urse the sheriff (*Vrso uicecomes*) with all the soldiers of the shrievalty; Ordric the steward with all the court (*curia*) of the bishop; Alwine, the steward of the bishop; and Ordric, reeve of that estate and many of the estates of the bishop. *Latin charter with bounds in English and Latin.*

MSS: 1.   Worcester, Cathedral, B. 1680a (Latin only) (original; seal formerly preserved separately, now lost in a coalmine in Shropshire [*ex* info. Heslop 1980]) (Darlington 1968, pl. opp. p. 8)
      2.   London, BL, Cotton Charter XI. 51 (with bounds) (Darlington 1968, 9: 'contemporary copy')
      3.   London, BL, Cotton Tiberius A. xiii, 187r–188r (*olim* 184r–185r) (bounds on 188r) (s. xi²)

4. Oxford, Bodleian, Dugdale 39 (6527), 119v (incomplete) (A.D. 1583 x)
5. Oxford, Bodleian, Rawlinson B. 445 (*olim* 443) (15474), 297v–300v (s. xvii)
6. Worcester, Cathedral, Muniments, A. 2, pp. 84–5 (Latin only) (early s. xiv transcript of MS 1 or 'possibly' MS 7 [Darlington 1968, xliii])
7. Worcester, Cathedral, Muniments, A. 4, 2v (Latin only) (s. xiii med.; probably transcript of MS 1 [Darlington 1968, xliii])

Printed: Dodsworth & Dugdale 1655, I, 135–6 *ex* MS 3; Hearne 1723, II, 418–21 *ex* MS 3; *Monasticon* I, 599, no. XXIX *ex* MS 3; Hale 1865, 84–85a *ex* MS 6; Darlington 1968, 8, no. 3 *ex* MS 1.

References: Wanley 1705, 258, no. CXXXIV *ex* MS 3; Thomas 1736, 'An Account...', 87–8 (latter page illustrates seal formerly attached to MS 1); Hooper 1876, 210 (comments on seal on MS 1); Atkins 1940, 203; Ker 1948, 57 (= Ker 1985, 41) (hand of Scribe I of MS 3 is 'very like' that of MS 1); Darlington 1968, xliii (MS 2 'is a contemporary copy almost certainly in the hand of the scribe who wrote that part of Hemming's Cartulary [Cott. Tib. A, xiii] in which the transcript of it occurs [fos. 187, 188]. This is the work of one of the three main scribes responsible for most of fos. 119–200. Another of these three scribes almost certainly wrote the original at Worcester.' On p. xliii n. 1 he states: 'Professor Wormald agrees with the opinions expressed above concerning the scribes of the original and the contemporary copy.' See also Darlington 1968, 8–9.); Healey & Venezky 1980, 72, no. B15.8.648; Heslop 1980, 12–13 and pl. IIB (on the lost seal formerly attached to MS 1).

Note: Impressions of Wulfstan's lost seal are London, BL, Seal LXXVII.6 and London, Society of Antiquaries, Seal Impressions, C. 31 (Wulfstan).

64

A.D. 1099 x 1100 or 1106 x *c*. 1122 (NPS I, 45[c]: 1106 x 1128). Writ of R(annulf Flambard), bishop (of Durham), to his thegns and drengs of Islandshire (*of Ealondscire*) and Norhamshire (*of Norhamscire*) (near Norham) declaring that he has granted Allerdean (*in Elredene*) and (the fishery of) Hallowstell (*Haliwarestelle*) (near the mouth of the Tweed) to St Cuthbert's Church (i.e., Cathedral, Durham). (All readings from MS 1.)

MSS: 1.   Durham, Prior's Kitchen, D & C Muniments 2.1, Pontificalium no. 9 (s. xi/xii) (Raine 1852, 219; NPS I, pl. 45[c])
2.   Durham, Prior's Kitchen, 'Cartuarium Vetus' of the monastery of Durham, 134v (s. xiii^2)
3.   Durham, Prior's Kitchen, 'Cartuarium Secundum' of the monastery of Durham, 9r (s. xv^1)
4.   Durham, Prior's Kitchen, 'Cartuarium Quartum' of the monastery of Durham, 1v–2r (s. xvi in.)
5.   Durham, Prior's Kitchen, 'Cartuarium Quartum' of the monastery of Durham, 23v (s. xvi in.)

Printed: Hickes 1703, II, 149 *ex* transcript of MS 1; Surtees 1816, I, i, App. no. I, p. cxxv *ex* MS 1; Raine 1839, App. no. XIX, p. xxix *ex* MS 1; Raine 1852, App. no. DCCXXVII, p. 129 *ex* MS 1; Greenwell 1872, 98n *ex* MS 1;

Liebermann 1903a, 283, no. III *ex* MS 1; NPS I, 45(c) *ex* MS 1; Offler 1968, 89 *ex* MS 1.
Translated: Hickes 1703, II 150 (translation into Latin); Liebermann 1903a, 283, no. III (translation into German).
References: Wanley 1705, 298; Stevenson 1896, 735 n. 10; Liebermann 1903a, 283–4; NPS I, 45(c); Offler 1968, 90–1 (place-name identifications); Healey & Venezky 1980, 72, no. B15.3.61; Chaplais 1987, 76.

DOCUMENTS ISSUED BY OTHER ECCLESIASTICS

65

A.D. ?1086 x c. 1104. Writ of Gilbert (*Gisilberd*) (Crispin), abbot (of Westminster), and the brethren of Westminster (*Westmeynstr'*) (Abbey) to Wigmund (*Wymond*), sheriff of Surrey (*on Suðeya*), declaring that Deormann of *Clarton* (*Deorman of Clar'ton'*) had sought Christ, St Peter, King Edward's resting-place (*Eadward' kynges rste*) and all the relics (*haligdom*); they request that he might take pity and forgive him for whatever his guilt is.
MS: London, BL, Cotton Faustina A. iii, 259r (s. xiii/xiv)
Printed: *Monasticon* I, 310, no. LXIV; Mason 1988, 110, no. 238.
References: Stevenson 1896, 735 n. 10; Morris 1927, 61; Honeybourne 1932–3, 324–32 and pl. III (on the sanctuary boundaries); Mason 1988, 110–11, no. 238.

66

A.D. ?1085 x 1117/8. Writ of G(ilbert Crispin), abbot (of Westminster), and all the brethren of Westminster (*on Westmynstr'*), to N., sheriff of Essex (*on Estsex'*), declaring that a man, R., has sought Christ, St Peter, King Edward's resting-place (*reste*) and all the relics (*haligdom*) which are within the minster; they request that he take pity and forgive him for whatever his guilt is.
MS: London, Westminster Abbey, Muniment Bk 11, 79v (*olim* 82v) (s. xiv, after A.D. 1308)
Printed: Robinson 1911, 37; Mason 1988, 111, no. 239.
References: Robinson 1911, 37; Morris 1927, 61; Honeybourne 1932–3, 324–32 and pl. III (on the sanctuary boundaries).

67

A.D. 1142 x 1143 or 1146 x 23 July 1189. Writ of Ralph (*Radulfus*), prior of (St Mary's) Church, Worcester (either Ralph of Bath or Ralph of Bedford), to all the faithful holding tenure of him declaring that he has granted to Folcwig of Horseley Hills (dative: *Fulquio de Horselega*) (in Wolverly, Glos.), that land which his father and he developed as an assart from the bishop's wood in return for an annual render of a sester of honey, over and above the two due from Horseley; should there be a shortage of honey, he must pay two pence per annum; if through royal intervention the land cannot be cultivated, the rent will cease for the period it cannot be cultivated; to prevent controversy over the limits between the bishop's wood and the aforementioned land, bounds are appended. *Charter in Latin with English bounds.*

MSS: 1.   London, BL, Cotton Tiberius A. xiii, 191v–192r (*olim* 188v–189r)
             (s. xii med.)
       2.   Oxford, Bodleian, Rawlinson B. 445 (*olim* 443) (15474), 307v–308v
             (s. xvii)
Printed: Hearne 1723, II, 429–30 *ex* MS 1.
References: Wanley 1705, 258, no. CXXXV *ex* MS 1; Ker 1948, 61 (= 1985,
45), no. L iv; Healey & Venezky 1980, 72, no. B15.8.649.
Note: Ker associates the document with Ralph of Bath, stating 'It is in a
contemporary hand' (*loc. cit.*). Mr Peter Kitson has pointed out (*pers. comm.*)
that it could, however, have been issued by Ralph of Bedford.

WILLS

68

November 1066 x 1068. Will of Ulfr (*Ulf*) and his wife Madselin (1 *Madselin*, 2
Madselm) made on their departure for Jerusalem (*Ier'l'm*) with bequests of land at
Carlton (*æt Carlatune*) (probably Carlton-le-Moorland, Lincs.), to Peterborough
(Abbey) (*into Burh*), Pytham (*æt Bytham*) (probably Castle Bytham, Lincs.), to
St Guthlac's (i.e., Crowland Abbey, Lincs.), and Sempringham (*æt Sempringa-
ham*), (Lincs.), to St Benedict's (Abbey), Ramsey (*to Ramesege*); Ealdræd,
(arch)bishop (of York), can purchase estates at Lavington (*æt Lofintune*),
(Lincs.), and Hardwick (*hæt Heordewican*) (possibly near Wellingborough,
Northants.), and he has a mortgage of eight marks of gold on estates at Skilling-
ton (*æt Scillintune*), (Lincs.), Hoby (1 *æt Houcbig*, 2 *æt Hovebig*), (Leics.), and
Morton (*æt Mortune*), to be repaid on the testators' return, and if they fail to do
so, the bishop is to pay the balance of their value in gold to charity with a
reversion to Brandr (*Brand*), abbot (of Peterborough), on the same terms if the
bishop not survive; the estate at Manthorpe (*æt Mannethorp*), (Lincs.), is granted
to Brandr (dative: *Brande*), at Wilby (1 *æt Willabyg*, 2 *æt Willabig*), (?Northants.),
to Siferth (dative: *Siferðe*), Ulfr's kinsman, at Stoke Rochford (*æt Stoce*),
(Lincs.), to Leofgifu (dative: 1 *Lyfgyfan*, 2 *Lyfgafan*), Madselin's kinswoman; she
has granted the estate at Stroxton (*æt Stroðistune*), (Lincs.), to Ingimundr (dative: *I[n]gemunde*) in return for the west hall at Winterton (*æt Wintringatune*);
the estate at Overton (*æt Ofertune*) (probably Cold Overton, Leics.), is to be sold
with the proceeds going to charity; Ulfr has granted his mother Kettleby (*Kit-
lebig*) (near Drawky, Leics.), and Keelby Cotes (or Nun Coton, Lincs.) (*Cotum*),
and she has granted him Messingham (*Mæssingaham*), (Lincs.), and Kettleby
(*Kytlebi*), (Lincs.); if he does not return Ingimundr (*Ingemund*) is to have the
estate at ?Kirmington (*æt Coringatune*), (Lincs.); he grants the estate at Claxby
(*æt Cleaxbyg*) (by Normanby, Lincs.), to his brother Halfdan (dative: 1 *Healþene*,
2 *Healwene*) and at North Ormsby (*æt Vrmesbyg*), (Lincs.), and its possessions to
St Mary's Monastery (*into Sc'e Marian Stowe*), (Stow, Lincs.); his servants
(*cnihtas*) are to have Limber (1 *Lindbeorhge*, 2 *Lindsbeorhge*), (Lincs.), if he does
not return and Madselin's estate there at *Lohtun* (*æt Lohtune*) is to go to Thorney
(Abbey, Cambs.) (*into Þornege*).

MSS: 1.   London, Society of Antiquaries, 60, 50v–51r (*olim* xlv–xlvi) (s. xii
            med.)
       2.   London, Society of Antiquaries, 131, 22 (*olim* pp. 43–4) (s. xviii
            transcript of MS 1)
Printed: Kemble 1839, IV, 287–8, no. 953 *ex* MS 1; Thorpe 1865, 594–5 *ex*
MS 1; Whitelock 1930, 94–6, no. XXXIX *ex* MS 1.
Translated: Thorpe 1865, 594–6; Whitelock 1930, 95–7.
References: Whitelock 1930, 207–12 (place-name identifications); Healey &
Venezky 1980, 72, no. B15.6.53.

69

A.D. 1088. Will of Robert of Stafford in which he grants for the sake of his soul
and those of his lord, William II, king of England, his wife and his son, Nicholas,
land at Wrottesley (*Wroteslea*) and Loynton (*Levuntona*), (Staffs.), to the monastery of Evesham into the hand of Walter (1077 – 20 January 1104), his faithful
friend, together with woods, meadows and pastures. In the same year he, his wife,
his son and his barons agreed they were to be buried in the monastery; he made
these gifts and undertakings with the agreement and testimony of Peter, bishop
of Chester (genitive: *Cestrei*) (died before April 1084), who imposed them as a
penance on him. Robert, having become a monk in the same monastery during
his illness, confirms the grant with the sign of the cross in his own hand.
Confirmed by Nicholas (*Nicholaus*), their son, Warin ?'Bad Corn' or 'Cruel Horn'
(*Warine Malcorne*), Brian (*Brien*) and Carnegode. The bounds of the two hides of
Wrottesley are appended. *Will in Latin with bilingual bounds.*
MS: Wrottesley, Lord Wrottesley, Muniments (destroyed by fire in 1897).
      ('From an ancient copy on parchment – in a hand of the fourteenth
      century – at Wrottesley' [Eyton 1881, 182]; 'one of the transcripts of five
      deeds, written on a small roll of parchment in a hand of the fifteenth
      century, formerly preserved at Wrottesley' [Wrottesley 1903, 6 n. 1])
Source: Eyton 1881, 182–3; Wrottesley 1898–9 (= Wrottesley 1903, 6–7)
References: Eyton 1881, 183–5; Wrottesley 1903, 6–7.

MISCELLANEOUS

Bath

70

A.D. x 1075 x 1087. List of relics inventoried by Ælfsige (*Ælsige*), abbot (of
Bath), and the monks (of Bath). *Bilingual.*
MS: Cambridge, CCC, 111, p. 7 (s. xi^2)
Printed: Hunt 1893, lxxv–lxxvi.
References: Wanley 1705, 149, no. I.1; James 1909–12, 236, no. 1; Ker 1957, 48,
no. 35.7; Cameron 1973, 188, no. B16.2.4; Healey & Venezky 1980, 165,
no. B16.2.4.

71

A.D. x 1075 x 1087. List of relics which Heorstan gave to St Peter's Minster at Bath (*on Baðon*). *Bilingual.*
MS: Cambridge, CCC, 111, p. 7 (s. xi^2)
Printed: Hunt 1893, lxxvi.
References: Wanley 1705, 149, no. I.2; James 1909–12, 236, no. 2; Ker 1957, 48, no. 35.7; Cameron 1973, 188, no. B16.2.4; Healey & Venezky 1980, 165, no. B16.2.4.

72

A.D. x 1075 x 1087. List of relics which Wulfwine of Reading (*Wulwine on Readingon*), (Berks.), gave to the Minster at Bath (*on Baðon*). *Bilingual.*
MS: Cambridge, CCC, 111, p. 7 (s. xi^2)
Printed: Hunt 1893, lxxvi.
References: Wanley 1705, 149, no. I.3; James 1909–12, 236, no. 3; Ker 1957, 48, no. 35.7; Cameron 1973, 188, no. B16.2.4; Healey & Venezky 1980, 165, no. B16.2.4.

73

A.D. x 1075 x 1087. Record of the purchase of release by Leofnoth, Æthelnoth's son at Corston (*Leofenoð, Ægelnoðes sunu æt Korstune*), (Somerset), of himself and his offspring from Ælfsige, abbot (of Bath), and all the (monastic) community at Bath (*on Baðon*) for five *oras* and twelve sheep in the presence of Kascill, the portreeve, and all the citizenry of Bath (*on ealre þære burhware on Baðon*).
MS: Cambridge, CCC, 111, p. 8 (s. xi^2)
Printed: Kemble 1839, IV, 270, no. 933; Kemble 1849 (= 1876), I, 497–8; Thorpe 1865, 640–1; Earle 1888, 268, no. 1; Hunt 1893, lxxvi.
Translated: Kemble 1849 (= 1876), I, 497–8; Thorpe 1865, 640–1.
References: Wanley 1705, 149, no. I.4; Turner 1852, III, 83; James 1909–12, 236, no. 4; Ker 1957, 48, no. 35.8; Cameron 1973, 188, no. B16.2.3; Healey & Venezky 1980, 165, no. B16.2.3; Davies 1982, 260 n. 7.

74

A.D. x 1075 x 1087. Record of the purchase of freedom by Æthelsige at Lyncombe (*Ægelsige æt Linncume*), (Somerset), of Wilsige, his son, from Ælfsige, abbot of Bath (*on Baðon*), and all the (monastic) community.
MS: Cambridge, CCC, 111, p. 8 (s. xi^2)
Printed: Kemble 1839, IV, 271, no. 934; Kemble 1849 (= 1876), I, 498; Thorpe 1865, 641; Earle 1888, 268, no. 2; Hunt 1893, lxxvii.
Translated: Kemble 1849 (= 1876), I, 498; Thorpe 1865, 641.
References: Wanley 1705, 149, no. I.5; Turner 1852, III, 83; James 1909–12, 236, no. 5; Ker 1957, 48, no. 35.8; Cameron 1973, 188, no. B16.2.3; Healey & Venezky 1980, 165, no. B16.2.3.

75

A.D. x 1075 x 1087. Record of the purchase of freedom by Æthelsige (*Ægelsige*), Byttic's son, of Hildesige, his son, from Ælfsige (*Ælsige*), abbot of Bath, and all the (monastic) community for sixty pence.
MS: Cambridge, CCC, 111, p. 8 (s. xi^2)

Printed: Kemble 1839, IV, 271, no. 935; Kemble 1849 (= 1876), I, 498; Thorpe 1865, 641; Earle 1888, 268, no. 3; Hunt 1893, lxxvii.
Translated: Kemble 1849 (= 1876), I, 498; Thorpe 1865, 641.
References: Wanley 1705, 149, no. I.6; James 1909–12, 236, no. 6; Ker 1957, 48, no. 35.8; Cameron 1973, 188, no. B16.2.3; Healey & Venezky 1980, 165, no. B16.2.3.

76

A.D. x 1075 x 1087. Record of the purchase of freedom by Godwig the Goat (*se bucca*) of Leofgifu the dairymaid of North Stoke (accusative: *Leofgife þa dægean æt Norðstoke*), (Somerset), and her offspring for half a pound from Ælfsige (*Ælsige*), abbot (of Bath), in the presence of the (monastic) community of Bath (*on Baðon*).
MS: Cambridge, CCC, 111, p. 8 (s. xi^2)
Printed: Kemble 1839, IV, 271, no. 936; Kemble 1849 (= 1876), I, 498; Thorpe 1865, 641; Earle 1888, 268, no. 4; Hunt 1893, lxxvii.
Translated: Kemble 1849 (= 1876), I, 498; Thorpe 1865, 641.
References: Wanley 1705, 149, I.7; James 1909–12, 236, no. 7; Ker 1957, 48, no. 35.8; Cameron 1973, 188, no. B16.2.3; Healey & Venezky 1980, 165, no. B16.2.3.

77

A.D. x 1075 x 1087. Record of the freeing by Ælfsige (*Ælsige*), abbot (of Bath), of Godwine Back or Fat (*Bace*) of Stanton Prior (*æt Stantune*), (Somerset), for himself and all the (monastic) community at Bath (*on Baðan*) witnessed by (all in the genitive case) Sæmann (*Sæmannes*); Wulfwig of Priston, (Somerset) (*Wulwiges æt Prisctune*); and Ælfric Cry or Shout (*Ælfrices Cermes*).
MS: Cambridge, CCC, 111, p. 8 (s. xi^2)
Printed: Kemble 1839, IV, 271, no. 937; Kemble 1849 (= 1876), I, 498–9; Thorpe 1865, 641; Earle 1888, 269, no. 5; Hunt 1893, lxxvii.
Translated: Kemble 1849 (= 1876), I, 498–9; Thorpe 1865, 641.
References: Wanley 1705, 149, no. I.8; James 1909–12, 236, no. 8; Tengvik 1938, 285–6, s.v. 'Bace'; Ker 1957, 48, no. 35.8; Cameron 1973, 188, no. B16.2.3; Healey & Venezky 1980, 165, no. B16.2.3.

78

A.D. 1077. Agreement of confraternity between Wulfstan (*Wulstan*), bishop (of Worcester), and Æthelwig (*Ægelwig*), Wulfweald (*Wulfwold*), Ælfsige, Eadmund, Ralph (*Rawulf*), Serlo (*Særle*), respectively abbots of Evesham (*on Eofesham*), Chertsey (*on Ceortesige*), Bath (*on Baðan*), Pershore (*on Perscoran*), Winchcombe (*on Wincelcumbe*) and Gloucester (*on Gleweceastre*), and Ælfstan, dean of Worcester (*on Wigraceastre*), with lists appended of the brethren at Evesham, Chertsey and Bath.
MS: Cambridge, CCC, 111, pp. 55–6 (s. xi^2)
Printed: Hickes 1703, V, 19–20; Thomas 1736, Appendix, p. 3, no. 2 (*ex* Hickes); Hart 1863, III, xviii–xx; Thorpe 1865, 615–7; Hunt 1893, 3–4; Atkins 1940, 216 (names only) *ex* Hart.
Translated: Thorpe 1865, 615–17.
References: Wanley 1705, 149, no. II; Thomas 1736, 'An Account', 100; Hart

1863, III, xvii–xviii; *DNB* XXI, 1090; James 1909–12, 238, no. 13; Westlake
1919, 7–8; Shelly 1921, 60 and 84; Darlington 1933, 4 n. 3; Atkins 1940, 35 and
216–17; Ker 1957, 48, no. 35.9; Darlington 1968, xliv; Cameron 1973, 188,
no. B16.2.2; Healey & Venezky 1980, 165, no. B16.2.2.

79

A.D. x 1075 x 1087. Record of the purchase of release by Ælfwig the Red (*se
Red*) of himself from Ælfsige, abbot (of Bath), and the (monastic) community (at
Bath) with a second pound (*mid anon punde*) in the presence of the congregation
of Bath (*on Baðan*).
MS: Cambridge, CCC, 140, 1r (s. xi^2)
Printed: Madox 1702, 416, no. DCCLII; Lye 1772, II, App. V, no. 1; Kemble
1839, VI, 209, no. 1351; Kemble 1849 (= 1876), I, 507; Earle 1888, 269, no. 6.
Translated: Madox 1702, 416, no. DCCLII (translation into Latin); Lye 1772,
II, App. V, no. 1 (translation into Latin); Kemble 1849 (= 1876), I, 507.
References: Wanley 1705, 116, no. II.1; Turner 1852, III, 83; James 1909–12,
324, no. 2; Ker 1957, 47, no. 35.2; Cameron 1973, 188, no. B16.2.3; Healey &
Venezky 1980, 165, no. B16.2.3.

80

A.D. x 1075 x 1087. Record of the purchase of freedom by Eadric at Bathford
(*Edric æt Fordan*), (Somerset), of his daughter Sægifu (*Sægyfu*) and her offspring
from Ælfsige, abbot (of Bath) and the (monastic) community at Bath (*on
Baðan*).
MS: Cambridge, CCC, 140, 1r (s. xi^2)
Printed: Madox 1702, 416, no. DCCL; Lye 1772, II, App. V, no. 2; Kemble
1839, VI, 209, no. 1351; Kemble 1849 (= 1876), I, 507; Earle 1888, 269, no. 7.
Translated: Madox 1702, 416, no. DCCL (translation into Latin); Lye 1772, II,
App. V, no. 2 (translation into Latin); Kemble 1849 (= 1876), I, 507.
References: Wanley 1705, 116, no. II.2; Turner 1852, III, 83; James 1909–12,
324, no. 3; Ker 1957, 47, no. 35.2; Cameron 1973, 188, no. B16.2.3; Healey &
Venezky 1980, 165, no. B16.2.3.

81

A.D. x 1075 x 1087. Record of the freeing of Ælfric Scot and Æthelric (*Ægelric*)
Scot for the soul of Ælfsige (genitive: *Ælsiges*), abbot (of Bath), in the presence
of all the (monastic) community.
MS: Cambridge, CCC, 140, 1r (s. xi^2)
Printed: Madox 1702, 416, no. DCCLI; Lye 1772, II, App. V, no. 3; Kemble
1839, VI, 209, no. 1351; Kemble 1849 (= 1876), I, 507; Earle 1888, 269, no. 11.
Translated: Madox 1702, 416, no. DCCLI (translation into Latin); Lye 1772, II,
App. V, no. 3 (translation into Latin); Kemble 1849 (= 1876), I, 507.
References: Wanley 1705, 116, no. II.3; Turner 1852, III, 83; James 1909–12,
324, no. 4; Ker 1957, 47, no. 35.2; Cameron 1973, 188, no. B16.2.3; Healey &
Venezky 1980, 165, no. B16.2.3.

82

(July 1088) x 1090 x 1122. Record of the purchase of freedom by Sigewine,
Leofwig's son at Lyncombe (*Siwine Loofwies* [sic] *sunu æt Lincumbe*), (Somerset),
of Siduflæd (accusative: *Sydeflæde*) from John (*æt Iohanne*) (de Villula), bishop

(of Wells until 1090, when he transferred the see to Bath) and the (monastic) community at Bath (*on Baþon*) for fifty shillings in pennies, witnessed by Godric Lad (*Codric Ladda*); Sæweald (*Sæwold*) and his two sons; Scirweald (*Scirewold*); and Beorhtweald (*Brihtwold*).

MS: Cambridge, CCC, 140, 1r (s. xi/xii)

Printed: Lye 1772, II, App. V, no. 10; Kemble 1839, VI, 210, no. 1351; Kemble 1849 (= 1876), I, 509; Earle 1888, 269–70, no. 13.

Translated: Lye 1772, II, App. V, no. 10 (translation into Latin); Kemble 1849 (= 1876), I, 509; Turner 1852, III, 82–3 *ex* Lye.

References: Wanley 1705, 116, no. II.4; James 1909–12, 324, no. 5; Ker 1957, 47, no. 35.2; Cameron 1973, 188, no. B16.2.3; Healey & Venezky 1980, 165, no. B16.2.3.

83

(July 1088) x 1090 x 1122. Record of the purchase by John (*Iohann*) (presumably de Villula, bishop of Wells until 1090, when he transferred the see to Bath) of Gunnhildr (accusative: *Gunnilde*), Thorketill's (*Þurkilles*) daughter, from Gode (*æt Gode*), Leofnoth's (*Leofenaðes*) widow, for half a pound in the presence of the (monastic) community (of Bath); he has entrusted her to Christ and St Peter (presumably the monastery at Bath) for the sake of his mother's soul.

MS: Cambridge, CCC, 140, 1v (s. xi/xii)

Printed: Lye 1772, II, App. V, no. 4; Kemble 1839, VI, 209, no. 1351; Kemble 1849 (= 1876), I, 507–8; Earle 1888, 270, no. 14.

Translated: Lye 1772, II, App. V, no. 4 (translation into Latin); Kemble 1849 (= 1876), I, 507–8.

References: Wanley 1705, 116, no. II.5; James 1909–12, 324, no. 6; Ker 1957, 47, no. 35.2; Cameron 1973, 188, no. B16.2.3; Healey & Venezky 1980, 165, no. B16.2.3; Insley 1985, 30 (on Gunnhildr) and 39 (on Thorkell).

84

A.D. x 1075 x 1087. Record of the release by Sæwig Belly of Withycombe (*Sæwi Hagg æt Widecume*), (Somerset), of his two sons from Ælfsige, abbot (of Bath), in the presence of all the (monastic) community.

MS: Cambridge, CCC, 140, 1v (s. xi²)

Printed: Lye 1772, II, App. V, no. 5; Kemble 1839, VI, 209, no. 1351; Kemble 1849 (= 1876), I, 508; Earle 1888, 270, no. 8.

Translated: Lye 1772, II, App. V, no. 5 (translation into Latin); Kemble 1849 (= 1876), I, 508.

References: Wanley 1705, 116, no. II.6; James 1909–12, 324, no. 7; Ker 1957, 47, no. 35.2; Cameron 1973, 188, no. B16.2.3; Healey & Venezky 1980, 165, no. B16.2.3.

85

(July 1088) x 1090 x 1122. Record of the freeing of Leofgyth at Bathford (*Lifgith æt Forda*), (Somerset), and her two children for John (*Iohann*) (de Villula), bishop (of Wells until 1090, when he transferred the see to Bath), and all the (monastic) community at Bath (*on Baðon*) witnessed by Ælfræd of Épaignes (*on Ælfredes g'witnesse Aspania*), (Eure).

MS: Cambridge, CCC, 140, 1v (s. xi/xii)

Printed: Lye 1772, II, App. V, no. 11; Kemble 1839, VI, 211, no. 1351; Kemble 1849 (= 1876), I, 509; Earle 1888, 270, no. 15.
Translated: Lye 1772, II, App. V, no. 11 (translation into Latin); Kemble 1849 (= 1876), I, 509.
References: Wanley 1705, 116, no. II.7; Turner 1852, III, 82; James 1909–12, 324, no. 8; Ker 1957, 47, no. 35.2; Cameron 1973, 188, no. B16.2.3; Healey & Venezky 1980, 165, no. B16.2.3.

86

A.D. 1106 or later. Record of an agreement between the prior and brotherhood of the monastery (of St Peter), Bath, and Sæwig (*Sæwi*) and his wife, Theodgifu (*Theodgyfu*), whereby the monastery offers them brotherhood, prayer and land for their lifetime from the road (*stræt*) that was the monastery's for them to enlarge their house; in return they agree to be obedient and faithful to the monastery, and after their deaths to give their house and land to 'Christ and St Peter' (i.e., the monastery).
MS: Cambridge, CCC, 140, 1v (s. xii[1])
Printed: Lye 1772, II, App. V, no., 6; Kemble 1839, VI, 209–10, no. 1351; Thorpe 1865, 436–7; Earle 1888, 270, no. 16.
Translated: Lye 1772, II, App. V, no. 6 (translation into Latin); Thorpe 1865, 436–7.
References: Wanley 1705, 116, no. II.8; James 1909–12, 324, no. 9; Ker 1957, 47, no. 35.3; Cameron 1973, 188, no. B16.2.1; Healey & Venezky 1980, 165, no. B16.2.1.

Bodmin

87

s. xi[2]. Record of purchase by Æthelsige (*Æilsig*) of Ongynethel (*Ongyneþel*) and her son Gythiccael (*Gyðiccael*) from Thorketill (*æt Purcilde*) for half a pound at the church door in Bodmin (*on Bodmine*), (Cornwall). He gave four pence as toll to Æthelsige (dative: *Æilsige*) the portreeve and Maccos (dative: *Maccosse*) the hundredman. He subsequently freed them at the altar of St Petroc's (Church, Bodmin) (*uppan Petrocys weofede*), witnessed by the mass-priests Isaac, Blethcuf (*Bleðcuf*), Wunning, Wulfgar (*Wulfger*), Grifiuth (*Grifiuð*), Noah (*Noe*) and Wurthicith (*Wurþicið*); Æthelsige (*Æilsig*) the deacon; Maccos; Tethion, Modræd's son (*Teðion Modredis sunu*); Cynehelm (*Kynilm*); Beornlaf (*Beorlaf*); Dierling (*Dirling*); Gratcant; and Talan.
MS: London, BL, Add. 9381, 8r (s. xi[2])
Printed: Gilbert 1838, III, 412, no. 27; Kemble 1839, IV, 313, no. 981; Oliver 1846, 432, no. 27; Kemble 1849 (= 1876), I, 501–2; Thorpe 1865, 627; Haddan & Stubbs 1869, I, 679–80, no. 28; Stokes 1870–2, 335; Earle 1888, 273, no. 27; Förster 1930, 91–2, no. 30.
Translated: Kemble 1849 (= 1876), I, 501–2; Thorpe 1865, 627.
References: Oliver 1846, 433–6; Ker 1957, 159, no. 126 (*contra* Förster 1930, 92 on the date); Cameron 1973, 188, no. B16.4; Healey & Venezky 1980, 166, no. B16.4; Davies 1982, 260 n. 6; Insley 1982, 88–9; Olson 1989, 71–2 and n. 95.

88

s. xi². Record of a payment at the church door in Bodmin (*æt Bodmine*) to avoid debt-enslavement by Putrael to Ælfric, Ælfwine's son, through the intercessions of his brother, Boia, to whom Putrael gave sixty pence and eight oxen for his advocacy, witnessed by Isaac the mass-priest; the priests Wunning and Sæwulf (*Sewulf*); Godric the deacon; Cufure the provost; Wincuf; Wulfweard (*Wulfwerd*); Gestin, the bishop's steward; Artaca; Cynehelm (*Kinilm*); Godric Son (*Map*); Wulfgar (*Wulfger*); and other good men (*ma godra manna*).

MS: London, BL, Add. 9381, 8v (s. xi²)

Printed: Gilbert 1838, III, 412–13, no. 30; Kemble 1839, IV, 314, no. 981; Kemble 1849 (= 1876), I, 502–3; Oliver 1846, 433, no. 30; Thorpe 1865, 628; Haddan & Stubbs 1869, I, 680, no. 31; Stokes 1870–2, 336; Earle 1888, 274, no. 30; Förster 1930, 93, no. 33.

Translated: Kemble 1849 (= 1876), I, 502–3; Thorpe 1865, 628.

References: Oliver 1846, 433–6; Ker 1957, 159, no. 126 (*contra* Förster 1930, 93 on the date); Cameron 1973, 188, no. B16.4; Healey & Venezky 1980, 166, no. B16.4; Olson 1989, 71–2 and n. 95.

89

s. xi/xii. Record of the freeing by Ælfweald (*Ælwold*) of Hwatu at Petroc's place (*a P'trocys stow*), (i.e., Bodmin, Cornwall), witnessed by Algar (genitive: *Ælgerys*); Godric; Wulfnoth (*Wulloð*); Grifyith (*Gryfyið*); Bleithcuf (*Bleyðcuf*); and Salomon (*Salaman*).

MS: London, BL, Add. 9381, 133v (s. xi/xii)

Printed: Gilbert 1838, III, 413, no. 34; Kemble 1839, IV, 315, no. 981; Oliver 1846, 433, no. 34; Kemble 1849 (= 1876), I, 503; Thorpe 1865, 629; Haddan & Stubbs 1869, I, 681, no. 35; Stokes 1870–2, 336–7; Earle 1888, 274, no. 34; Förster 1930, 94, no. 37.

Translated: Kemble 1849 (= 1876), I, 503; Thorpe 1865, 629.

References: Oliver 1846, 433–6; Förster 1930, 94–5; Ker 1957, 159, no. 126; Cameron 1973, 188, no. B16.4; Healey & Venezky 1980, 166, no. B16.4; Davies 1982, 260 n. 6; Olson 1989, 71 and n. 90.

Canterbury, Christ Church

90

A.D. 1093 x 1109. Record of an agreement between the convent of Christ Church and the members (*cnihtas*) of a merchant guild at Canterbury (*Cantwarebyrig*), whereby the former exchange seven hawes within Burgate (*wiðinnan Burhgate*) for nine hawes, two outside Ridingate (*utan Readingaten*) occupied by Ælfric and Brunmann (*Bruman*), and seven within Newingate (*innan Niwingate*) occupied by Sigeweard (*Siword*), Cuthfrith (*Cutfert*), Wulfgifu (*Wulfgeue*) and Ælfwine, witnessed by Archbishop Anselm; the convent of Christ Church; Calveal the portreeve; and the elders (*yldesta men*) of the society (*heap*). The convent has one copy of the document (*gewrit*) and the society the other.

Source: Canterbury, D & C, K–27–16, William Somner's personally annotated copy of his *Antiquities of Canterbury* (London, 1640), p. 365

Printed: Battely 1703, 179; Gross 1890, II, 37 *ex* Battely; Urry 1955, II, 219, Charter no. I *ex* Somner; Urry 1967, 385, no. I *ex* Somner.
Translated: Somner 1640, 365–6; Battely 1703, 179; Gross 1890, II, 37.
References: Somner 1640, 365; Gross 1890, I, 5 and 183–8 (on the meaning of *cniht*); Maitland 1897, 191 (= 1960, 233); Westlake 1919, 11; Stenton 1932, 134 n. 3 (= 1961, 135 n. 1) (on the meaning of *cniht*); Tait 1936, 120–3; Urry 1955, I, 153–9 (on William Calveal and his family), 525–9, 533 and II, 219–20; Urry 1958, 133–6 (= 1959, 14–17) (on William Calveal); Urry 1967, 126–8 and 385; Clark 1976a, 5, 9–10 and 28 n. 11; Urry 1978, 6–7 (on William Calveal).

Exeter

91

A.D. 1069 x 1072. Record of the gifts made by Leofric, bishop (of Exeter), to St Peter's Minster, Exeter (*into Sc'e Petres mynster on Exanceastre*), viz., estates (all in Devon) that had been alienated at Culmstock (*æt Culmstoke*), Branscombe (*æt Brancescumbe*), Salcombe Regis (*æt Sealtcumbe*) (near Sidmouth), St Mary Church (*æt Sc'e Maria circea*), Staverton (*æt Stofordtune*), Sparkwell (*æt Spearcanwille*), Marshall Farm (*æt Morceshille*) (near Ide), St Sidwell's holding (*Sidefulla hiwisc*) (in Exeter St Sidwell's parish), *æt Brihtricesstane* (either a lost Brightston or Treasbeare Farm in the parish of Clyst Honiton), Topsham (*æt Toppeshamme*), unjustly taken by Harold, Stoke Canon (*æt Stoke*), Sidbury (*æt Sidebirig*), Newton St Cyres (*æt Niwantune*) (near Crediton), Norton (*æt Norðtune*) and the estate at Clyst (*æt Clist*) held by Wid; from his own possessions he has endowed the minster for the support of the monks with estates at Bampton (*æt Bemtune*), Aston (*æt Esttune*), and Chimney (*æt Ceommenige*) (all in Oxon.), Dawlish (*æt Doflisc*), Holcombe (*æt Holacumbe*) and Southwood (*æt Supwuda*) (all in Devon); he also grants various ecclesiastical objects and vestments and a number of books (itemized) to the minster; after his death he grants his *capella* to the minster. (All readings from MS 1.)

MSS: 1.   Exeter, Cathedral, 3501, 1r–2v (original) (Chambers 1933, 1a–2b) (s. xi²)
       2.   Oxford, Bodleian, Auct. D. 2. 16 (2719), 1r–2v (original) (s. xi²)
       3.   Cambridge, CCC, 101, pp. 447–50 (s. xvi transcript of MS 2)
       4.   Exeter, Cathedral, Charter 2570 (s. xv transcript of a lost s. xiii version in Middle English)
       5.   Exeter, Cathedral, 3501, 3r (Latin abstract of MS 1) (Chambers 1933, 3a) (s. xii¹)
       6.   London, BL, Add 9067, 2r, 3r, 4r, 5r (A.D. 1831; transcript of MS 1)
       7.   London, BL, Harley 258, 125v–126v (s. xvii transcript of MS 3)

Printed: Parker ?1567, The Preface to the Christian Reader, [xxiii–xxiv] (extracts) *ex* MS 1; Dodsworth & Dugdale 1655, I, 221–2 *ex* MS 2; Wanley 1705, 80–1 *ex* MS 2 (incomplete); Conybeare 1826, 198 n. 1 (English on p. 199) *ex* Wanley; Kemble 1839, IV, 274–6, no. 940 *ex* MSS 2 and 7; *Monasticon* II, 527, no. IV *ex* MS 2; Pedler 1856, 136–8 *ex* Kemble; Thorpe 1865, 428–32 *ex* MS 6; Warren 1883, xxi–xxiii *ex* MS 2 (incomplete); Earle 1888, 249–51 *ex* MSS 1, 2 and 7; Edmonds 1899, 48–9 *ex* Warren; Kershaw 1922, 206–7 *ex* MS 1; Förster

1933, 18–30 *ex* MS 1 with variants from MSS 2, 3 and 7 noted, 30–2 *ex* MS 4 and 32 *ex* MS 5; Robertson 1939 (= 1956), 226–30 *ex* MS 2; Gatch 1977, 42–3, extracts *ex* Förster 1933; Lapidge 1985, 65–6 *ex* MSS 1 and 2.

Translated: Parker ?1567, Preface, [xxiv–xxv]; Dodsworth & Dugdale 1655, I, 222 (translation into Latin by William Somner); *Monasticon* II, 527–8, no. IV (translation into Latin by W. Somner); Wright 1842, 38–9 *ex* MSS 1 and 7; Pedler 1856, 138–40; Thorpe 1865, 428–32; Davidson 1881, 127–8 (partial translation); Edmonds 1899, 48; Robertson 1939 (= 1956), 227–31.

References: Parker ?1567, Preface, [xxii and xxv]; Wanley 1705, 279, no. 1 *ex* MS 1; Oliver 1861, 7–8; Wright 1862, 220–4; Freeman 1867, II, 562–3; Macray 1868, 23–4 (= 1890, 29) *ex* MS 2; Davidson 1881, 128; Earle 1888, 251–2; Edmonds 1899, 26–36; James 1909–12, 195, no. 62 *ex* MS 3; Chanter 1914–15, 175, no. 147; Rose-Troup 1914–15, 208, no. 170; Boggis 1922, 43–4; Förster 1933, 10–32; Robertson 1939 (= 1956), 473–80 (place-name identifications); Bishop 1955, 193; Ker 1957, 30, no. 20(6) and (8) *ex* MS 1 and 351, no. 291*a ex* MS 2; Lloyd 1972, 32–42; Cameron 1973, 192, no. B16.10.1; Gatch 1977, 199 n. 17; Drage 1978, 41–61, 67–70, 162–7 and 163 n. 1 *ex* MS 1, 206–55, 342–3, no. 4 *ex* MS 1, 343, no. 5d *ex* MS 5 and 380, no. 3 *ex* MS 2; Grant 1978, 32 and 123 n. 4 *ex* MS 2; Healey & Venezky 1980, 167, no. B16.10.1; Lapidge 1985, 64–9.

92

A.D. 1069 x 1072. Inscription of donation made by Leofric, bishop (of Exeter), to St Peter's Minster, Exeter (3, 7 *into Exanceastre*, 5, 9 *into Exancestre*, 2 *on Exancestr'*, 1, 6, 10 *on Exancestre*, 8 omits). *Latin and English versions.*

MSS: 1. Cambridge, CCC, 41, p. 488 (s. xi^2)
        2. Cambridge, Trinity College, B. 11. 2 (241), 121v (s. xi^2)
        3. Cambridge, Univ. Lib., Ii. 2. 11, 1r (s. xi^2)
        4. London, BL, Harley 2961 (*leaf now missing*)
        5. Oxford, Bodleian, Auct. D. 2. 16 (2719), 6v (s. xi^2)
        6. Oxford, Bodleian, Auct. F. 1. 15 (2455), 77v (Drage 1978, pl. IIIB) (s. xi^2)
        7. Oxford, Bodleian, Auct. F. 1. 15 (2455), 78r (s. xi^2)
        8. Oxford, Bodleian, Auct. F. 3. 6 (2666), 2v (s. xi^2)
        9. Oxford, Bodleian, Bodl. 579 (2675), 1r (s. xi^2)
      10. Oxford, Bodleian, Bodl. 708 (2609), 113r (s. xi^2) (Lloyd 1956 [= 1967], [pl. 2])

Printed: Wanley 1705, 81 *ex* MS 5, 114 *ex* MS 1 and 152 *ex* MS 3; Macray 1868, 23 (= 1890, 28–9) *ex* MS 10; Warren 1883, 1 *ex* MS 9; Earle 1888, 252 *ex* MS 5 and 253 *ex* MS 9; Miller 1890, xvii *ex* MS 1 (English version only); Schipper 1897, xxvii *ex* MS 1; James 1900, I, 327, no. 241 *ex* MS 2; James 1909–12, I, 81 *ex* MS 1; Savage 1911, 110 *ex* MS 1 (Latin version only); Nicholson 1913, lxi–lxii *ex* MSS 5–10; Madan & Craster 1922, II, 374, no. 2455 *ex* MSS 6 and 7 (Latin version only), 450, no. 2609 *ex* MS 10 (Latin version only), 481, no. 2666 *ex* MS 8 (Latin version only), 488, no. 2675 *ex* MS 9 (Latin version only), 512, no. 2719 *ex* MS 5 (Latin version only); Förster 1932, 230 n. 1 *ex* MS 1; Förster 1933, 11–12 n. 3 *ex* MSS 1–3 and 5–10; Lloyd 1956 (= 1967), 1 *ex* MS 10 (Latin version only; final word 'fiat' omitted); Lloyd 1972, 40 *ex* MS 8 (Latin version only).

Translated: Lloyd 1956 (= 1967) 1 *ex* Latin of MS 10; Lloyd 1972, 40 n. 2 *ex* Latin.

References: Hardwick 1856–67, III, 384 *ex* MS 3; James 1900–2, I, 327, no. 241 *ex* MS 2; Savage 1911, 110–11 *ex* MSS 1 and 5; Nicholson 1913, lx–lxi; Boggis 1922, 44–5; Lloyd 1956 (= 1967), 1 (incorrectly refers to MS 9 instead of MS 10); Ker 1957, 45, no. 32.19 *ex* MS 1, 129, no. 84 *b ex* MS 2, 30, no. 20.10 *ex* MS 3, 308, no. 236 *ex* MS 4, 351, no. 291 *b ex* MS 5, 353, no. 294 *b ex* MSS 6 and 7, 354, no. 296 *c ex* MS 8, 378, no. 315 *b ex* MS 9, 379, no. 316 *ex* MS 10; Cameron 1973, 193, no. B16.10.5 *ex* MSS 1–10; Drage 1978, 29–41 *ex* MSS 1–3, 5–10, 119 *ex* MS 9, 150–4 *ex* MSS 2, 5, 6, 8 and 9, and 162–7 *ex* MSS 1, 3, 7 and 10; Grant 1978, 32 and 123 n. 3 *ex* MS 9; Healey & Venezky 1980, 167–8, nos. B16.10.5.1–5, B16.10.5.6.1–2 and B16.10.5.7–9; Lapidge 1983, 23–4 *ex* MS 9 (on the scribe).

93

s. xii[1]. Record that Robert of Powderham (*Rotberd a Poldraham*), (Devon), has declared free from subjection to the estate at Powderham (*of Poldraham lande*) and from every claim (*cwæð saccles . . . of elcre craurigge*) William (*Willelm*), his brother's son, witnessed by Ragnaldr the priest (*Reinald preost*); Dunning (*Dunnig*); Dalfin; Sæfari (*Seuara*); Sæwig (*Sewi*); Girard; William the Marshall (*Willelm merescald*); Richard of Cowick Barton (*Ricard a Cuic*), (Devon); Wulfric Pig (*Wulfricc Pig*); Ralph Shoulder (*Rau Sculdur*); Richard (*Ricard*) *Gealdulesc*; Herbert (*Herberd*); Sægar (*Segar*); Algar ?'Inner Cottage' or 'In (the) Cottage' (*Alger Inna Bure*); Algar the weaver (*Alger se webba*); William the weaver (*Willelm se webba*); Roger the steward (*Rogere se stiwerd*); Robert, (son of) Winihard (*Rotberd Wianard*); Richard, Osanne's son (*Ricard Osanna sune*); Sæmær Pleasant Skin (*Semer Swetleder*); Joel of Upcott (*Iohel Uppa Cote*), (Devon); Asketill (*Ascetill*); Robert, Eadwig's kinsman (*Rotberd Edwies meg*). (All readings from MS 1.)

MSS: 1. Exeter, Cathedral, 3501, 4r (NPS I, pl. 10; Chambers 1933, 4a) (s. xii[1])
      2. London, BL, Add. 9067, 8r (A.D. 1831; transcript of MS 1)

Printed: Hickes 1703, V, 15–16 *ex* MS 1; Thorpe 1865, 645–6 *ex* MS 2; Earle 1888, 257 *ex* MS 1; NPS I, page opp. pl. 10 *ex* MS 1.

Translated: Thorpe 1865, 645–6.

References: Wanley 1705, 279, no. 6 *ex* MS 1; Förster 1933, 47, no. 6 and 50 n. 35 *ex* MS 1; Rose-Troup 1937, 428, no. 6 and 433 *ex* MS 1; Ker 1957, 30, no. 20.13 *ex* MS 1; Cameron 1973, 193, no. B16.10.6; Healey & Venezky 1980, 168, no. B16.10.6.2; Insley 1982, 87 (on Sæfari) and 82 (on Askell).

94

s. xii[1]. Record that Ottarr (*Oter*) and his child has declared Ælfric the Red (*Aluric þane Reda*) and his offspring free from obligation (*cwede saccles*), witnessed by the priests Alweard (*Alword*) and Ælfræd (*Alured*); Walter the priest and canon (*Waltere p' se can'*); Theobald (*Theodbald*); Sæmær, Cippspon's son (*Semer Cipspones sune*); Walter the Fleming (*Waltere se Flemig*); Geoffrey, Hoel's (son) (*Gesfrei Hoel*); Randolph the cordwainer (*Randolf se cordewan'*); Alwine Brave (*Alwine Modi*); Alwig Daw (*Alwi Kya*); Algar Oxbelly (*Alger Oxawamb*); Æthelweard (*Ailwerd*); Jordan (*Iordan*); Martinus (*Martin*); Osbern, (son of)

Heafoc (*Osbern Hauoc*); and Willemot Clubfoot (*Crukeuot*). Richard the Fleming (*Ricard se Flemig*) took fourpence as toll. (All readings from MS 1.)
MSS: 1.   Exeter, Cathedral, 3501, 4r (NPS I, pl. 10; Chambers 1933, 4a)
            (s. xii[1])
       2.   London, BL, Add. 9067, 8r (A.D. 1831; transcript of MS 1)
Printed: Hickes 1703, V, 16 *ex* MS 1; Thorpe 1865, 646 *ex* MS 2; Earle 1888, 257–8 *ex* MS 1; NPS I, page opp. pl. 10 *ex* MS 1.
Translated: Thorpe 1865, 646.
References: Wanley 1705, 279, no. 7 *ex* MS 1; Turner 1852, III, 83; Förster 1933, 47–8, no. 7 *ex* MS 1; Rose-Troup 1933, 35–6, 39 (identification of persons); Rose-Troup 1937, 428, no. 7 *ex* MS 1; Ker 1957, 30, no. 20.13 *ex* MS 1; Cameron 1973, 193, no. B16.10.6; Healey & Venezky 1980, 168, no. B16.10.6.2.
Note: Most editors have read *Willemot Quikeuot* 'Quickfoot' (cf. Tengvik 1938, 330, s.v. 'Quikeuot') but this is a misreading.

95

s. xii[1]. Record that Geoffrey (*Gesfrei*) Foliot has declared Sæmær, Ælfræd's kinsman (*Semer Aluredes mæg*), and all his offspring free from obligation (*cweð saccles*), witnessed by Richard the portreeve (*Ricard se portreua*); Ralph, Theobald's (son) (*Rau Theodb'*); Walter of ?Saint-Ouen (*Waltere de s' odin'*); William Shield (*Willem Pafard*); William ?'Saliva' or 'Representative, Deputy' (*Willelm Spalla*); Æthelweard Saddlehook (*Ailwerd Sadelhack'*); Sæfari (*Seuara*); and Eadmær, Burgweald's son (*Edmer Burhwolles s'*). (All readings from MS 1.)
MSS: 1.   Exeter, Cathedral, 3501, 4r (NPS I, pl. 10; Chambers 1933, 4a)
            (s. xii[1])
       2.   London, BL, Add. 9067, 8r (A.D. 1831; transcript of MS 1)
Printed: Thorpe 1865, 648 *ex* MS 2; Earle 1888, 258 *ex* MS 1; NPS I, page opp. pl. 10 *ex* MS 1.
Translated: Thorpe 1865, 648.
References: Wanley 1705, 279, no. 8 *ex* MS 1; Förster 1933, 48, no. 8 *ex* MS 1; Rose-Troup 1933, 35–6, 39 (identification of persons); Rose-Troup 1937, 428, no. 8 *ex* MS 1; Ker 1957, 30, no. 20.13 *ex* MS 1; Cameron 1973, 193, no. B16.10.6; Healey & Venezky 1980, 168, no. B16.10.6.2; Insley 1982, 87 (on Sæfari).

96

s. xii[1]. Record that Alice (*Aðelicc*), sister of Richard (genitive: *Ricardes*) the sheriff, has declared Hrothwulf, Sæwig's son of Alphington (*Hrodolf Sewies sune an Alfintune*), (Devon), free from every claim (*saccles of elcre crauigge*), witnessed by Richard the portreeve (*Ricard se portreua*); William, (son of) Lambert (*Willelm Lambr'*); Dunning (*Dunnig*); Herlewin (*Eorlawine*); Rainer (*Reiner*); Ælfric Spot (*Aluric Spoe*); Robert Pudding (*Rotb'd Puddig*); Wighere (*Wiggere*); Dalfin; Goscelin Dung-Hawk (probably the Red Kite, *Milvus milvus*) (*Gotselin Gorpittel*); Leggefot; John (*Iohan*); Osbern Jaw (*Osb'n Ceaca*); Rotbeorn Shank (*Rotb'n Sceanca*); Beorhtric (*Brihtric*); Æthelweard, Algar's son (*Ailword Algar' s'*); Richard Cutter (*Ricard Trencard*); Jordan the priest (*Iordan se prb'*); Richard (*Ricard*); and all the Hundred of Alphington (*Alfint'*). (All readings from MS 1.)
MSS: 1.   Exeter, Cathedral, 3501, 4r (NPS I, pl. 10; Chambers 1933, 4a)
            (s. xii[1])

2.   London, BL, Add. 9067, 8r (A.D. 1831; transcript of MS 1)
Printed: Hickes 1703, V, 15 *ex* MS 1; Thorpe 1865, 645 *ex* MS 2; Earle 1888, 258 *ex* MS 1; NPS I, page opp. pl. 10 *ex* MS 1.
Translated: Hickes 1703, V, 15 (partial translation into Latin); Thorpe 1865, 645.
References: Wanley 1705, 279, no. 9 *ex* MS 1; Förster 1933, 48, no. 9 *ex* MS 1; Rose-Troup & Watkin 1930–1, 370–3 (mis-numbered as 6 instead of 9); Rose-Troup 1932, 403 (mis-numbered); Rose-Troup 1937, 425–6 (on Alphinton) and 428–9, no.9 *ex* MS 1; Anderson 1939, 75; Cam 1944, 108; Ker 1957, 30, no. 20.13 *ex* MS 1; Cameron 1973, 193, no. B16.10.6; Healey & Venezky 1980, 168, no. B16.10.6.2; Insley 1982, 84 (on Hrothwulf).

97

s. xii[1]. Record that Walter, Wulfweard's son (*Waltere Wulwordes sune*) freed Æthelgifu (*Aþeluue*) in St Peter's Minster (*minstre*), (Exeter), over his father's body for the redemption of his father's soul and his own, witnessed by (all names in the genitive case) Vivianus (*Viuienes*); Master Oda (*Mestre Odes*); Master Leofwine (*Mestre Leowines*); Godwine the priest (*Godwines p'*); Eadwacer (*Edwakeres*) and his son; and all the clergy and laity who were there. (All readings from MS 1.)
MSS: 1.   Exeter, Cathedral, 3501, 4v (Chambers 1933, 4b) (s. xii[1])
        2.   London, BL, Add. 9067, 9r (A.D. 1831; transcript of MS 1)
Printed: Hickes 1703, V, 15 *ex* MS 1; Thorpe 1865, 632 *ex* MS 2; Earle 1888, 258–9 *ex* MS 1.
Translated: Hickes 1703, V, 15 (partial translation into Latin); Thorpe 1865, 632.
References: Wanley 1705, 279, no. 10 *ex* MS 1; Förster 1933, 48, no. 10 *ex* MS 1; Rose-Troup 1933, 24–6 (on Oda and Leofwine); Rose-Troup 1937, 421–2 (on Walter and his son) and 429, no. 10 *ex* MS 1; Ker 1957, 30, no. 20.13 *ex* MS 1; Cameron 1973, 193, no. B16.10.6; Healey & Venezky 1980, 168, no. B16.10.6.2.

98

s. xii[1]. Record that Geoffrey, Feala's son (*Gesfræg Feala sune*), bought Edith, Eadwig's daughter (*Gidiþ Edwiges docter*), from Ælfstan of Wonford (*at Alpsta on Wunforda*), (Devon), and Neæle, ?'Pinca's son' or 'the butler' (*at Neæle pinceune* [*sic*], probably a scribal error either for *Pince sune* or *pincerne*), for ten shillings (to be) free and without obligation to Wonford (*ut of Wunforda*), (Devon); ?'Ealdbeorht' or possibly 'Golden Beard' (*Gyldeberd*) the portreeve took the toll on the king's behalf, witnessed by Eadmær of Cowick Barton (*Gedmær on Cuike*), (Devon); Sægar the priest at Heavitree (*Sægær p' on Hefatriwe*), (Devon); Randolph from Hayes (*Randolf de Hage*, (Devon); Roger of Pinhoe (*Roggere on Pynnoc*), (Devon); Morin at the East Gate (*Morin at Gest Gate*); Richard, Ælfstan's son (*Riceard Alpstanes sune*); Wulfweard (*Wlfword*), his brother; Godwine, Leofwine's son (*Leowines sune*); Goda, his brother; Gytha (*Geda*); Sægar (*Sægær*); Richard (*Riceard*) *Kykebeauw*; and Eadmær, Northmann's son (*Edmær Nordman' sun* [*sic*]). (All readings from MS 1.)
MSS: 1.   Exeter, Cathedral, 3501, 4v (Chambers 1933, 4b) (s. xii[1])
        2.   London, BL, Add. 9067, 9r (A.D. 1831; transcript of MS 1)

Printed: Hickes 1703, V, 15 *ex* MS 1; Thorpe 1865, 631–2 *ex* MS 2; Earle 1888, 259 *ex* MS 1.
Translated: Hickes 1703, V, 15 (partial translation into Latin); Thorpe 1865, 631–2.
References: Wanley 1705, 279, no. 11 *ex* MS 1; Gover *et al.* 1931 (on place-names); Förster 1933, 48, no. 11 *ex* MS 1; Rose-Troup 1933, 39 (on Eadmær, Northmann's son); Rose-Troup 1937, 430, no. 11 *ex* MS 1; Tengvik 1938, 328 (on *pinceune*) and 390 (*Kykebeauw*); Ker 1957, 30, no. 20.13 *ex* MS 1; Cameron 1973, 193, no. B16.10.6; Healey & Venezky 1980, 168, no. B16.10.6.2.

99

s. xi/xii. Record that Hubert of Clyst (*Huberd on Clist*) (either Bishop's Clyst or Clyst Satchvil, Devon) released Edith (*Edit*), Leofgar's (*Liuegeres*) wife, and all her offspring from an unjust summons (*leosende . . . far his unriht cræfinge*) because Leofgar had released her from Geoffrey (*Gosfreige*), bishop (of Coutances), for thirty pence as was right in those days to free a woman, witnessed by William of ?Les Buhots (*Will'm de Buhuz*); ?'Hroaldr' the knight (*Ruold se cniht*); Osbern (?his) uncle; ?'Humphrey' of Tedburn St Mary (*Unfreig de Tettaborna*), (Devon); Alweard the portreeve (*Alword portgereua*); John the knight (*Iohan se cniht*); and Ralph, Fulcard's son (*Rau Folcard*). This suit (*spæc*) was heard within the house (*bure*) of William of ?Les Buhots (*Vill'mes de Buhuz*) in Exeter (*on Excestre*). (All readings from MS 1.)
MSS: 1.   Exeter, Cathedral, 3501, 4v (Chambers 1933, 4b) (s. xi/xii)
       2.   London, BL, Add. 9067, 9r (A.D. 1831; transcript of MS 1)
Printed: Hickes 1703, V, 18 *ex* MS 1; Thorpe 1865, 633 *ex* MS 2; Earle 1888, 259 *ex* MS 1.
Translated: Thorpe 1865, 633–4.
References: Wanley 1705, 279, no. 12 *ex* MS 1; Gover *et al.* 1931, II, 586 and 451 (on *Clist* and *Tettaborna*); Förster 1933, 48, no. 12 *ex* MS 1 and 52 n. 61 (on *Clist*); Rose-Troup 1937, 423–4 (on *Willelm* and *Ruold*) and 430–1, no. 12 *ex* MS 1; Ker 1957, 30, no. 20.13 *ex* MS 1; Cameron 1973, 193, no. B16.10.6; Healey & Venezky 1980, 168, no. B16.10.6.2.

100

s. xii[1]. Record that William of Bruyère (*Willelm de la Brugere*), (Calvados), declared Wulfweard the weaver (*Wulwærd se webba*) free of obligation from every claim (*saccles ... of elce crafigge*) within the town and without, witnessed by Ralph, Theobald's son (*Rau Teodb' sune*); Theobald (*Teodb'*), his son; Azur the White (*Atsun se Hwita*); Hrothwulf (*Hroðolf*), Alca's son; Aimeri (*Hemeri*) *cuta k***; Philip, Paganus's son (*Philippe Pagenes s'*); Richard, Alca's son (*Ricard Alkas'*); Geoffrey (*Gesfrei*) (son of) Hoel; Herbert (*Herb'd*); 'Goldwine' or possibly 'Goslen' (*Gollein*); Æthelweard the smith (*Ailwerd faber*) and his brother; Ralph of Sassy, (Calvados), or Sacey, (Manche) (*Rau de Salcei*); Herlewin (*Herlawine*); and Beorhtmær (*Brihtmer*) *Vidic*. (All readings from MS 1.)
MSS: 1.   Exeter, Cathedral, 3501, 4v (Chambers 1933, 4b) (s. xii[1])
       2.   London, BL, Add 9067, 9r (A.D. 1831; transcript of MS 1)
Printed: Hickes 1703, V, 15 *ex* MS 1; Thorpe 1865, 648 *ex* MS 2; Earle 1888, 259–60 *ex* MS 1.
Translated: Thorpe 1865, 648.

References: Wanley 1705, 279, no. 13 *ex* MS 1; Förster 1933, 48, no. 13 *ex* MS 1; Rose-Troup 1933, 35 and 38–9 (*Rau* and *Atsun*); Rose-Troup 1937, 431, no. 13 *ex* MS 1; Tengvik 1938, 112 (on *Salcei*); Ker 1957, 30, no. 20.13 *ex* MS 1; Cameron 1973, 193, no. B16.10.6; Healey & Venezky 1980, 168, no. B16.10.6.2; Insley 1982, 83 (on *Atsun*) and 84 (on Hrothwulf).

101

11 June 1096 x 18 June 1102. Notification of Osbern, bishop of Exeter (*Execestres biscop*), that the monks of St Nicholas' Minster (*on Sc'e Nicholaus Minstre*), (Exeter), may continue ringing their bells following their earlier practice. (All readings from MS 1.) *English and Latin versions.*
MSS: 1.   Exeter, Cathedral, 3501, 5r (Chambers 1933, 5a) (s. xi/xii) (English version only)
     2.   London, BL, Add. 9067, 10r (A.D. 1831; transcript of MS 1)
     3.   London, BL, Cotton Vitellius D. ix, 29 (s. xiii)
Printed: Hickes 1703, V, 18 *ex* MS 1; Oliver 1846, 113 n. 6 *ex* MS 1; Thorpe 1865, 437 *ex* Hickes; Earle 1888, 260 *ex* MS 1; Blake 1970, 230 *ex* MSS 1 and 3.
Translated: Thorpe 1865, 437.
References: Wanley 1705, 279, no. 15; Phillipps 1834, 61, no. 14 *ex* MS 3; Oliver 1846, 113; Clarke 1912, 193–4; Boggis 1922, 52; Förster 1933, 49, no. 15 *ex* MS 1; Rose-Troup 1937, 432, no. 15 *ex* MS 1; Ker 1957, 30, no. 20.12 *ex* MS 1; Blake 1970, 84–5; Cameron 1973, 193, no. B16.10.7; Healey & Venezky 1980, 168, no. B16.10.7.
Note: See Anselm's letter in connection with this matter in Schmitt 1938, IV, 53–4, no. 172 or Migne 1844, CLIX, cc. 47–8 (Lib. III, epis. 20).

102

s. xii[1]. Record that Ælfric (*Aluric*) the canon of Exeter (*of Execestre*) released Ragnaldr (*Reinold*) from Herbert (*at Herberde*) and from his children and their offspring for two shillings and declared him free and without obligation (*freoh 7 saccles*) in town and out of town, witnessed by John, Ælfric's son (*Iohan Alurices sune*); Nicholas (*Nicole*); Æthelric (*Ailric*); Randolph (*Randolf*); Alweard Child (*Alword Cild*); Osbern, Cloppel's son (*Osb'n Clopeles sun'*); Richard of Paul's Street, (*Ricard a Paules Stret*), (Exeter); Richard, Theobald's kinsman (*Ricard Theodbaldes meg*); Andrew (*Andreu*); Serlo (*Serle*); Selewine (*Saluin*); Særic (*Seric*); Hubert (*Huberd*); Randolph, Cote's son (*Randolf Cotes sune*) (possibly a scribal error for *coces sune*, 'son of [the] cook' or 'Cock's son'); Osbern Hood (*Osb'n hod*); Pilgrim (*Pilegrim*); Ialebriht (cf. Ealubeorht 112); Geoffrey the cook (*Gesfrei se coc*); Pierres the wafer-baker (*se niulier*); Æthelric (*Ailric*); and Gales. (All readings from MS 1.)
MSS: 1.   Cambridge, Univ. Lib., Ii. 2. 11, 202v + Exeter, Cathedral, 3501, 5v (Chambers 1933, 5b *ex* Exeter, Cathedral, 3501, 5v; Dickins 1950, pl. XII[*b*] opp. 366) (s. xii[1])
     2.   London, BL, Add. 9067, 11r (A.D. 1831; transcript of Exeter, Cathedral, 3501, 5v)
Printed: Hickes 1703, V, 152 *ex* Cambridge, Univ. Lib., Ii. 2. 11, 202v; Thorpe 1865, 622 (partial) *ex* Cambridge, Univ. Lib., Ii. 2. 11; Förster 1938, 40 fn. *ex* MS 1; Dickins 1950, 366 *ex* MS 1.

Translated: Turner 1852, III, 83 (partial translation); Thorpe 1865, 622 (partial translation); Dickins 1950, 366–7.
References: Wanley 1705, 279, no. 16 *ex* Exeter, Cathedral, 3501, 5v ('cujus pars prior ab aliqua nefaria manu exscinditur'); Hardwick 1856–67, III, 384 *ex* MS 1 (Cambridge, Univ. Lib., Ii. 2. 11); Förster 1933, 49–50, no. 16 (partial) *ex* MS 1 (Exeter, Cathedral, 3501, 5v); Rose-Troup 1937, 418 and 432–3, no. 16 *ex* MS 1; Förster 1938, 39–41 n. 5 *ex* MS 1; Dickins 1950, 363–7 *ex* MS 1; Bishop 1955, 193; Ker 1957, 30, no. 20.13 *ex* MS 1; Cameron 1973, 193, no. B16.10.6; Healey & Venezky 1980, 168, no. B16.10.6.2.

103

2 July 1133 (Blake 1972, 28–9; Rose-Troup 1933: 3 x 13 June 1133). Record that William (*Willelm*) (Warelwast), bishop of Exeter (*of Execestre*), declared Wulfric Pig (*Pig*) free and without obligation (*freoh 7 saccles*) to the estate (*lande*) at Bishop's Teignton (*a' Teigtune*), (Devon), on the day when (the remains of) Bishop Osbern and Bishop Leofric were moved from the old cathedral to the new, witnessed by Algar, bishop of Coutances (*of Constance*); the priors of Plympton (*of Plimtune*), Taunton (*of Tantune*), St Nicholas' Minster (*Sc'es Nichol' minst'*) and St Andrew's (*Sc'es Andreas*); Leofwine (*Leowine*) the canon; Walter (*Waltere*) the priest; William (*Will'm*) the priest; Robert the White (*Rodb'd se blund*); Ælfric (*Aluric*); Osbern (*Osb'n*) the priest and chaplain; William (*Will'm*); Osbern (*Osb'n*) the deacon; William (*Will'm*) the treasurer; Bartholomew (*Barthol'*); Odo; Hugh of Eu (*Hugo Ou*), (Seine-Maritime); Geoffrey (*Gesfreg*); Hugh of Orbec (*Hugo Or*), (Calvados); William, Eadwig's son (*Willelm Edw s'*); Algar, Leofflæd's son (*Alger Liffl' s'*); Jordan (*Iordan*), his son; Randolph (*Randolf*); Ralph, Mathilda's son (*Rau Mahtille s'*); Walter, Daniel's (son) (*Waltere Dan'*); Osbern, (son of) Heafoc (*Osbern Hauoc*); Asketill Outside the Gate (*Ascetill Buta Port*); Sæfari, Ialewa's son (*Seuara Ialewa s'*); Dunning (*Dunnig*); Ralph, Theobald's (son) (*Rau Theodb'*); Theobald (*Teodbald*); William, Selewig's son (*Willelm Selewies s'*); and many others who cannot be named (*fela oðra þe ma nemna ne mæg*). (All readings from MS 1.)
MSS: 1.   Exeter, Cathedral, 3501, 5v (Chambers 1933, 5b; Dickins 1950, pl. XII[c] opp. 366 [partial]) (s. xii[1])
       2.   London, BL, Add. 9067, 11r (A.D. 1831; transcript of MS 1)
Printed: Hickes 1703, V, 16 *ex* MS 1; Thorpe 1865, 646–7 *ex* MS 2; Earle 1888, 260–1 *ex* MS 1; Rose-Troup 1933, 17 *ex* MS 1 (partial).
Translated: Hickes 1703, V, 16 and 18 (translation into Latin); Thorpe 1865, 646–7.
References: Wanley 1705, 279, no. 17 *ex* MS 1; Rose-Troup 1926–7, 97 and 304; Bishop 1928–9, 53–4; Rose-Troup 1928–9, 107–8; Förster 1933, 50, no. 17 *ex* MS 1; Rose-Troup 1933, *passim*, and 1937, 419–20 and 433, no. 17 *ex* MS 1 (dating, etc.); Ker 1957, 30, no. 20.13 *ex* MS 1; Blake 1970, 119–20; Blake 1972, 28–9; Cameron 1973, 193, no. B16.10.6; Healey & Venezky 1980, 168, no. B16.10.6.2; Insley 1982, 82 (on Askell).

104

s. xi/xii. Record that Bruning, Cola's son, purchased the release of Roting from Colewine (*æt Colewyne*) and Leofe (*æt Leofa*) (to be) free and without obligation (*freoh 7 sacleas*) to Shebbear (*ut of Sceftbeara*), (Devon), witnessed by (all names

in the genitive case) Serlo (*Særla*) the portreeve; Hubert (*Huberdes*); Alweard
(*Ælwerdes*); Algar Tramp (*Ælgares Paiardes*); William (*Wyllelmes*), his son;
Godwine, Colewine's son (*Godwynes Colwines suna*); and Asbjorn, Alweard's son
(*Esb'nes Ælwerdes suna*). (All readings from MS 1.)
MSS: 1.   Exeter, Cathedral, 3501, 6r (Chambers 1933, 6a) (s. xi/xii)
       2.   London, BL, Add. 9067, 12r (A.D. 1831; transcript of MS 1)
Printed: Thorpe 1865, 635 *ex* MS 2; Earle 1888, 261 *ex* MS 1.
Translated: Thorpe 1865, 635.
References: Wanley 1705, 279, no. 18 *ex* MS 1; Förster 1933, 50, no. 18 *ex*
MS 1; Rose-Troup 1937, 433–4, no. 18 *ex* MS 1; Ker 1957, 30, no. 20.13 *ex* MS
1; Cameron 1973, 193, no. B16.10.6; Healey & Venezky 1980, 168,
no. B16.10.6.2.

105

s. xi/xii. Record that Teolling bought Alweard Stammerer (*Ælword Stamera*) and
Eadwine (*Edwine*), his brother, from Colewine (*Coluwine*) for seven mancuses as
purchase price and toll (*to cepe 7 to tolle*). Alweard (*Ælword*) the portreeve took
the toll. Witnessed by Vitalis of Cullompton (*Viðel æt Culumtune*), (Devon);
Sæwulf; Vitula; Eadmund the priest; Snelling, Tulling's son; Leofwine,
Leofweard's brother (*Leowine Leowerdes broðor*); Ælfgar Hell Bull (*Hellebula*).
(All readings from MS 1.)
MSS: 1.   Exeter, Cathedral, 3501, 6r (Chambers 1933, 6a) (s. xi/xii)
       2.   London, BL, Add. 9067, 12r (A.D. 1831; transcript of MS 1)
Printed: Hickes 1703, V, 15 *ex* MS 1; Thorpe 1865, 633 *ex* MS 2; Earle 1888,
261–2 *ex* MS 1.
Translated: Thorpe 1865, 633 *ex* MS 1.
References: Wanley 1705, 279, no. 19 *ex* MS 1; Förster 1933, 50, no. 19 *ex* MS
1; Rose-Troup 1937, 434, no. 19 *ex* MS 1; Ker 1957, 30, no. 20.13 *ex* MS 1;
Cameron 1973, 193, no. B16.10.6; Healey & Venezky 1980, 168, no. B16.10.6.2.

106

s. xi/xii. Record that Leofwine the Londoner (*Leowine Lundenisca*) and Edith
(*[E]aldgið*), his wife, bought Ælfhild (*Ælfilde*) from Tofi (*Touie*) for sixty-four
pence. Ælfric Neck (*Hals*) took the toll within Tofi's dwelling (*innan Touies
bure*) on the king's behalf. Witnessed by Roscelin (*Roðsalin*) the priest; Æthel-
weard (*Ailword*) the deacon; Alwine the deacon; Dunstan *Peoning*. (All readings
from MS 1.)
MSS: 1.   Exeter, Cathedral, 3501, 6r (Chambers 1933, 6a) (s. xi/xii)
       2.   London, BL, Add. 9067, 12r (A.D. 1831; transcript of MS 1)
Printed: Thorpe 1865, 635 *ex* MS 2; Earle 1888, 262 *ex* MS 1.
Translated: Thorpe 1865, 635.
References: Wanley 1705, 279, no. 20 *ex* MS 1; Förster 1933, 50–1, no. 20 *ex*
MS 1; Rose-Troup 1937, 434, no. 20 *ex* MS 1; Tengvik 1938, 144–5, s.v. 'Peon-
ing'; Ker 1957, 30, no. 20.13 *ex* MS 1; Cameron 1973, 193, no. B16.10.6; Healey
& Venezky, 168, no. B16.10.6.2; Insley 1982, 87 (on Tofi).

107

s. xi/xii. Record that Wulfweard (*Wulword*) bought Leofede (*Leouede*) from
Hearding, Eadnoth's son (*æt Hierdinge, Eadnoðes sune*), for five shillings as pur-

chase price and toll (*to cepe 7 to tolle*). Garwig (*Garwi*), the reeve at Topsham (*to Toppeshamme*), (Devon), took the toll. Witnessed by (all names in the genitive case) Smeawine (*Smewines*) the priest; Alwine the priest; Æthelweard of Ottery St Mary (*Ailwordes æt Oteri*), (Devon); Dunning Cut Iron (*Dunninges Tailiferes*) (cf. Tailifer 109); Æthelweard, Lyfing's son (*Ailwordes Liuinges suna*); Dunewine; Godwine of Clyst Honiton (*æt Hinatune*), (Devon); Hearding (*Hierdinges*); Beorhtmær, Ælfgar's son (*Brihtmares Alfgares suna*). (All readings from MS 1.)
MSS: 1.   Exeter, Cathedral, 3501, 6r (Chambers 1933, 6a) (s. xi/xii)
       2.   London, BL, Add. 9067, 12r (A.D. 1831; transcript of MS 1)
Printed: Thorpe 1865, 648–9 *ex* MS 2; Earle 1888, 262 *ex* MS 1.
Translated: Thorpe 1865, 648–9.
References: Wanley 1705, 279, no. 21 *ex* MS 1; Förster 1933, 51, no. 21 *ex* MS 1; Rose-Troup 1937, 434–5, no. 21 *ex* MS 1; Ker 1957, 30, no. 20.13 *ex* MS 1; Cameron 1973, 193, no. B16.10.6; Healey & Venezky 1980, 168, no. B16.10.6.2.

108

s. xi/xii. Record that Regenhere (*Regenere*) bought Ælfgyth (*Alfiðe*) from Regenweald (*at Regenolde*) the monk of Cowick Barton (*at Cuicu*), (Devon), for five shillings (to be) free and without obligation to the estate at Cowick (*freoh 7 sacles [u]ppan Cuiclan[d]e*), to be at liberty (*to beonde on fridome*), witnessed by (all names in the genitive case) Eadmær (*Edmæres*) the priest; Eadwine (*Edwines*) the reeve; Robert (*Rodberdes*); Æthelric of Stallenge Thorne (*Agelrices at Stanlince*), (Devon); and all the hundred at Cowick (*on Cuicu*). Ælfric Neck (*Alfric Hals*) took the toll. (Readings from MS 1.)
MSS: 1.   Exeter, Cathedral, 3501, 6r (Chambers 1933, 6a) (s. xi/xii)
       2.   London, BL, Add. 9067, 12r (A.D. 1831; transcript of MS 1)
Printed: Thorpe 1865, 637 *ex* MS 2; Earle 1888, 262 *ex* MS 1.
Translated: Thorpe 1865, 637.
References: Wanley 1705, 280, no. 22 *ex* MS 1; Förster 1933, 51, no. 22 *ex* MS 1; Rose-Troup 1937, 435, no. 22 *ex* MS 1; Anderson 1939, 74; Ker 1957, 30, no. 20.13 *ex* MS 1; Cameron 1973, 193, no. B16.10.6; Healey & Venezky 1980, 168, no. B16.10.6.2.

109

s. xi/xii. Record that Sæwine ?'Finch' or possibly '(son of) Pinca' (cf. 98) (*Sewine Pinca*) bought himself for ten shillings from William (*Willelme*), witnessed by (all names in the genitive case) Eadmær (*Edmæres*) the priest; Eadwine (*Edwines*); Tailifer (cf. Dunning Tailifer 107); Robert (*Rodb'es*); and all the hundred at Cowick Barton (*on Cuicu*), (Devon). Ælfric Neck (*Alfric Hals*) took the toll. (All readings from MS 1.)
MSS: 1.   Exeter, Cathedral, 3501, 6r (Chambers 1933, 6a) (s. xi/xii)
       2.   London, BL, Add. 9067, 12r (A.D. 1831; transcript of MS 1)
Printed: Hickes 1703, V, 15 *ex* MS 1; Thorpe 1865, 632 *ex* MS 2; Earle 1888, 262–3 *ex* MS 1.
Translated: Thorpe 1865, 632.
References: Wanley 1705, 280, no. 23 *ex* MS 1; Förster 1933, 51, no. 23 *ex* MS 1; Rose-Troup 1937, 435, no. 23 *ex* MS 1; Anderson 1939, 74; Cam 1944, 108; Ker 1957, 30, no. 20.13 *ex* MS 1; Cameron 1973, 193, no. B16.10.6; Healey & Venezky 1980, 168, no. B16.10.6.2.

110

A.D. 1072 x 1103. Record that when Osbern (fitz Osbern), bishop (of Exeter), consecrated St Mary's Porch (*portic*), Fulcard (*Folcard*) freed Æthelwine (*Agelwine*), his man, and his offspring, there to the glory of Christ and St Mary and for the redemption of his soul; he may choose a lord wherever he wishes to look (*let him ceosa hlaford, loc hwær hig wolde*). (All readings from MS 1.)
MSS: 1.   Exeter, Cathedral, 3501, 6r (Chambers 1933, 6a) (s. xi/xii)
        2.   London, BL, Add. 9067, 12r (A.D. 1831; transcript of MS 1)
Printed: Thorpe 1865, 634 *ex* MS 2; Earle 1888, 263 *ex* MS 1.
Translated: Thorpe 1865, 634.
References: Wanley 1705, 280, no. 24 *ex* MS 1; Förster 1933, 51, no. 24 *ex* MS 1; Rose-Troup 1937, 435–6, no. 24 *ex* MS 1; Ker 1957, 30, no. 20.13 *ex* MS 1; Cameron 1973, 193, no. B16.10.6; Healey & Venezky 1980, 168, no. B16.10.6.2.

111

A.D. 1048 x 4 February 1093. Record that Leofgar the baker at Exeter (*Liueger se bacestere on Excestre*) released a woman called Edith, daughter of Godric Cock's Throat (*Ediþ hatte Godrices doht' cocraca*), and all her offspring from Bishop's Clyst (*ut of Clistlande*), (Devon), from Geoffrey (*æt Gosfreige*), bishop (of Coutances), for thirty pence to be forever free and without obligation (*æfre ma freoh 7 saccles*); 'and Bishop Geoffrey was lord over the estate at Clyst in those days' (*7 Gesfreig bisceop wæs hlaferd ofer Clistland on þam dagum*). Witnessed by Kolsveinn (*Colswein*); Roger of Bovey Tracy (*Roger on Buui*), (Devon); Herebert of Clyst (*Hereberd on Clist*); and Eadric the merchant (*Edric se cipa*). (All readings from MS 1.)
MSS: 1.   Exeter, Cathedral, 3501, 6r (Chambers 1933, 6a) (s. xi/xii)
        2.   London, BL, Add. 9067, 12r (A.D. 1831; transcript of MS 1)
Printed: Thorpe 1865, 637–8 *ex* MS 2; Earle 1888, 263 *ex* MS 1.
Translated: Thorpe 1865, 637–8.
References: Wanley 1705, 280, no. 25 *ex* MS 1; Förster 1933, 52, no. 25 *ex* MS 1; Rose-Troup 1937, 436, no. 25 *ex* MS 1; Le Patourel 1944, 152 (on Geoffrey's landholdings); Ker 1957, 30, no. 20.13 *ex* MS 1; Cameron 1973, 193, no. B16.10.6; Healey & Venezky 1980, 168, no. B16.10.6.2; Insley 1982, 85 (on Kolsveinn).

112

s. xi/xii. Record that Huscarl released himself from Ealubeorht (*Eal[u]wb[r]***) (cf. Ialebriht **102**) for forty pence witnessed by (all names in the genitive case) Godwine the priest; Alweard (*Alwordis*) the portreeve; Ealdræd (*Ealdrides*), his son; Osbern (*Osb'*); Walter, his brother; Sæmær (*Sæmæris*); and Godwine the priest. Sveinn (*Swegn*) and Wulfgeat (*Wulfet*) took the toll on the king's behalf and for Særle, who was the portreeve. (All readings from MS 1.)
MSS: 1.   Exeter, Cathedral, 3501, 6v (Chambers 1933, 6b) (s. xi/xii)
        2.   London, BL, Add. 9067, 13v (A.D. 1831; transcript of MS 1)
Printed: Thorpe 1865, 635–6 *ex* MS 2; Earle 1888, 263 *ex* MS 1.
Translated: Thorpe 1865, 635–6.
References: Wanley 1705, 280, no. 26 *ex* MS 1; Förster 1933, 52, no. 26 *ex* MS 1; Rose-Troup 1937, 436–7, no. 26 *ex* MS 1; Ker 1957, 30, no. 20.13 *ex* MS 1;

Cameron 1973, 193, no. B16.10.6; Healey & Venezky 1980, 168, no. B16.10.6.2;
Insley 1982, 84 (on Huscarl) and 86–7 (on Sveinn).

113

s. xi/xii. Record that Leofwine, Feala's son (*Leowine Feala sunu*), bought himself
and his offspring from Wulfweard, Ælfric's (*æt Wulfworde Alfrices sunu*) son at St
James' Church (*æt Iacobes Cyrca*), (Wonford Hundred, Devon), for half a pound
to choose a lord for himself and his offspring wherever he wished (*to ceosende him
hlaford 7 his ofspring, swa hwær swa hig woldon*), witnessed by (all names in the
genitive case) the priests William, Godwig (*Godwies*), Arnold and Eadwine
(*Edwines*); Bartholomew, Flothar's son (*Barth[o]lomeus Floheres suna*); Algar
Tramp (*Pagardes*); Conan (*Cona*); Algar, Leofflæd's (*Leoflæde*) son; Haim;
Ottarr, Dierling's son (*Oter Dirlinges sunu*); Eadwacer (*Edwacer*); Alweard, Ælfstan's son (*A[g]elword, *[l]lfstanes sunu*); Osbern, Alweard's son (*Osber[n] Alwor-
des sunu*); Ælfstan of Wonford (*Alfsta on Wunforda*), (Devon); Eadwig Nobol
(*Edwi Nobol**); King (*Cing*); Æthelweard (*Agelword*) Pudding the deacon; and all
the hundred at Exeter (*on Excestre*). Alweard (*Alword*) the portreeve and Alwine
(*Alwine*), Dierling's son-in-law (or brother-in-law) (*Dirlinges aþum*), took the toll
on the king's behalf. (All readings from MS 1.)
MSS: 1.   Exeter, Cathedral, 3501, 6v (Chambers 1933, 6b) (s. xi/xii)
          2.   London, BL, Add. 9067, 13r (A.D. 1831; transcript of MS 1)
Printed: Thorpe 1865, 636 *ex* MS 2; Earle 1888, 264 *ex* MS 1.
Translated: Thorpe 1865, 636.
References: Wanley 1705, 280, no. 27 *ex* MS 1; Rose-Troup & Watkin 1930–1,
370; Förster 1933, 52, no. 27 *ex* MS 1; Rose-Troup 1937, 437, no. 27 *ex* MS 1;
Ker 1957, 30, no. 20.13 *ex* MS 1; Cameron 1973, 193, no. B16.10.6; Healey &
Venezky 1980, 168, no. B16.10.6.2.

114

s. xi/xii. Record that Edith (*Ediþ*), daughter of Leofric Lock (genitive: *Locces*),
bought herself and her offspring from Hubert (*H[uberd]*) for twenty-four pence,
witnessed by (all names in the genitive case) William the steward; Æthelweard
Pudding (*Agilwerdes Pudinges*); Eadmær (*Edmeres*) the priest; Eadwig (*Edwies*),
Hreawa's son; Huscarl; Algar Wreocg (*Algeres [W]r[eo]cge[s]*); Godwine the
priest; and Leofwine the Londoner (*Leowines Lundeniscea*). (All readings from
MS 1.)
MSS: 1.   Exeter, Cathedral, 3501, 6v (Chambers 1933, 6b) (s. xi/xii)
          2.   London, BL, Add. 9067, 13r (A.D. 1831; transcript of MS 1)
Printed: Thorpe 1865, 636–7 *ex* MS 2; Earle 1888, 264 *ex* MS 1.
Translated: Thorpe 1865, 636–7.
References: Wanley 1705, 280, no. 28 *ex* MS 1; Förster 1933, 52, no. 28 *ex* MS
1; Rose-Troup 1937, 437, no 28 *ex* MS 1; Ker 1957, 30, no. 20.13 *ex* MS 1;
Cameron 1973, 193, B16.10.6; Healey & Venezky 1980, 168, no. B16.10.6.2;
Insley 1982, 84 (on Huscarl).

115

s. xii. List of witnesses of land bought by Ælfric Paz from Freawine's widow (*at
Frewines laue*) on Paul's Street (*on Paules Stret*), (?Exeter). (All readings from
MS 1.)

MSS: 1.   Exeter, Cathedral, 3501, 6v (Chambers 1933, 6b) (s. xii^1)
         2.   London, BL, Add. 9067, 13r (A.D. 1831; transcript of MS 1)
Unprinted.
References: Wanley 1705, 280, no. 29 *ex* MS 1; Förster 1933, 52, no. 29 *ex* MS
1; Rose-Troup 1937, 438, no. 29 *ex* MS 1; Ker 1957, 30, no. 20.14 *ex* MS 1;
Cameron 1973, 194, no. B16.10.10; Healey & Venezky 1980, 168,
no. B16.10.10.

116

s. xii. Lists of witnesses of Eadgifu, (daughter of) Ealdgyth (*Ieduue Ialdit*), wife of
Reinfrei (*Reinfreis wif*), and of Iale Ire. (All readings from MS 1.)
MSS: 1.   Exeter, Cathedral, 3501, 6v (Chambers 1933, 6b) (s. xii^1)
         2.   London, BL, Add. 9067, 13r (A.D. 1831; transcript of MS 1)
Unprinted.
References: Förster 1933, 52–3, no. 30 *ex* MS 1; Rose-Troup 1937, 438–9,
no. 30 *ex* MS 1; Ker 1957, 30, no. 20.14 *ex* MS 1; Cameron 1973, 194,
no. B16.10.10; Healey & Venezky 1980, 168, no. B16.10.10.

117

s. xii. List of witnesses of land bought by Ælfric (*Alfric*) from Æthelweard
(*Ailword*). (Both readings from MS 1.)
MSS: 1.   Exeter, Cathedral, 3501, 6v (Chambers 1933, 6b) (s. xii^1)
         2.   London, BL, Add. 9067, 13r (A.D. 1831; transcript of MS 1)
Unprinted.
References: Wanley 1705, 280, no. 30 *ex* MS 1; Förster 1933, 53, no. 31 *ex* MS
1; Rose-Troup 1937, 439, no. 31 *ex* MS 1; Ker 1957, 30, no. 20.14 *ex* MS 1;
Cameron 1973, 194, no. B16.10.10; Healey & Venezky 1980, 168,
no. B16.10.10.

118

s. xii. List of witnesses of land bought outside the East Gate (*but* Gestete*),
(presumably at Exeter), by Ælfric (*Alfric*) from Richard (*at Ricerde*). (All read-
ings from MS 1.)
MSS: 1.   Exeter, Cathedral, 3501, 6v (Chambers 1933, 6b) (s. xii^1)
         2.   London, BL, Add. 9067, 13r (A.D. 1831; transcript of MS 1)
Unprinted.
References: Förster 1933, 53, no. 32 *ex* MS 1; Rose-Troup 1937, 439, no. 32 *ex*
MS 1; Ker 1957, 30, no. 20.14 *ex* MS 1; Cameron 1973, 194, no. B16.10.10;
Healey & Venezky 1980, 168, no. B16.10.10.

119

s. xii. List of witnesses of land on Martin's Street (*a Martines Stræt*), (presumably
at Exeter), bought by Ælfric (*Alfric*) from Ragnhildr (*at Ragenilde*). (All readings
from MS 1.)
MSS: 1.   Exeter, Cathedral, 3501, 6v (Chambers 1933, 6b) (s. xii^1)
         2.   London, BL, Add. 9067, 13r (A.D. 1831; transcript of MS 1)
Unprinted.
References: Förster 1933, 53, no. 33 *ex* MS 1; Rose-Troup 1937, 439–40, no. 33
ex MS 1; Ker 1957, 30, no. 20.14 *ex* MS 1; Cameron 1973, 194, no. B16.10.10;
Healey & Venezky 1980, 168, no. B16.10.10; Insley 1982, 86 (on Ragnhildr).

120

A.D. 1072 x 1103. Record of the membership and obligations of a guild at Woodbury (*on Wudebiriglande*), (Devon), adopted in fellowship by Osbern (*Osb'n*), bishop (of Exeter), and the canons of St Peter's Minster, Exeter (*innan Sc's Petrus Minstre on Excestre*). (All readings from MS 1.)

MSS: 1.   Exeter, Cathedral, 3501, 7r (Chambers 1933, 7a) (s. xi/xii)
      2.   London, BL, Add. 9067, 14r (A.D. 1831; transcript of MS 1)
Printed: Hickes 1703, V, 18 *ex* MS 1; Thorpe 1865, 608–609 *ex* Hickes; Earle 1888, 264–5 *ex* MS 1.
Translated: Hickes 1703, V, 18–19 (translation into Latin); Thorpe 1865, 608–609.
References: Wanley 1705, 280, no. 31 *ex* MS 1; Westlake 1919, 4–6; Förster 1933, 53, no, 34(a) *ex* MS 1; Rose-Troup 1937, 440, no. 34 *ex* MS 1; Ker 1957, 29, no. 20.4 *ex* MS 1; Barlow 1963 (= 1979), 196–8; Cameron 1973, 192, no. B16.10.2; Campbell 1979, 133–4 (= 1986, 152); Healey & Venezky 1980, 167, no. B16.10.2 = 170, no. B16.30.

121

A.D. ?1072 x 1103. Record of the membership and obligations of a second guild at Woodbury (*on Wudebiriglande*), (Devon). (Place-name from MS 1.)

MSS: 1.   Exeter, Cathedral, 3501, 7r (Chambers 1933, 7a) (s. xi/xii)
      2.   London, BL, Add. 9067, 14r (A.D. 1831; transcript of MS 1)
Printed: Hickes 1703, V, 19 *ex* MS 1; Thorpe 1865, 609 *ex* Hickes (incomplete); Earle 1888, 265 *ex* MS 1 (incomplete).
Translated: Thorpe 1865, 609.
References: Wanley 1705, 280, no. 32 *ex* MS 1; Westlake 1919, 5–6; Förster 1933, 53, no. 34(b) *ex* MS 1; Rose-Troup 1937, 440, no. 34 *ex* MS 1; Ker 1957, 29, no. 20.4 *ex* MS 1; Barlow 1963 (= 1979), 196–8; Cameron 1973, 192, no. B16.10.2; Campbell 1979, 133–4 (= 1986, 152); Healey & Venezky 1980, 167, no. B16.10.2.

122

A.D. ?1072 x 1103. Record of the membership of a guild at Colaton Raleigh (genitive: *Colatunes*), (Devon). (Place-name from MS 1.)

MSS: 1.   Exeter, Cathedral, 3501, 7r (Chambers 1933, 7a) (s. xi/xii)
      2.   London, BL, Add. 9067, 14r (A.D. 1831; transcript of MS 1)
Printed: Hickes 1703, V, 19 *ex* MS 1 (incorrectly recorded after no. **124** below); Thorpe 1865, 609 *ex* Hickes (incomplete); Earle 1888, 265 *ex* MS 1 (incomplete).
Translated: Thorpe 1865, 609.
References: Wanley 1705, 280, no. 33 *ex* MS 1; Westlake 1919, 5; Förster 1933, 53, no. 34(c) *ex* MS 1; Rose-Troup 1937, 440, no. 34 *ex* MS 1; Ker 1957, 29, no. 20.4 *ex* MS 1; Barlow 1963 (= 1979), 196–8; Cameron 1973, 192, no. B16.10.2; Campbell 1979, 133–4 (= 1986, 152); Healey & Venezky 1980, 167, no. B16.10.2.

123

s. xi/xii. Record that Eadmær (*Gedmer*), Spernægl's son, released Leofhild, his kinswoman (*Leofilde his magu*), from the estate at Topsham, (Devon) (*ut of*

Toppeshamlande), for twenty-four pence from Ceolric, Hearding's (*Heordinges*) reeve, Eadnoth's (*Eadnoðes*) son, witnessed by Alwine (*Ælwine*) the priest; Æthelweard (*Ailword*) Pudding; Hearding (*Heording*) and his brothers; Wulfweard of St James' Church (*Wulword at Iacobes circan*), (Wonford Hundred, Devon); Hugh the Red (*Huga se Ræda*); and all the hundred at Topsham (*at Toppeshamme*). (All readings from MS 1.)

MSS: 1.   Exeter, Cathedral, 3501, 7r (Chambers 1933, 7a) (s. xii[1])
      2.   London, BL, Add. 9067, 14r (A.D. 1831; transcript of MS 1)
Printed: Thorpe 1865, 634 *ex* MS 1.
Translated: Thorpe 1865, 634.
References: Wanley 1705, 280, no. 33 *ex* MS 1; Förster 1933, 54, no. 35 *ex* MS 1; Rose-Troup 1937, 440–1, no. 35 *ex* MS 1; Anderson 1939, 75; Cam 1944, 108; Ker 1957, 29, no. 20.5 *ex* MS 1; Cameron 1973, 193, no. B16.10.6; Healey & Venezky 1980, 168, no. B16.10.6.1.

124

A.D. ?1072 x 1103. Record of the membership of a guild at Broad Clyst (genitive: *Clisttunes*), (Devon). (Place-name from MS 1.)
MSS: 1.   Exeter, Cathedral, 3501, 7r (Chambers 1933, 7a) (s. xi/xii)
      2.   London, BL, Add. 9067, 14r (A.D. 1831; transcript of MS 1)
Printed: Hickes 1703, V, 19 (incorrectly recorded before no. **122** above); Thorpe 1865, 609 *ex* Hickes (incomplete); Earle 1888, 265 *ex* MS 1 (incomplete).
Translated: Thorpe 1865, 609.
References: Wanley 1705, 280, no. 34 *ex* MS 1; Westlake 1919, 5; Förster 1933, 53, no. 34(d) *ex* MS 1; Rose-Troup 1937, 440, no. 34 *ex* MS 1; Ker 1957, 29, no. 20.4 *ex* MS 1; Barlow 1963 (= 1979), 196–8; Cameron 1973, 192, no. B16.10.2; Campbell 1979, 133–4 (= 1986, 152); Healey & Venezky 1980, 167, no. B16.10.2.

125

A.D. ?1072 x 1103. Record of the membership of Alwine's (*Alwines*) guild at Woodbury (*on Wudebirig*), (Devon). (Both readings from MS 1.)
MSS: 1.   Exeter, Cathedral, 3501, 7r (Chambers 1933, 7a) (s. xi/xii)
      2.   London, BL, Add. 9067, 14r (A.D. 1831; transcript of MS 1)
Printed: Hickes 1703, V, 19 *ex* MS 1; Thorpe 1865, 610 *ex* Hickes (incomplete); Earle 1888, 265 *ex* MS 1 (incomplete).
Translated: Thorpe 1865, 610.
References: Wanley 1705, 280, no. 34 *ex* MS 1; Westlake 1919, 5; Förster 1933, 53, no. 34(e) *ex* MS 1; Rose-Troup 1937, 440, no. 34 *ex* MS 1; Ker 1957, 29, no. 20.4 *ex* MS 1; Barlow 1963 (= 1979), 196–8; Cameron 1973, 192, no. B16.10.2; Campbell 1979, 133–4 (= 1986, 152); Healey & Venezky 1980, 167, no. B16.10.2.

126

A.D. ?1072 x 1103. Record of the membership of a guild at Bridford (genitive: *Bridafordes*), (Devon). (Place-name from MS 1.)
MSS: 1.   Exeter, Cathedral, 3501, 7v (Chambers 1933, 7b) (s. xi/xii)
      2.   London, BL, Add. 9067, 15r (A.D. 1831; transcript of MS 1)

Printed: Hickes 1703, V, 19 *ex* MS 1; Thorpe 1865, 610 *ex* Hickes (incomplete); Earle 1888, 265 *ex* MS 1 (incomplete).
Translated: Thorpe 1865, 610.
References: Wanley 1705, 280, no. 34 *ex* MS 1; Westlake 1919, 5; Förster 1933, 54, no. 34(g) *ex* MS 1; Rose-Troup 1937, 440, no. 34 *ex* MS 1; Ker 1957, 29, no. 20.4 *ex* MS 1; Barlow 1963 (= 1979), 196–8; Cameron 1973, 192, no. B16.10.2; Campbell 1979, 133–4 (= 1986, 152); Healey & Venezky 1980, 167, no. B16.10.2.

127

A.D. ?1072 x 1103. Record of the membership of a guild at Clyst St George (*of Clistwike*), (Devon). (Place-name from MS 1.)
MSS: 1.   Exeter, Cathedral, 3501, 7v (Chambers 1933, 7b) (s. xi/xii)
        2.   London, BL, Add. 9067, 15r (A.D. 1831; transcript of MS 1)
Printed: Hickes 1703, V, 19 *ex* MS 1; Thorpe 1865, 610 *ex* Hickes (incomplete); Earle 1888, 265 *ex* MS 1 (incomplete).
Translated: Thorpe 1865, 610.
References: Wanley 1705, 280, no. 34 *ex* MS 1; Westlake 1919, 5; Förster 1933, 54, no. 34(h) *ex* MS 1; Rose-Troup 1937, 440, no. 34 *ex* MS 1; Ker 1957, 29, no. 20.4 *ex* MS 1; Barlow 1963 (= 1979), 196–8; Cameron 1973, 192, no. B16.10.2; Campbell 1979, 133–4 (= 1986, 152); Healey & Venezky 1980, 167, no. B16.10.2.

128

A.D. ?1072 x 1103. Record of the membership of a guild at Leigh (*on Lege*), (Devon). (Place-name from MS 1.)
MSS: 1.   Exeter, Cathedral, 3501, 7v (Chambers 1933, 7b) (s. xi/xii)
        2.   London, BL, Add. 9067, 15r (A.D. 1831; transcript of MS 1)
Printed: Hickes 1703, V, 19 *ex* MS 1; Thorpe 1865, 610 *ex* Hickes (incomplete); Earle 1888, 265 *ex* MS 1 (incomplete).
Translated: Thorpe 1865, 610.
References: Wanley 1705, 280, no. 34 *ex* MS 1; Westlake 1919, 5; Förster 1933, 54, no. 34(i) *ex* MS 1; Rose-Troup 1937, 440, no. 34 *ex* MS 1; Ker 1957, 29, no. 20.4 *ex* MS 1; Barlow 1963 (= 1979), 196–8; Cameron 1973, 192, no. B16.10.2; Campbell 1979, 133–4 (= 1986, 152); Healey & Venezky 1980, 167, no. B16.10.2.

129

A.D. ?1072 x 1103. Record (presumably of the membership of a guild at) Nutwell Court (*of Hnutwille*), (Devon). (Place-name from MS 1.)
MSS: 1.   Exeter, Cathedral, 3501, 7v (Chambers 1933, 7b) (s. xi/xii)
        2.   London, BL, Add. 9067, 15r (A.D. 1831; transcript of MS 1)
Printed: Hickes 1703, V, 19 *ex* MS 1; Thorpe 1865, 610 *ex* Hickes (incomplete); Earle 1888, 265 *ex* MS 1 (incomplete).
Translated: Thorpe 1865, 610.
References: Wanley 1705, 280, no. 34 *ex* MS 1; Westlake 1919, 5; Förster 1933, 54, no. 34(k) *ex* MS 1; Rose-Troup 1937, 440, no. 34 *ex* MS 1; Ker 1957, 29, no. 20.4 *ex* MS 1; Barlow 1963 (= 1979), 196–8; Cameron 1973, 192,

no. B16.10.2; Campbell 1979, 133–4 (= 1986, 152); Healey & Venezky 1980, 167, no. B16.10.2.

130
A.D. ?1072 x 1103. Record (presumably of the membership of a guild at) Colaton Raleigh (*of Colatune*), (Devon). (Place-name from MS 1.)
MSS: 1.   Exeter, Cathedral, 3501, 7v (Chambers 1933, 7b) (s. xi/xii)
          2.   London, BL, Add. 9067, 15r (A.D. 1831; transcript of MS 1)
Printed: Hickes 1703, V, 19 *ex* MS 1; Thorpe 1865, 610 *ex* Hickes (incomplete); Earle 1888, 265 *ex* MS 1 (incomplete).
Translated: Thorpe 1865, 610.
References: Wanley 1705, 280, no. 34 *ex* MS 1; Westlake 1919, 5; Förster 1933, 54, no. 34(l) *ex* MS 1; Rose-Troup 1937, 440, no. 34 *ex* MS 1; Ker 1957, 29, no. 20.4 *ex* MS 1; Barlow 1963 (= 1979), 196–8; Cameron 1973, 192, no. B16.10.2; Campbell 1979, 133–4 (= 1986, 152); Healey & Venezky 1980, 167, no. B16.10.2.

131
A.D. ?1072 x 1103. Record (presumably of the membership of a guild at) Sidmouth (*of Sidemuða*), (Devon). (Place-name from MS 1.)
MSS: 1.   Exeter, Cathedral, 3501, 7v (Chambers 1933, 7b) (s. xi/xii)
          2.   London, BL, Add. 9067, 15r (A.D. 1831; transcript of MS 1)
Printed: Hickes 1703, V, 19 *ex* MS 1; Thorpe 1865, 610 *ex* Hickes (incomplete); Earle 1888, 265 *ex* MS 1 (incomplete).
Translated: Thorpe 1865, 610.
References: Wanley 1705, 280, no. 34 *ex* MS 1; Westlake 1919, 5; Förster 1933, 54, no. 34(m) *ex* MS 1; Rose-Troup 1937, 440, no. 34 *ex* MS 1; Ker 1957, 29, no. 20.4 *ex* MS 1; Barlow 1963 (= 1979), 196–8; Cameron 1973, 192, no. B16.10.2; Campbell 1979, 133–4 (= 1986, 152); Healey & Venezky 1980, 167, no. B16.10.2.

132
A.D. ?1072 x 1103. Record (presumably of the membership of a guild at) Halsfordwood (*of Halsforda*), (Devon). (Place-name from MS 1.)
MSS: 1.   Exeter, Cathedral, 3501, 7v (Chambers 1933, 7b) (s. xi/xii)
          2.   London, BL, Add. 9067, 15r (A.D. 1831; transcript of MS 1)
Printed: Hickes 1703, V, 19 *ex* MS 1; Thorpe 1865, 610 *ex* Hickes (incomplete); Earle 1888, 265 *ex* MS 1 (incomplete).
Translated: Thorpe 1865, 610.
References: Wanley 1705, 280, no. 34 *ex* MS 1; Westlake 1919, 5; Förster 1933, 54, no. 34(n) *ex* MS 1; Rose-Troup 1937, 440, no. 34 *ex* MS 1; Ker 1957, 29, no. 20.4 *ex* MS 1; Barlow 1963 (= 1979), 196–8; Cameron 1973, 192, no. B16.10.2; Campbell 1979, 133–4 (= 1986, 152); Healey & Venezky 1980, 167, no. B16.10.2.

133
A.D. ?1072 x 1103. Record (presumably of the membership of a guild at) Whitestone (*of Hwitastane*), (Devon). (Place-name from MS 1.)
MSS: 1.   Exeter, Cathedral 3501, 7v (Chambers 1933, 7b) (s. xi/xii)
          2.   London, BL, Add. 9067, 15r (A.D. 1831; transcript of MS 1)

Printed: Hickes 1703, V, 19 *ex* MS 1; Thorpe 1865, 610 *ex* Hickes (incomplete); Earle 1888, 266 *ex* MS 1 (incomplete).
Translated: Thorpe 1865, 610.
References: Wanley 1705, 280, no. 34 *ex* MS 1; Westlake 1919, 5; Förster 1933, 54, no. 34(o) *ex* MS 1; Rose-Troup 1937, 440, no. 34 *ex* MS 1; Ker 1957, 29, no. 20.4 *ex* MS 1; Barlow 1963 (= 1979), 196–8; Cameron 1973, 192, no. B16.10.2; Campbell 1979, 133–4 (= 1986, 152); Healey & Venezky 1980, 167, no. B16.10.2.

134

A.D. ?1072 x 1103. Record (presumably of the membership of a guild at) Axmouth (*of Axamuða*), (Devon). (Place-name from MS 1.)
MSS: 1.   Exeter, Cathedral, 3501, 7v (Chambers 1933, 7b) (s. xi/xii)
          2.   London, BL, Add. 9067, 15r (A.D. 1831; transcript of MS 1)
Printed: Hickes 1703, V, 19 *ex* MS 1; Thorpe 1865, 610 *ex* Hickes (incomplete); Earle 1888, 266 *ex* MS 1 (incomplete).
Translated: Thorpe 1865, 610.
References: Wanley 1705, 280, no. 34 *ex* MS 1; Westlake 1919, 5; Förster 1933, 54, no. 34(p) *ex* MS 1; Rose-Troup 1937, 440, no. 34 *ex* MS 1; Ker 1957, 29, no. 20.4 *ex* MS 1; Barlow 1963 (= 1979), 196–8; Cameron 1973, 192, no. B16.10.2; Campbell 1979, 133–4 (= 1986, 152); Healey & Venezky 1980, 167, no. B16.10.2.

135

xi/xii. Record of the freeing at Exeter (*on Execstre*) by Alwynn Hook (*Halwun Hoce*) of her woman, Æthelflæd (accusative: *Hægelflæde*), whom she had bought and paid toll for.
MS: Oxford, Bodleian, Bodl. 579 (2675), 1r (Rose-Troup 1937, pl. 57 [reduced; incorrect foliation]) (xi/xii)
Printed: Hickes 1703, V, 12; Thorpe 1865, 638; Haddan & Stubbs 1869, I, 688, no. 1; Warren 1883, 1; Earle 1888, 253, no. 5.
Translated: Hickes 1703, V, 12 (translation into Latin); Thorpe 1865, 638; Haddan & Stubbs 1869, I, 688, no. 1 *ex* Thorpe 1865; Boggis 1922, 49–50 *ex* Haddan & Stubbs.
References: Turner 1852, III, 82; Rose-Troup 1937, 441–2, no. L.M. 1; Ker 1957, 378, no. 315c; Cameron 1973, 193, no. B16.10.6; Drage 1978, 73 and 119; Healey & Venezky 1980, 168, no. B16.10.6.4; Davies 1982, 260 n. 7.

136

s. xi ex. Record of the freeing by Æthelgifu Good (*Æilgyuu Gode*) of Hig and Dunna and their offspring from Manegot (*Mangode*) for thirteen mancuses; Einulf (*Æignulf*) the portreeve and Godric Buttock (*Gupa*) took the toll, witnessed by (all names in the genitive case) Manleof (*Manlefes*); Leofweard Lame (*Leowerdes Healtes*); Leofwine (*Leowines*), his brother; Ælfric, son of Happ (*Maphappes*); and Sveinn the shieldmaker (*Sweignis scyldwirhta*).
MS: Oxford, Bodleian, Bodl. 579 (2675), 1r (Rose-Troup 1937, pl. 57 [reduced; incorrect foliation]) (s. xi ex.)
Printed: Hickes 1703, V, 12–13; Thorpe 1865, 638; Haddan & Stubbs 1869, I, 688–9, no. 2; Warren 1883, 1; Earle 1888, 253, no. 4.

Translated: Hickes 1703, V, 13 (translation into Latin); Thorpe 1865, 638; Haddan & Stubbs 1869, I, 688–9, no. 2 *ex* Thorpe.
References: Turner 1852, III, 83; Rose-Troup 1937, 442 no. L.M. 2; Tengvik 1938, 378 (on *Maphappes*); Ker 1957, 378, 315c; Cameron 1973, 193, no. B16.10.6; Drage 1978, 73 and 119; Healey & Venezky 1980, 168, no. B16.10.6.4; Davies 1982, 260 n. 7; Insley 1982, 86–7 (on Sveinn).

137

s. xi ex. Record of the purchase (?of release) by Godwine Black (*Blaca*) of himself, his wife and his offspring from William Booted (*æt Wyllelme Hosethe*) for fifteen shillings, witnessed by (all names in the genitive case) Eadmær (*Edmæres*) the priest; Alwig (*Ælwies*); Dunning; Sæmær; Almær (*Ælmæres*); and the hundred at Cowick Barton (*on Cuiclande*), (Devon). Ælfric Neck (*Hasl* [sic]) took the toll on the king's behalf (*for þæs kynges hand*).
MS: Oxford, Bodleian, Bodl. 579 (2675), 1v (Rose-Troup 1937, pl. 58 [reduced; incorrect foliation]) (s. xi ex.)
Printed: Hickes 1703, V, 13; Thorpe 1865, 639; Haddan & Stubbs 1869, I, 689, no. 3; Warren 1883, 1; Earle 1888, 253, no. 1.
Translated: Hickes 1703, V, 13 (translation into Latin); Thorpe 1865, 639; Haddan & Stubbs 1869, I, 689, no. 3 *ex* Thorpe; Boggis 1922, 50 *ex* Haddan & Stubbs.
References: Turner 1852, III, 83; Rose-Troup 1937, 442, no. L.M. 3; Ker 1957, 378, 315c; Cameron 1973, 193, no. B16.10.6; Drage 1978, 73 and 119; Healey & Venezky 1980, 168, no. B16.10.6.4; Davies 1982, 260 n. 7.

138

c. A.D. 1045. Record of the release by Eadwig, Beornheah's son (*Edwy Beorneges sunu*), of himself, his wife and his child(ren) from Hunwine, Heca's son (*æt Hunewine Hega suna*), from the estate at Topsham (*ut of Toppeshammlande*), (Devon), in the time of King Edward the Confessor (*on Edwerdes dæge cynges*), witnessed by (all names in the genitive case) Cynestan (*Kynstanes*) the priest; Leofsunu at Wonford (*Leofsuna a Wunforda*), (Devon); Ælfric White (*Hwita*); Vikingr Boatswain (*Wycinges batswegenes*); Sæwine, Lufa's son; Leofsige (*Leofsies*); and Ælfsige (*Ælfsies*).
MS: Oxford, Bodleian, Bodl. 579 (2675), 1v (Rose-Troup 1937, pl. 58 [reduced; incorrect foliation]) (s. xi ex.)
Printed: Hickes 1703, V, 13; Thorpe 1865, 638–9; Haddan & Stubbs 1869, I, 689, no. 4; Warren 1883, 1; Earle 1888, 254, no. 3.
Translated: Hickes 1703, V, 13 (translation into Latin); Thorpe 1865, 638–9; Haddan & Stubbs 1869, I, 689, no. 4 *ex* Thorpe.
References: Rose-Troup 1937, 442–3, no. L.M. 4; Ker 1957, 378, no. 315c; Cameron 1973, 193, no. B16.10.6; Drage 1978, 73 and 119; Healey & Venezky 1980, 168, no. B16.10.6.4; Davies 1982, 260 n. 7.
Note: Though this document refers to an act performed under Edward the Confessor, the wording indicates the record was composed after his reign.

139

s. xi ex. Record of the purchase by Eadgifu, Sæfugul's widow (*Ediuuu Sæuugeles laf*), of Gladu from Colewine for half a pound as purchase price and toll; Alweard

(*Ælword*) the portreeve received the toll, witnessed by Leofwine, Leofweard's
brother (*Leowine Leowordes broðor*); Alwig Black (*Ælwi Blaca*); Alwine the King
(*Ælwine se Cyng*); Landbeorht (*Landbyriht*); Alca; and Sæweard (*Sæwerd*).
MS: Oxford, Bodleian, Bodl. 579 (2675), 1v (Rose-Troup 1937, pl. 58 [re-
        duced; incorrect foliation]) (s. xi ex.)
Printed: Hickes 1703, V, 13; Thorpe 1865, 639; Haddan & Stubbs 1869, I,
689–90, no. 5; Warren 1883, 1; Earle 1888, 254, no. 2.
Translated: Hickes 1703, V, 13 (translation into Latin); Turner 1852, III, 79 *ex*
Hickes; Thorpe 1865, 639; Haddan & Stubbs 1869, I, 689–90, no. 5 *ex* Thorpe.
References: Rose-Troup 1937, 443, no. L.M. 5; Ker 1957, 378, no. 315c;
Cameron 1973, 193, no. B16.10.6; Drage 1978, 73 and 119; Healey & Venezky
1980, 168, no. B16.10.6.4; Davies 1982, 260 n. 7.

140

s. xi ex. Record of the purchase of freedom by Beorhtmær of Holcombe
(*Brihtmær æt Holacumbe*), (Devon), of himself and Ælfgifu, his wife, and their
children and their offspring from Roger (*æt Rocgere*) *Derindig* for two pounds,
witnessed by (all names in the genitive case) Duddemann (*Dudemannes*), the
priest at Exeter (*on Exancestre*); Leofwine, the priest at Whitstone (*on Hwitastane*), (Devon); the portreeves, Ælfgar (*Ælfgæres*) and Ælfweard (*Ælfwærdes*),
who received the toll on the king's behalf; the latter's brother, Leofweard (*Leof-
wærdes*); Eadwine (*Edwines*), Leofede's son; Ottarr, Dierling's son (*Oteres Dyr-
linges suna*); Ælfgar (*Ælfgæres*), Ælfric's son; Blæcmann (*Blakemanes*); Leofric,
Sæwine's son; Dunstan, Sæwine's son; Randolph (*Randolfes*); Albeald (*Alboldes*);
Smeawine of Holcombe (*Smewines on Holacumbe*), (Devon); Æthelweard, Ælf-
sige's son (*Ægilwærdes Ælfsies suna*); Ælfmær, Cyng's son; Ælfsige With the
Beard (*mid þam berde*); Eadwine (*Edwine*), Leofric's son; Eadwine, Eadmær's son
(*Edwine Edmæres suna*); Eadric at Ramridge (*Edric on Hrennahricge*), (Devon);
and all the hundred at Holcombe (*on Holacumbe*), (Devon), and at Exeter (*on
Exancestre*).
MS: Oxford, Bodleian, Bodl. 579 (2675), 377v (Rose-Troup 1937, pl. 59
        [reduced]) (s. xi ex.)
Printed: Hickes 1703, V, 13; Thorpe 1865, 639–40; Haddan & Stubbs 1869, I,
690, no. 6; Warren 1883, 269; Earle 1888, 256–7.
Translated: Hickes 1703, V, 13 (translation into Latin); Thorpe 1865, 639–40;
Haddan & Stubbs 1869, I, 690, no. 6 *ex* Thorpe.
References: Turner 1852, III, 83; Rose-Troup 1937, 443–4, no. L.M. 6; Ander-
son 1939, 74; Cam 1944, 108; Ker 1957, 378, 315d; Cameron 1973, 193,
no. B16.10.6; Drage 1978, 82; Healey & Venezky 1980, 168, no. B16.10.6.4;
Davies 1982, 260 n. 7.

Lambourn

141

?Post A.D. 1066. Record of dues rendered to the church at Lambourn (*into þam
minstre on Lambourne*), (Berks.), including those from lands (all in Berks.) at Up
Lambourn (*on vp hæme toune*), Chipping Lambourn (*on byrihæme tune*), Coppington (*Cobbaudoune*) (either Coppington Down or Coppington Hill), East-

bury, and Bockhampton (*on Bokhamtoune*). This was made known within the
parish (*scire*) and hundred of Lambourn, witnessed by the priests Croc, Hearding
(*Heardyng*), Werman (*Perman* [sic]), Walter (*Wattear*) and Theodric (*Þeodric*);
Walter the deacon (*Wealtear diacon*); Ansfrid (*Anffrig*); Ralph of West Bock-
hampton (*Rauf ou b'*), (Berkshire); Oda; Vikingr of *Trawe* (*Wikyng ou Traue*);
Æthelwine of Membury (*Ægelwine on Minbiry*), (Wilts.); Cafi; Ælfric (*Ealfric*)
Lif; Ælfric (*Ealri*) *km'* and Ælfwine *b'*.
MS: London, Guildhall, 25, 516, 40v (*olim* 36v) (A.D. ?1299)
Printed: Footman 1894, Appendix A, 183–4; Robertson 1939 (= 1956), 240,
App. I, no. 5.
Translated: Birch in Footman 1894, 17–19; Robertson 1939 (= 1956), 241,
App. I, no. 5.
References: Footman 1894, 16–17 and 19–20; Robertson 1939 (= 1956), 490–3
(place-name identifications); Gelling 1973, II, 336 (on *Traue*); Hoad 1975, 323;
Healey & Venezky 1980, 72, no. B15.5.39.

Northamptonshire

142
A.D. 1066 x 1083 (probably 1072 x 1078; Finn 1970: no later than 1075).
Northamptonshire geld roll listing the hidage in the time of King Edward and in
that of William and the geld paid for the following hundreds: King's Sutton (*into
Suttunes hundred*), Chipping Warden (*into Werdunes hundret*), Cleley (*into
Klegele*), (*into*) *Grauesende* (later part of Fawsley), (*into*) *Eadboldesstowe* (later part
of King's Sutton), (*into*) *Egelweardesle* (later part of Fawsley), Foxley (*into Uoxle*)
(later Green's Norton), Towcester (*into Uyceste*, probably a scribal error for *into
Touyceste*), Huxloe (*into Hocheshlawa*), Willybrook (*into Wilebroce*), Upton
Green (*to Uptunegrene*) (double hundred, later Nassaborough), (*into*) *Naueres-
lund* (double hundred, later part of Huxloe), Navisford (*into Næresforda*), Pole-
brook (*into Pocabroc*), Nobottle Grove (*into Neowbotlegraue*) (hundred and a
half), Guilsborough (*into Gildesburh*), Spelhoe (*into Spelhoh*), Witchley West
(*into Hwiccleslea West*) (later part of Wrangdike hundred, Rutland), Witchley
East (*into Hwicceslea East*) (later part of Wrangdike hundred, Rutland), (*into*)
Stotfalde (later part of Rothwell), Stoke (*into Stoce*) (later part of Corby), Higham
(*into Hchham*) (hundred and a half; later Higham Ferrers), Mawsley (*into Males-
læ*) (later part of Orlingbury), Corby (*into Corebi*), Rothwell (*into Roðewelle*),
Hamfordshoe (*into Anduerðeshoh*), Orlingbury (*into Ordlingbære*) and Wymersley
(*into Wimereslea*) (hundred and a half). (All readings from MS 1.)
MSS: 1. London, Society of Antiquaries, 60, 52r–54v (*olim* xlvii–xlix) (s. xii
           med.)
       2. London, Society of Antiquaries, 131, 22v–24r (olim pp. 44–47)
           (s. xviii transcript of MS 1)
Printed: Ellis 1833, I, 184–7; Robertson 1939 (= 1956), 230–6, App I, no. 3.
Translated: Cockayne 1864, 205–207; Robertson 1939 (= 1956), 231–7, App. I,
no. 3; EHD II, 517–20, no. 61.
References: Cockayne 1864, 207–8 (meanings of certain terms used); Round
1895, 147–56 (= 1964, 124–30); Maitland 1897, 457–8 and 468–9 (= 1960, 24–5

and 26–7); Round 1900, 78–86; Baring 1902, 76–83; Round 1902, I, 258–61; Robertson 1939 (= 1956), 481–4 (place-name identifications); Stenton 1943 (= 1947), 636 n. (= 1971, 644 n. 3); Galbraith 1961, 45, 92, 95–6 and 98; Hart 1970, 16–21; Finn 1971, 235 and 239–40; Galbraith 1974, xxxiii and 92–5; Campbell 1975, 41–2 (= 1986, 157–8); Hoad 1975, 323; Campbell 1980, 120 (= 1986, 174); Healey & Venezky 1980, 170, no. B16.26.4; Clarke 1985, 54 and nn. 16–17; Chaplais 1987, 71.

Shaftesbury

143

After A.D. 1086 x 1156; 'the first decade of the reign of Henry I seems likely; the closing decade of the reign of William II is also a possibility' (Williams 1986, 226). List of estates supporting knights owing military service for the Benedictine nunnery of Shaftesbury (*of Shaftesbury*), (Dorset) (consisting of nine full fees and ten fractions). The lands are at Chicklade (*Chiklad*), Dinton (*at Donyntone*), Nippard (*at Nypred*) and Fernhill (*at Fernhulle*) (in Tisbury parish), Hazledon (*at Haseldene*), Easton (*Estone*) (in Donhead St Andrew parish), East Hatch (*at Yscahche*) (in Tisbury parish) (all in Wilts.), Gussage St Andrew (*at Gyssyh*) (in Handley, Dorset), Linley (*at Imlege*) and Bridzor (*at Brudesperde*) (in Tisbury parish, Wilts.), Dudleys (*at Dudele se yne þan home of Bradeforde*) (in Holt, Bradford Hundred, Wilts.), Sedgehill (*by þare Seggþe hylle þe þan home of Tysse-bury*) (in Tisbury parish, Wilts.), Preston (*at Prestone*) (in Iwerne Minster, Dorset), Bedchester (*at Bedeshurste*) (in Fontmell Magna, Dorset), Iwerne (*at Iwerne*) (in Iwerne Minster, Dorset), Hartgrove (*at Haregraue*) (in Orchard, Dorset), Pimperne (*at Pimperne*) (later Hyde Farm in Pimperne, attached to Tarrant Hinton, Dorset), Kingston Abbess (*at Kyngstone*), (Dorset), Atworth (*at Atte-worþe þne þan home of Bradeforde*) (in Bradford-on-Avon, Wilts.), Cheselbourne (*at Cheselburne*) and Shilvinghampton (*at Sylfhamptone*), (Dorset), Handley (*at Henlege*), (Dorset), Oakley (*at Oclege*) (in Dinton, Wilts.), Apshill (*at Apshulle*) (in Tisbury parish, Wilts.), and Felpham (*at Falgham*), (Sussex).

MS: London, BL, Harl. 61, 22 (s. xv in.) (Williams 1986, 234–5)
Printed: Palgrave 1832, II, ccclxxiv n. 26 (= 1919, VII, 716 note a) (partial); *Monasticon* II, 477; Hutchins 1861, III, 22–3; Williams 1986, 233.
Translated: Williams 1986, 236–7.
References: Palgrave 1832, II, ccvii n. 104 (= 1919, VII, 287 note b); Douglas 1932, ci n. 2; Harvey 1970, 19; Williams 1986, 214–32 and Tables I–V.

Taunton

144

A.D. 1066 x 1086. Record of dues rendered to the manor of Taunton (*into Tantvne*), (Somerset), at King Edward's (*Eadwerd cing*) death, including those from lands (all in Somerset) at Nynehead Flory (*æt Nigonhidon*), Oake (*æt Acon*), Tolland (*of Taalande*), the two Cheddons (*of twam Cedenon, of Cedon*) (Upper and Lower Cheddon Fitzpaine), Ford (*of Eaforde*) (in Norton Fitzwarren), Hele (*æt Hele*), Bagborough (*æt Baggabeorgan, of Baggabeorge*), Lydeard St Lawrence (*of Lidigerde*), Hillfarrance (*of Hylle*) and the two Holfords (*æt twam Holaforda*) (Rich's Holford in Lydeard St Lawrence and Treble's Holford in Combe Florey), witnessed by Giso (*Gisa*), bishop (of Wells); Ælfsige (*Ælfsie*), abbot (of Bath); Wulfgeat (*Wulgeat*), abbot (?of Athelney); Ælfnoth (*Ælfnod*), prior of Taunton; Wulfweard White (*Wulfwerd Wita*); Godwine, Eadwig's son (*Eadwies sunu*); Ælfmær (*Ælmer*), the abbot's brother; Æthelric of Halsway (*Ælgelric æt Healswege*), (Somerset); Hearding, Eadnoth's son (*Heardinc Eadnoðes sunu*); Garmund; Ælfric ?'Trace' or 'Tile' (*tigel*); Ordgar the White (*se wite*); Ælfweard, Leofsunu's son; Beorhtric the Bald (*Brichtric se calewa*); Dodda of Curry Rivel (*æt Cyri*), (Somerset); Ælfmær (*Ælmer*) *werl*; Sæweald (*Sæwold*) *æt Iliacum*; Wulfric of Poleshill (*æt Pauleshele*), (?Devon); Ealdræd of Monksilver (*Ealdred æt Sulfhere*), (Somerset); Wulfgar of Hewish (*Wulger æt Hiwerc*), (in Yatton, Somerset); and Æthelwine (*Æilwine*) *wunge* (possibly a scribal error for *iunge*, 'Young').

MS: London, BL, Add. 15350, 27 (*olim* 25) (s. xii)

Printed: Kemble 1839, IV, 233–4, no. 897; Thorpe 1865, 432–4; Robertson 1939 (= 1956), 236–8, App. I, no. 4 (heading in English omitted).

Translated: Thorpe 1865, 432–4; Robertson 1939 (= 1956), 237–9, App. I, no. 4.

References: Robertson 1939 (= 1956), 485–90 (place-name identifications); Hoad 1975, 323; Healey & Venezky 1980, 72, no. B15.5.38.

King William I

145

A.D. 1066 x 1087. Regulations of King William I regarding exculpation. *English and Latin versions.*

MSS: 1. Cambridge, CCC, 96, 106v (= Quire 9, 10v) (Latin version only) (s. xv)

    2. ?Cheltenham, Phillipps 26641 (*olim* 2777; present location untraced) (Latin version only) (s. xiii)

    3. London, BL, Add. 47680, 95v (Latin version only) (*c.* A.D. 1230 [Liebermann 1903, I, 483 note *a*])

    4. London, BL, Cotton Claudius C. ix, 73r (*olim* 70r) (Latin version only) (s. xiii)

    5. London, BL, Cotton Claudius D. ii, 44r (*olim* 41r), no. 2 (Latin version only) (s. xvi)

    6. London, BL, Cotton Julius C. ii, 60r (English version only) (s. xvi/xvii transcript of MS 19)

    7. London, BL, Cotton Tiberius C. xiii, 98v–99r (*olim* 96v–97r) (Latin version only) (s. xiii)

    8. London, BL, Cotton Titus A. xxvii, 148v (*olim* 147v) (Latin version only) (s. xiii in. [Liebermann 1892, 63])

    9. London, BL, Cotton Vitellius A. xiii, 7r–8r (*olim* 6r–7r) (Latin version only) (s. xiii)

10. London, BL, Hargrave 313, 99v (Latin version only) (s. xiii)
11. London, BL, Harl. 261, 71 (Latin version only) (s. xiii)
12. London, BL, Harl. 311, 39r (*olim* 189r) (Latin version only) (s. xvii transcript of MS 17 made by Simon D'Ewes)
13. London, BL, Harl. 596, 41v (English version only) (s. xvii transcript of MS 19 made at the request of Simon D'Ewes)
14. London, BL, Harl. 6523, 47 (English version only) (s. xvii transcript of MS 19 made by E. Elstob)
15. London, BL, Royal 11 B. II, 166 (Latin version only) (s. xii)
16. London, BL, Royal 13 A. XVIII, 109r (Latin version only) (s. xiv[1])
17. London, PRO, 'Liber Rubeus Scaccarii', 163r (Latin version only) (s. xiii)
18. London, Society of Antiquaries, 177, 41r (s. xviii transcript of MS 19)
19. Maidstone, Kent County Archives Office, DRc/R1, 47 (Sawyer 1957, I, 47) (s. xii[1])
20. Manchester, John Rylands, 420, 33r (*olim* 78r) (s. xii)
21. Oxford, Bodleian, Gough Kent 1 (17947), pp. 21–2 (s. xviii transcript of MS 19)
22. Oxford, Bodleian, Hatton 54 (4072), 192 (Latin version only) (s. xiv[1])

Printed: Selden 1623, 193–4 *ex* MS 7; Twysden 1652, 982–3 *ex* MSS 1 and 7; Hearne 1720, I, 16 *ex* MS 21; Wilkins 1721, 230 *ex* MS 17 (Wilkins notes on p. 230 n. a: 'In codice rubeo f. cxlii a. haec reperitur Inscriptio: Carta ejusdem Regis Willelmi de appellatis pro aliquo maleficio Franco vel Anglico'); Clarke *et al*. 1816, I, 2 *ex* MS 17; Schmid 1832, I, 188–9 (= 1858, 352–3) *ex* Hearne (English version) and MS 17 (Latin version); Hardy 1840, II, 473 n. 2 *ex* MSS 2, 4 and 11; Thorpe 1840a, 210–11, no. II (= Thorpe 1840b, I, 488–9) *ex* MSS 3, 17 and 19; Migne 1844, CXLIX, c. 1321–2 *ex* Selden; Klipstein 1849, I, 299 *ex* Thorpe 1840; Stubbs 1887, II, 348 *ex* MSS 4, 11 and 22; Liebermann 1892, 144–5 (partial) *ex* MSS 1, 3, 5, 8 and 15; Liebermann 1903b, I, 483–4 *ex* MSS 1, 3–5, 7–8, 10–11, 15, 17, 19–20 and 22; Robertson 1925, 232 *ex* MS 19.
Translated: Schmid 1832, I, 188–9 (= 1858, 353) (translation into German); Liebermann 1903b, I, 483–4 (translation into German); Stubbs 1906, 78; Robertson 1925, 233.
References: Selden 1623, 193; Wanley 1705, 186, no. XIII *ex* MS 6 and 274, no. XIX *ex* MS 19; Klipstein 1849, I, 429; Liebermann 1893, 322; Round 1894, 838; Pollock & Maitland 1895, I, 75 (= 1898, I, 98); Brunner 1896a, 537; Brunner 1896b, 128 (= Brunner 1931, II, 620); Hall 1896, I, xcvi, no. 116; Liebermann 1903b, III, 271–3; Stubbs 1906, 77–81; James 1909–12, 184 *ex* MS 1; *Regesta* I, 63, no. 238 ('spurious'); Warner & Gilson, I, 343–4, no. 8 *ex* MS 15 and II, 85, no. 6 *ex* MS 16; Robertson 1925, 223–4 and 360–1; Goebel 1937, 409–16; Ker 1957, 445, no. 373 A.20 *ex* MS 19; Oakley 1970 , I.2, 1005–6 *ex* MS 19; Cameron 1973, 140–1, no. B14.57; Healey & Venezky 1980, 121, no. B14.57; Garnett 1986b, 117 n. 59 and 130–5.

Worcester

146

A.D. ?1084. Record of payments made by the Church (of Worcester) to King William I.

MS: London, BL, Cotton Tiberius A. xiii, 177r (*olim* 176r; 174 in Hearne 1723) (s. xi ex)

Printed: Hearne 1723, II, 393 (see also 392); Thorpe 1865, 439–40; Robertson 1939 (= 1956), 242, App. I, no. 6.

Translated: Thorpe 1865, 439–40; Robertson 1939 (= 1956), 243, App. I, no. 6; Atkins 1940, 35 *ex* Thorpe.

References: Wanley 1705, 257, no. CXXVII; Robertson 1939 (= 1956), 493; Atkins 1940, 34–5; Ker 1948, 57, no. 2, 62 (N.ii) and pl. II (= Ker 1985, 41, no. 2, 46 [N.ii], 56 and pl. 4); Ker 1957, 251, No. 190 B (*a*); Cameron 1973, 196, no. B16.23, 3; Healey & Venezky 1980, 169, no. B16.23.3.

147

A.D. 1096 x 4 October 1113. Record (composed by Thomas, prior of Worcester Cathedral,) of how Wulfstan (*Wulstan*) attained the bishopric (of Worcester) and of lands granted to him at Blackwell (*Blækewællan*), (Worcs.), Wolverley (*Wulfweardiglea*), (Worcs.), Church Iccomb (*æt Ickacumbe*), (Worcs., later in Glos.), (*æt*) *Cullaclif* (later Cookley Wood, Worcs., cf no. 3 above), Alveston (*æt Ælfestune*), (Glos.), Mitton (*Myttun*), (Worcs.), White Ladies Aston (*Eastun*), (Worcs.), Lindridge (*Twegen Lindehrycgeas*), (Worcs.), Penn Hill (*Penhyll*), (Worcs.), Grimley (*Grimanleah*), (Worcs.) and Henwick (*Hinawican*), (Worcs.); his brother Ælfstan, prior (of Worcester Cathedral), acquired land (in Worcs.) at Rous Lench (*æt Lenc*), Dunhampstead (*æt Dunhamstyde*) and Peachley (*æt Pecesleage*); Wulfstan was also given the mill at Northwick (*æt Norðwican*), (Glos.) and a quarter of the land there and the monastery at Westbury-on-Trym in Gloucestershire (*æt Westbyrig on Gleawecestrescire*) which he re-established and endowed with vestments and land, assigning it to St Mary's Minster, (Worcester). (All readings from the English version of MS 1.) *English and Latin versions.*

MSS: 1.   London, BL, Cotton Tiberius A. xiii, 180v–182v (*olim* 177v–179v) (s. xi ex) (damaged)

       2.   London, BL, Harl. 4660, 11v–12r (Latin version with English *titulus in dorso* and opening words of English version) (s. xvii)

Source: Hickes 1703, II, fig. IIb opp. p. 144 (facsimile of opening six lines of the lost Worcester original of MS 2, reproduced by Atkins 1940, pl. XL opp. p. 225 *ex* Hickes)

Printed: Wharton 1691, I, 541–2 *ex* MS 1 (Latin version only); Hickes 1703, II, 175–6 *ex* a lost Worcester MS; Hearne 1723, II, 403–408 *ex* MS 1; *Monasticon* I, 599–600 *ex* MS 2; Thorpe 1865, 445–7 *ex* MS 1 (English version only); Atkins 1940, 208 *ex* Hickes (endorsement only).

Translated: Thorpe 1865, 445–7 (translation of English version); Atkins 1940, 208–9.

References: Wanley 1705, 257, no. CXXVIII *ex* MS 1; Keller 1906, pl. XI (on hand); Atkins 1940, 36 and 208; Ker 1948, 57 (= 1985, 41) (on hand); Ker 1957, 251, no. 190 B (*b*).

York

148

A.D. 1070 x 1100. Powers and laws (*þa gerihto 7 þa la[g]a*) of T(homas I), archbishop (of York), over York (*Euerwic*), both inside and outside the city. Witnesses: Arngrimr (*Arngrim*) the monk; Authgrimr (Eng.: *Oudergrim*, Lat.: *Oudgrim*); Clibern (or Clibjorn) (Eng.: *Clibern*, Lat.: *Clibernus*); Wulfstan (Eng.: *Wlfstan*, Lat.: *Wlstanus*); Authulfr (*Oudolf*); Ulfketill (*Ulfkil*); Authbjorn (Eng.: *Ouderbern*, Lat.: *Oudbern*); Heardwulf (Eng.: *Haryolf*, Lat.: *Hardolf*); Lithulfr an Gl'uneorn (Eng.: *Lisolf an Gl'uneorn*, Lat.: *Hulfus Gluneorn*); Beornwulf (or Bjornulfr) (Eng.: *Beornolf*, Lat.: *Beornulfus*); Ulfr (*Ulf*); all the citizens of York (Eng.: *eal [s]eo bur[hw]are on Euerwic*, Lat.: *tota civilis communio Eboraci*); the archbishop's congregation (Eng.: *hirde*, Lat.: *familia*); Hugh the sheriff (Eng.: *Hu[g]a scirgreuan*, Lat.: *Hugo scire prepositus*); William of Nottingham (Eng.: *Yillem of Snotingham*, Lat.: *Willelmus de Notingham*); Berengar (Eng.: *Beringar*, Lat.: *Berengar*), the king's messenger (Eng.: *arendracan*, Lat.: *nuncius*); Ilbeard of ?Whitewood (Eng.: *Ilbeard of Hittayuda*, Lat.: *Ilbertus de Hiwitawda*); William of Percy (Eng.: *Yilelm de P'cid*, Lat.: *Willelmus de Percy*), (Manche); William Firebrand (Eng.: *Yilelm Tysun*, Fr.: *Willelmus Tisun*); and all the king's men. *English and French versions, the latter with Latin witness clause and anathema.*

MS: York, Borthwick Institute, 'Magnum Registrum Album, pt I', 61r
        (English), 61v (French) (s. xiv, *temp.* Edw III)

Printed: Liebermann 1903a, 279–81, no. II *ex* transcript of MS.

Translated: Liebermann 1903a, 280–1 (translation into German).

References: Liebermann 1903a, 278–9 and 282–3; Tengvik 1938, 382, s.v. Tison; Healey & Venezky 1980, 72, no. B15.3.60

INDICES

A. PERSONS

b. = brother; CG = Continental Germanic; d. = daughter; f. = father; (f) = female; Fr. = French; s. = son; Scand. = Scandinavian; sist. = sister; t-r = receiver of toll; w. = witness. All references are to the text numbers.

B. PLACES

Only names appearing in the original texts are cited in this index. The counties are those
that were in existence up to A.D. 1974.

C. SELECTED SUBJECTS